CW01402011

Hollywood Inside & Out: The Kenny Miller Story

by Kenny Miller with
Donald Vaughan

Hollywood Inside & Out: The Kenny Miller Story

by Kenny Miller with
Donald Vaughan

BearManor Media
2005

Hollywood Inside & Out: The Kenny Miller Story
© 2005 Kenny Miller, Donald Vaughan

All rights reserved.

For information, address:

BearManor Media
P. O. Box 750
Boalsburg, PA 16827

bearmanormedia.com

Cover design by John Teehan

Typesetting and layout by John Teehan

Published in the USA by BearManor Media

ISBN—1-59393-039-9

Table of Contents

Foreword
by Nancy Streebeck

"Here, little lady, give 'em a roll!"

Elvis blew on the dice and handed them to me. Kenny Miller, a cluster of bodyguards, and a half-a-hundred strangers stared intently at my tightly-clenched fist.

Then, as if on cue, the strangers dropped stacks of different-colored chips on various sections of the crap table.

"Kenny," I whispered. "What are they doing?"

"They're placing bets on what they think you're going to roll. Throw the dice down to the other end of the table."

I did. The strangers hissed. They were not happy.

The croupier, a Hoagy Carmichael lookalike wearing a green translucent visor and matching casino apron, scooped up the dice with a short wooden rake and slid them toward me. "One more time, compliments of the house," he mumbled without emotion.

Elvis pointed to a spot on the table. One of his bodyguards put a tall stack of chips on the spot.

I rolled the dice again. The strangers hissed more loudly than before. They turned their backs on me and left the table en masse. The King shrugged. He motioned for Kenny and me to follow him.

As we weaved our way though blackjack tables, slot machines and roulette wheels, I quietly asked Kenny why everyone had left the table.

"They all lost their money when you crapped out."

"Elvis, too?"

Kenny nodded in the affirmative.

"How much?"

"Seven hundred dollars."

Seven hundred dollars! And The King didn't seem to be the least bit upset about it.

Kenny and I walked a few paces behind Elvis and his four-man entourage. Two of the bodyguards cleared a path, another carried Elvis's "orange juice" (the vodka was never added in public view), and a fourth mostly strutted around wearing a six-pack of ballpoint pens clipped to his jacket pocket so that Elvis would always have a writing implement to sign autographs.

We were directed to a small, dimly-lit lounge. It was well after midnight, not yet dawn, and only a dozen or so patrons sat at the tiny square tables waiting for the next show to begin. Elvis, Kenny, the custodian of the orange juice, and I sat together at one table; the remaining three bodyguards sat at another table.

Exactly on the hour (an assumption because there were no clocks in the lounge and it was too dark to read our wristwatches), the DeMarco Sisters burst onto the stage above us. They were an energetic group. They sang loudly, spun around in unison, and gingerly sashayed across the stage from the left to right. As they made the crossing, one of them noticed Elvis sitting front and center. She squealed with delight, never missing a beat, and the sisters performed the rest of their act playing directly to our table. Elvis was cute—shucks, he was downright adorable!—flirting with the performers, pounding out rhythm on the tabletop; and all the while refusing repeated invitations to join the act on stage. "I don't wanna upstage 'em," he explained. "They're doin' real fine by themselves." Kenny and I thought it a very respectful gesture.

After the DeMarco Sisters finished their set, a lounge patron coyly approached Elvis and asked for an autograph. She was short, round and middle-aged. Elvis called her "ma'am," snapped his fingers for a ballpoint pen, and signed a cocktail napkin. (He dedicated it "To Lena" and misspelled sincerely as he usually did. A publicist friend of mine, who worked on many of Elvis's films, once burned fifty 8x10 photographs that Elvis had personally signed because he didn't want Elvis to be embarrassed about the misspelling. Those fifty glossies would bring at least $50,000 at auction today!)

Kenny Miller and I had ended up sitting there with Elvis quite by chance. Kenny, a darling of the fan-magazine editors, and I, a publicist for a handful of teen-favorite entertainers, had come to Las Vegas earlier that evening to prepare for a photo shoot with Frankie Avalon, Fabian, and Bobby Rydell for "TV Star Parade." The trio of heart-throb singers was staying in a residential complex with their manager, and they weren't yet old enough to gamble in the casinos, so Kenny and I had gone out seeking our own late-night adventures. That's when we wandered into the Stardust Casino where Elvis was holding court at a crap table. He recognized Kenny and sent one of his bodyguards over to fetch us.

Sharing that spontaneous night with The King, and watching the DeMarco Sisters perform, was just another routine happenstance for Kenny during the '50s. At the age of twenty-plus, Kenny was an up-and-coming, triple-threat talent with a smattering of solid credits behind him. Known to some, unknown to others, he was hovering on the edge of the big time. Anything might be everything, and everything might be anything. He was determined to be prepared; to utilize all possibilities, planned or un-planned.

The relentless drive, dedication and determination needed to suc-ceed in show business have traditionally perpetrated a "work hard, play hard" lifestyle for performers. By today's standards, play in the '50s was rather meek.

After beating twelve or fourteen nonstop, stressful hours to death, it was common for actors to unwind at one of the popular 24-hour coffee shops in Los Angeles. One of the most frequented was Googie's, a com-fortable Naugahyde-enhanced assemblage, wedged into the side of Schwab's Drugstore at the corner of Sunset Boulevard and Crescent Height. (No, Lana Turner wasn't discovered at Schwab's; she was discovered at a long-gone drugstore across the street from Hollywood High School.)

The management at Googie's catered to actors and liked having them on the premises. The atmosphere was nonchalant and on any given late night/early morning, you could run into the likes of Nick Adams, Hugh O'Brian, Bobby Van and Tab Hunter—or gangster Mickey Cohen, who enjoyed hanging around places where actors hung out.

James Dean was also a regular at Googie's. He generally sat hunched over and sprawled out, sometimes with a girlfriend or a boyfriend sitting beside him, in a rear booth that provided an unrestricted view of the entire restaurant. One evening, while Kenny and I were sitting in a booth next to Dean and a girlfriend, a lanky cowboy-type meandered by Dean's booth and tripped over one of the moody actor's feet. An accident or on purpose? It didn't matter. In a flash, Dean's fast lass bent over, rolled up her pant leg, and unstrapped a wooden leg! She whacked the cowboy's private anatomy with her wooden anatomy. He grabbed himself where it counted most and dropped to the floor. Someone called the cops. All of us were out of there—Dean and partner via his motorcycle which was parked outside; she riding behind him with the wooden leg tucked under arm—before the desk sergeant had time to pick up the phone receiver at West Hollywood Station.

This is about as unruly as it ever got for us. Life was our upper, sleep was our downer, and an occasional vodka cocktail was our drug of choice. We overdosed on enthusiasm and imagination. Was the world a better place in the '50s and '60s? Maybe yes. Maybe no. It certainly was a different place.

Although Kenny's upbringing was fiercely strict and often difficult, it provided a beneficial prerequisite for the social patterns of the '50s-'60s, and for the demanding profession he chose for himself. He inherited extroversion and showmanship from his preacher father. He inherited friendliness and openness from his mother. A sense of duty was a gift from both of them.

Two or three years after I met Kenny, I spent an afternoon with his mother at the family home in Springfield, Ohio. She was warm, simple, direct, somewhat shy—not a phony breath in her being.

"Sit here on the davenport beside me," she offered. "I'll bring some fresh lemonade from the kitchen and we can look at Ken's scrapbook."

Page by page, we slowly examined the album together: Kenny's original birth certificate (I hoped that she wasn't showing that to too many people, as we had cut off a couple of years for publicity purposes), faded newspaper articles from the early '40s, PFC. Kenneth L. Miller in uniform, Kenny romping with Hollywood beauties in magazine shoots that I myself had orchestrated. And the two side-by-side photographs of which she was most proud: Kenny before his nose surgery, and Kenny after his nose surgery.

I listened attentively as she spoke, and with each page I acted as if I had never seen any of the pictures before. And perhaps I hadn't. On that day, I saw them through the eyes of a loving mother who was in awe because a surgeon had reshaped her son's damaged nose; a woman who deemed it miraculous that she could watch her son's likeness singing and dancing on an enormous projection screen at the local cinema.

Kenny was instrumental in delivering two very important associations to my industry career. In 1958, he introduced me to Jimmie Rodgers. In 1959, he introduced me to Burt Reynolds. Individually, Jimmie and Burt both eventually hired me for long-term employment.

A short while after Kenny connected me with Burt Reynolds, the three of us were relaxing around the kitchen table at Burt's hillside house, indulging in Chinese take-out before Kenny was to leave for a casting call. Kenny finished eating first, wiped his mouth with a grand flourish, kissed me on the cheek, slapped Burt on the back, and tap-danced to the front door. He skipped down the steep outdoor steps singing a tune from "Finian's Rainbow."

Burt laughed out loud and shook his head. "There goes Mr. Show Business," he chuckled. "He looks like Danny Kaye, talks like Walter Winchell, and negotiates like one of the Warner brothers."

To me, Kenny remains Mr. Show Business. He has been a constant in my life for more than 40 years—always there, even if he isn't here.

One early morning during the mid-'80s, it happened that Broderick Crawford was attending a meeting in the office building where I was working. After completing his transactions, he asked me directions to the men's room. I indicated a door down the hall. By mistake, Crawford opened the door to a storage room. "Good gawd," he barked. "This entire closet is filled with Kenny Miller press clippings! Didn't anyone ever tell you that today's newspaper is tomorrow's cat litter?"

I smiled at the gruff-voiced star's crusty evaluation. "Oh, I think I'll save everything that's in there," I mused. "Perhaps Kenny will want to write a book someday."

And he has.

Introduction
by Don Vaughan

Kenny Miller was a part of my life long before I actually met him.

As a kid growing up in South Florida, I was a motion picture junkie. I saw as many new movies as I could talk my parents into taking me to, as well as whatever I could catch on television. I also made it a point to see every classic re-release that managed to find its way to my tiny home town. I fell madly in lust with Ingrid Bergman in "Casablanca," and watched wide-eyed as Atlanta burned in "Gone With The Wind."

The classics were fun, but like most young boys, my true movie loves were horror and science fiction. I enjoyed them all, but two of my absolute favorites were "I Was A Teenage Werewolf" and "Attack of the Puppet People," both of which co-starred a blond, impossibly cleft-chinned singer/dancer named Kenny Miller.

He wasn't the star, but Kenny definitely made a memorable impression. Who could forget the party scene in "Teenage Werewolf" in which an enraged Tony (Michael Landon) beats the hell out of Vic (Kenny Miller) following a silly prank? Or the heart-stopping sequence in "Puppet People" in which Stan (Kenny again) acts as lookout on the monster-sized door while his fellow "puppet people" work desperately to make themselves big again? To a 10 year old, this was absolute heaven, and I couldn't get enough.

I eventually grew up, but my love of movies remained stunted in adolescent awe (in fact, it's still there now). I became a journalist and took a job as a staff writer for "The Lake Worth Herald," a small South Florida weekly. One day I was assigned to interview a singer named Kenny Miller, who was premiering a new nightclub act in Palm Beach. His name didn't

1

ring a bell at the time, but as we talked, Kenny dropped occasional references to his movie career—including roles in "I Was A Teenage Werewolf" and "Attack of the Puppet People," as well as more mainstream cinema classics such as Cecil B. DeMille's "The Buccaneer" (directed by Anthony Quinn), "Rebel Without A Cause," "This Rebel Breed," "Battle Flame" and Orson Welles' "Touch of Evil." I fought to maintain my professional composure. This guy appeared in some of my all-time favorite movies! How much more cool could you get?

(A brief aside here to illustrate just what kind of a guy Kenny Miller really is: Shortly after the conclusion of his night club gig, Kenny did a stint on a Caribbean-bound cruise ship. Even though we had met only once and for a very brief time, Kenny went out of his way to send me a post card from the ship just to say hi. His was the first celebrity autograph I ever received, and I still have it today.)

Fast forward ten years. I'm now a full-time freelance writer. I discover a wonderful magazine called "Filmfax," which covers both the famous and the little known in motion pictures and television. I pitch a profile of Kenny Miller, noting his impressive filmography and extensive television work. I get the assignment, and spend nearly four hours interviewing Kenny about his wide-ranging career as an actor and entertainer. As we conclude our chat, Kenny gives me a huge stack of framed movie stills—most of them pulled off his living room wall—to run with the article.

And that's how our friendship started.

You'll understand as you read the following pages how Kenny's life was practically destined to become a book. He's known everyone, been everywhere and done everything. Other entertainers may be better known, but none of them taught Jackie Kennedy how to do the Twist, rode in a stretch limousine with Orson Welles as he attempted to find Latino extras in the toughest sections of Los Angeles, ditched the Secret Service to go club-hopping with the wife of Jordan's King Hussein, or nearly died climbing a wall-sized door for a movie as legendary film director Bert I. Gordon egged them on.

Indeed, the book you're holding in your hands is both a fascinating life story and a remarkable glimpse at back-stage Hollywood during a transitional era that never could be again.

It must be noted that I wasn't the first to help Kenny chronicle his life story. That honor goes to Susan Kennedy, a talented Palm Beach writer and long-time Kenny confidant who realized long ago how incredibly entertaining Kenny's life has been. Susan had just started transcribing several hours of interviews with Kenny when, sadly, she suddenly passed away.

Susan's death hit Kenny hard. They had known each other for many years and had become extremely close. With her passing, Kenny lost not only a gifted collaborator, but a kindred spirit and a dear friend. So I was honored and thrilled when, several months later, Kenny asked if I would be interested in picking up where Susan had left off and helping him complete his autobiography.

Of course, I said yes. The life-long film buff who grew up with Kenny's movies wouldn't let me do otherwise.

– Don Vaughan

Chapter 1

Remember Me?
I Used To Be Famous

The hotel is so crowded that it's difficult to breathe, much less move. Lines of people circle the hallways, intermingling again and again until, inevitably, they meld into a solid mass of humanity. It's total chaos, but in a good way.

A guy in his 30s steps up to my table and eyes the photographs I've meticulously laid out. He finally selects a still from "I Was A Teenage Werewolf" and asks me personalize it to him. His name is Bob. I smile and take pen to picture, signing my name in silver ink for what seems like the hundredth time that day.

"I love "Teenage Werewolf," Bob enthuses as he hands me $20 in exchange for the autographed photo. "What was Whit Bissell like? I thought he was great in "Time Tunnel." Bob catches me by surprise with that one; most people want to know about the film's star, Michael Landon.

I tell Bob that I didn't have any scenes with Whit Bissell in "I Was A Teenage Werewolf" so I didn't know him very well, but from what I had heard, Whit was a really nice man and a consummate professional. Bob seems disappointed that I don't have any personal anecdotes about Whit Bissell, but takes the news graciously. He shakes my hand, thanks me again for the autograph and walks away. The guy behind him in line steps up to my table and the whole process begins again.

The event is Chiller Theatre, a semi-annual nostalgia convention based in the Meadowlands of New Jersey and THE place to be if you're a celebrity who hasn't worked in front of the camera for a while. This show routinely attracts thousands of movie and television buffs and the guest list reads like a Who's Who of classic television, vintage cinema and general pop culture. Once considered superstars in television or motion pictures, many of my fellow thespians are now retired or semi-so. But rather than stay home waiting for royalty checks, they now spend their weekends traveling the country reliving the good old days with fans and friends. Some attend shows like Chiller Theatre because they need the money or see it as a way of raising funds for a favorite charity, others simply because they miss the public adulation. Celebrity can be a potent drug and one that many stars can't kick cold turkey.

Chiller Theatre is unique among shows in that it usually features a very eclectic line up of guests. It's not uncommon to see big Hollywood stars exchanging pleasantries with professional wrestlers, or porno actresses chatting up the cast members of some once-popular '60s science fiction series. You never know who your table mate might be, and that's half the fun.

Over the years, many nostalgia shows have found great success by adhering to a theme. "Star Trek" conventions, of course, are legendary for the enthusiasm of the fans they attract. Conventions dedicated to "Star Wars," "The X Files," "Lost In Space," "Batman" and almost any other popular television series with a hardcore fan base are also extremely common. So are comic book conventions, which got their start in a big way in the early '70s. Today, it's not uncommon for actors with a comic-book connection, such as Lou Ferrigno, who played "The Incredible Hulk" on television, to make well-received appearances at comic-book conventions. I often get invited to these theme conventions because of my appearance in a variety of films and television shows, and I enjoy them because they allow me to catch up with old friends like Mark Goddard or David Prowse (aka Darth Vader), who flies in from the United Kingdom.

A decade ago, I'm told, nostalgia shows like Chiller Theatre were few and far between. Science fiction and comic book conventions were relatively common, however, and the cast members of popular movies or television shows were often invited guests. Back then, though, their attendance was paid for by the convention and the stars graciously signed autographs free for eager fans.

But then, almost overnight, celebrity autographs became a marketable commodity. Signed photos started selling for big bucks on the Internet and celebrities realized that others were making money off their signatures, so why shouldn't they? The days of the free autograph were over. Now, at events like Cinema Wasteland or Ray and Sharon Court's Hollywood Collectible Show, every celebrity guest charges for his or her auto-graph. Coming from an era when movie stars happily signed anything for a fan, this commercial trend took me a bit by surprise, but I quickly ac-cepted it.

When I attended my first Chiller Theatre in 2002, I was a relative newcomer to the nostalgia show scene. My first show, just a couple of years earlier, had been a tiny affair in Fort Lauderdale. Buffalo Bob Smith of "Howdy Doody" fame was the star attraction, and what a wonderful man he was! Though getting on in years, he greeted every fan with heart-felt warmth and appreciation, his smile a passport back to a simpler time when a puppet named Howdy and a clown named Clarabell were a kid's best friends. It was genuinely heartwarming to watch crowds of Baby Boomers—many of them in their 40s or older—grinning like children as Buffalo Bob led them through the "Howdy Doody" theme song. ("What time is it, kids? It's Howdy Doody time!"…) That was the first time I met Buffalo Bob, and I was deeply saddened when he passed away a short time after.

Though that autograph show was relatively small, I did pretty well (though not nearly as well as Buffalo Bob, who was already riding high on the skyrocketing nostalgia craze). I had an eclectic array of photographs from "I Was A Teenage Werewolf," "Attack of the Puppet People," "Touch of Evil" and other film and television work, and my fans seemed delighted. So did the autograph dealers in attendance, many of whom bought sev-eral signed photos for resale later. I was new to the autograph scene—fresh meat—and they knew they could capitalize on that.

On my way home from that first show I realized I was missing out on a really good thing. More shows followed, some more successful than others, though I always managed to have a good time. Sometimes I was seated next to someone I knew, and we would spend our free time remi-niscing about the good old days. Other times I was seated next to some-one I had never heard of but who, judging from the long lines of people requesting his or her autograph, was still extremely popular with today's pop culture-crazed young people.

Take, for example, the Ladies of "The Evil Dead." I'll be honest with you—I've never watched Sam Raimi's cult horror classic. I know it helped make Bruce Campbell a star and Sam one of his generation's most ac-claimed directors, but horror movies like "The Evil Dead" just aren't my cup of tea (and yes, I know how silly that sounds coming from the star of

"Blood Stalkers"). However, when I met the movie's three leading ladies—Betsy Baker, Ellen Sandweiss and Theresa Tilly—at my first Chiller Theatre show, I just fell in love. They were incredibly nice to me and, being old hands at this, took me under their protective wings. Betsy, in particular, was full of advice for a show novice such as myself, and we've stayed in touch ever since, making each other aware of show opportunities and sharing stories, both good and bad, of the various events we've attended. It's always nice to see the Ladies of "The Evil Dead" because they know how to make an autograph show something special. They also love their fans, and never tire of telling stories about the harrowing filming of their biggest claim to fame.

Indeed, attending autograph shows, science fiction and horror conventions and related events has been a real education for me in so many ways, especially when it comes to cult films and popular culture. Particularly striking is the dedication of horror aficionados. Even though horror movies—especially gory horror movies—aren't my favorite, I've come to appreciate the people who star in them and the fans who never stop watching them.

Over the years I've shared memorable days with some of the biggest names in contemporary horror, including Michael Berryman, the formidable-looking but remarkably sweet star of "The Hills Have Eyes;" Dick Warlock, who played the delightfully evil Michael Meyers in "Halloween II;" Gunnar Hansen, who, despite his many film credits, will always be remembered as the terrifying Leatherface in Tobe Hooper's "Texas Chainsaw Massacre;" Reggie Bannister of the "Phantasm" series; Linda Blair, the vomit-spewing pixie from "The Exorcist;" Ken Foree, the zombie-busting hero of George Romero's "Dawn of the Dead," and the always amusing Conrad Brooks, whose proudest claim to fame is his work for cult filmmaker Ed Wood.

Though I may not have seen all of their movies, I've enjoyed meeting every single one of these people and I envy the relationship they have with their fans. Horror buffs are die-hard fans for life, no doubt about it. And even though I've hung out with many of these kind folks for only a weekend or two, I consider them dear, dear friends. That's the kind of camaraderie bred by shows like Chiller Theatre.

But while the horror stars are great fun to pal around with, I relate better to the more mainstream stars of television and movies, many of whom I worked and played with early in my career, such as Robert Fuller,

Edd "Kooky" Byrnes, Alex Cord, Tippi Hedren, Janet Leigh and Dale Robertson. Even though decades may have passed since last we saw each other, there are always plenty of grins and hugs and "do you remember whens" each time we run into each other.

(Occasionally, however, a friendship will die with the passing years. Recently, I was seated across from a gentleman with whom I had partied hard during our early days in Hollywood. It had been a long time since we'd chatted and I was quite pleased to see him, but he greeted me with an icy coldness that I couldn't understand. Later, a mutual friend told me that my former pal was jealous because time had been a little kinder to me than it had been to him. I was shocked and saddened, but luckily, encounters like that are pretty rare.)

Every show I attend adds more pages to the album of wonderful memories in my mind. I'll never forget, for example, the time I had to sneak my beloved schnauzer, Sassi, into a Hilton Hotel in New Jersey and having both Lee Meriwether and Will "Sugarfoot" Hutchins offer to take her for a walk. Or sharing recollections of filming "Attack of the Puppet People" with the legendary John Agar. Or being surprised with a hug and a kiss from my former "Little Laura and Big John" co-star, Karen Black. Or hearing my name shouted across a crowded hotel ballroom and turning to see the still-gorgeous Irish McCalla, the star of TV's "Sheena, Queen of the Jungle" and one of my fellow entertainers during a 1960 USO tour of the Far East. Or laughing with Buddy Hackett about the fabulous engagement party he hosted in New Jersey for my close friend Connie Stevens and her fiancé, Eddie Fisher.

I cherish these memories, and I have so many of them. But sometimes they sadden me, too, because so many of these dear friends are no longer with us. I hope those fans who got to meet them at various nostalgia shows treasure those encounters because they truly were in the presence of entertainment legends.

I've never thought of myself that way, of course. Though I have a good-sized ego (you have to, if you're going to succeed in Hollywood), I've always considered myself just an extremely lucky Ohio kid who happened to fulfill his wildest dreams. I never won an Academy Award, but I'm proud of the movies and television shows I've made over the years and I always enjoy discussing them with fans. And I'm happy to say that most of the people who approach my table at the various shows are kind, considerate, pleasant and fun. Sometimes they'll ask me to autograph a piece of memorabilia that I never knew existed or hadn't seen for decades, which is always a treat.

Sadly, there are exceptions. I've discussed this with many of my friends and colleagues, and we all agree that some fans are seriously lacking in both basic social skills and common courtesy. Take, for example, the Biographers. These are fans who want to know everything about you and often ask deeply personal, inappropriate questions or beg for your address or phone number. It's obvious that they don't view what they're doing as wrong, but to most celebrities Biographers are a major nuisance and more than once I've found myself answering one of their ridiculous questions with a clench-jawed "That's really none of your business!"

Then there are the Obsessive Collectors. These are fans who take forever deciding what photo they'd like us to sign for them. They go through our pics over and over, asking questions about each, until we want to scream, "Just pick one already!" These people never give a single thought to those in line behind them; it's almost as if they see themselves as the only fans in the room.

The Clingers, however, are the worst. These are fans who take their appreciation of our work to almost frightening extremes, hovering around our tables for hours at a time or pestering us with silly, inane questions that defy answer. No celebrity wants to appear rude so we tolerate the Clingers with a tight smile, hoping desperately that they'll eventually go away. The Clingers are especially troublesome because their hovering keeps other fans at bay, which can cost us sales, not to mention the opportunity to visit with old friends too polite to butt in.

Most celebrities stay in the hotel in which a show is held. This is convenient, but it also provides fans with a troublesome proximity. More than once I've had fans wrangle my room number from the front desk and call me late at night. Some have even pounded on my door in the hope of spending some personal time with me. But while I love all of my fans, at the end of a hectic day I'm usually too tired to do anything but have a quick dinner and go to bed. Needless to say, I learned early on not to answer the door once I've locked it for the night.

Amusingly, I've also had fans—both male and female—slip written propositions under my door. I'm flattered, but there's no way I'm going to hook up with a total stranger, no matter how much they loved my performance in "I Was A Teenage Werewolf" or "Touch of Evil."

Fans also tend to get a little overly friendly during costume parties, dances and other late-night show events. Apparently many of them feel that our attendance is an invitation to get touchy-feely, and I've been groped, fondled and manhandled numerous times. Now, if I go at all, I make an early appearance and bail before things get too weird.

The occasional moment of inappropriate behavior not withstanding, I really do enjoy meeting my fans, many of whom, it seems, are amateur filmmakers. I've been approached many times by budding Steven Spielbergs eager to have me in their projects, the majority of which have been horror movies. Most of the offers are for cameos, though a few have been for larger character parts. I always explain that I'm a member of the Screen Actors Guild, which has very strict rules about working in non-union films, but that doesn't seem to bother them. "Don't worry, we'll work it out with the Guild," or "Don't worry, we have a way around that" are two lines I hear often.

Despite their films' typically low budgets, I'm genuinely impressed by the passion shown by most of the young filmmakers who have approached me about being in their movies. Their knowledge of filmmaking and their dedication to the craft sometimes rivals that of Orson Welles, and I honestly wouldn't mind appearing in some of them if certain issues could be worked out.

The one time I did agree to appear in a low-budget film proved to be a truly interesting experience. It was a small cameo in a horror flick made by some very dedicated fans in Indiana, a short introductory scene that had me in a car putting the moves on a pretty girl. I had only a few lines so the shoot shouldn't have taken much time at all, but the weather refused to cooperate. It was unseasonably cold and very windy, which (a) caused my eyes to tear up like crazy and (b) wrecked havoc with the sound. Director Solomon Mortamur had several production assistants hold blankets around us in an attempt to buffer us from the wind, but it didn't help much. The whole thing took several long, chilly hours and I couldn't wait to get back to my comfy hotel room.

But as we filmed, something wonderful happened—carloads of fans (most of them friends of Solomon) kept arriving at the location to watch us work. When Solomon finally called a wrap, I happily lingered another half hour to sign autographs and pose for photos. The weather may have been on the cool side, but the love I felt from those who came to watch helped warm me up.

Ultimately, that's what autograph and nostalgia shows are really all about for those of us behind the table—that feeling of warmth and affection that comes from meeting someone who has very fond memories of something we did years if not decades earlier.

And how did I come to be behind the table? Well, that's an interesting story...

Chapter 2
Somewhere Over the Rainbow
Lies Hollywood

"You'll never amount to anything!"

Those were my father's last words to me as he lay dying from leukemia. I was 16 years old, and my deepest desire was to become a Hollywood movie star.

My parents, the Rev. James Miller and Bessie Lewis Miller, knew of my dreams, and vehemently opposed them. They were fundamentalist Christians in the mission field who felt my life would be better served in the name of God. To them, Hollywood was a modern incarnation of Sodom and Gomorrah, and anything even remotely connected to show business was the work of the devil.

Now, after some 40 years in the business, I'm not so sure they were wrong!

My dad's final words hurt me deeply; I couldn't believe he could say something so spiteful and bitter to his youngest child. But deep in my heart, I understood why he felt the way he did.

You see, my father spent most of his life helping the poor and indigent in Springfield, Ohio, and he simply couldn't understand why I didn't want to follow in his footsteps. He refused to listen when I tried to explain to him the burning desire I had to entertain—to make people happy with my God-given talents—and after a while I stopped trying. We were at polar opposites on the issue, and neither of us would budge. But I proved my father wrong regarding his death-bed claim. And, despite his fundamentalist views on Hollywood and entertaining, I think he would have been proud of the way my career turned out. I lived my dream and made it a reality.

The funny part is that my father was at least partially responsible for my need to be in front of an audience. As a child, I sang with my brothers, Dick and George, at the City Mission, which Mom and Dad ran in the worst part of Springfield. Across the street on the other corner was a Afro-American mission. I loved going there because the congregation really sang its heart out. The walls would literally shake as religious fervor overtook them. Best of all, they had a drummer and a sax player, which made performing there even more fun. Singing before a whooping, clapping crowd always made my Sundays brighter.

My parents weren't Holy Rollers, but that's not to say my father didn't work up a sweat behind the pulpit. He had a terrific voice and never failed to convey the spirit of God whenever he preached. He would shout his praises to the Lord, and his enthusiasm was contagious. His sermons were very emotional, heartfelt and always wonderful to watch. You could practically feel the heat from the fire and brimstone!

Dad closed the City Mission when times got tougher, and he became a minister in the Pilgrim Holiness Church. We moved to Fostoria, Ohio, for two years, and then to Bremen, Ohio, for another two years. My parents decided that moving all the time would be too hard on their children's education, so we moved back to Springfield, and Mom and Dad re-opened the Sunshine Mission in another downtrodden part of town. It was for derelicts and poor families who couldn't get out of bed in the morning after carousing all night. We had Sunday School and church in the afternoon so they could get their children there. On Sunday I had to attend six services. When my folks were holding a revival, I had to go to church twelve times in a single week! The visiting preachers often stayed with us and I usually had to give up my bed.

All of this religion got to me after a while, and as I grew older, I backed off going to church so frequently. In fact, when I finally left home and headed to Hollywood, I rarely went at all. I figured I had already gone to church enough for one lifetime, but I became more spiritual.

My father was a tough taskmaster, but then, he had eight children to contend with. And we were spaced out pretty well, to the point where many people couldn't believe we were brothers and sisters. I was the youngest, born October 15, 1931. My brother Henry and my sister Lucille were both married by the time I arrived, so they were more like surrogate parents to me than brother and sister. Another brother and sister died from scarlet fever before I was born, and my brother Given, who was always frail, passed away from heart problems when I was a small child. I have fond memories of sitting in his lap in our living room as he read to me and combing his hair with a fining comb. Then there were George and Dick with whom I was raised.

Because my parents were devout fundamentalists, we lived a relatively Spartan lifestyle. The women weren't allowed to wear makeup, and none of us were allowed to go dancing or to the movies. Those activities didn't promote the religious spirit in which they were grounded, so my parents saw them as a waste of time or, worse, the work of the devil.

We were far from rich, but we managed to get by, and I remember my childhood with great fondness. Our diet was basic—meat was a rarity because it was so expensive—but Mom was a whiz in the kitchen and she managed to make sure we all stayed fed, along with anyone who happened on our doorstep. It was often difficult, but she always came through. Mission work didn't pay very well, and much of what my parents did make went right back into the mission. It was important to my parents that we always help those who needed it, even if we were just one notch above the families who came to us for aid. That was the Christian way, Dad and Mom said, and they lived it as well as preached it.

When I was a kid, Saturday night was the big night at home—we would get a bath! My mother would heat water on the coal stove in the kitchen and pour it into the galvanized tub in which she also did the washing. It sounds funny today, but back then it was a big deal. We all got a bath whether we needed it or not!

My father was a very strict disciplinarian, and doled out punishment in the form of a whipping whenever he felt he had been disobeyed. That might be considered a form of abuse these days, but I never saw it that way. There was no doubt my parents loved us very much, but Dad was a firm believer in the adage: Spare the rod and spoil the child. The list of offenses for which we could be punished was rather extensive, so my brothers and I learned it was just easier to tell a small fib whenever we did something our parents might not approve of. Not that we were bad kids, but we just never knew what might set Dad off.

For example, he once beat me silly merely for dancing with some friends at the local YMCA. The Club Coed was on the YMCA roof, and they had a live band that I was dying to hear. Unfortunately, the Club Coed was open only to upperclassmen, and I was a lowly freshman. But I wasn't about to let that stop me! I snowed the people at the front door into believing I was a sophomore, and in I went. I hooked up with a pair of twins named Wanda and Wuanita Miller, and quickly proved to the crowd that we were, without a doubt, the best dancers in Springfield. Whenever the girls and I hit the dance floor, the other dancers would form a circle and watch us do the latest dances. No one could touch us.

Somehow my father found out that I was sneaking away to go to the YMCA, and one night he came to get me. There I was, dancing my heart out to the sounds of the Eddie Kadel Band, when who should I see wading through the crowd but my father. He grabbed me in front of all my friends and whipped me out of the room and down the stairs, lecturing me the whole time. He thought what I had done was an affront to him and his ministry, even though absolutely nothing wrong was going on there. We weren't drinking alcohol or smoking or doing anything bad; all we were doing was drinking soda and dancing. But to my father, we were all guilty of the worst kinds of sin. He kept saying, "Why would you ever come to a place like this? You know who I am and you're my son!" I tried to explain, but it did no good; he didn't want to hear it. His behavior embarrassed me so much that I never went back. I just couldn't face the kids there after that horrible scene.

I lied to my parents a lot as a child and a teenager, especially when I learned that I had a talent for song and dance—and that people would pay to see me. I became an entertainer early on, but had to hide the fact from my parents because they never would have understood. It was just easier to fib than try to explain. More importantly, I was afraid they would try to stop me, and I couldn't let that happen. I was having too much fun.

So strict were my parents when it came to show business that I didn't see my first movie until I was eight years old—and even that was a fluke. We were living in Fostoria, Ohio, at the time, and my mother was in the hospital with pneumonia. "The Wizard of Oz" was playing at the local theater, and I wanted to see it so badly that I could taste it. So I decided to sneak downtown, watch the movie and return home before anyone knew I was gone. But my mother came home from the hospital unexpectedly, and I just couldn't lie to her. I told Mom that I was going to see "The Wizard of Oz" with some friends, and to my astonishment she grudgingly said okay, only because admission was a can of food for charity. "But I want you home immediately after," Dad said. "No dawdling."

I can't begin to describe how deeply affected I was by "The Wizard of Oz." I was mesmerized by the whole picture, and stunned by its breathtaking beauty. When the film transformed from black and white to color, I was so shocked I peed my pants! I had never seen anything like it, and I couldn't wait to see it again. I ducked into the men's room and stood on a commode in a stall so no one could see me until the second show started, then snuck back in and found a seat.

It was midway through the second show that my father came marching down the aisle looking for me. I had forgotten that he wanted me home right after the first show, and he was so mad you could practically see the steam coming out of his ears. He grabbed me by the arm, yanked me to my feet and smacked me up the aisle, through the lobby and down the street. It was a lousy way to end the day, but I'll never forget the excitement of sitting in that darkened theater and watching the screen turn into vivid Technicolor. That was one of the most inspiring moments of my life, and one of the main reasons I later wanted to live in Hollywood and be a movie star. I wanted to live the glamorous life. I actually thought Hollywood was somewhere up in the heavens. Boy, was I naive! Only later would I find out what a hell of a lot of hard work it would require.

When I was in junior high school, I worked at the Majestic Theater just so I could see the movies. I vacuumed the floors, took tickets—anything to hang around. The manager couldn't actually hire me because I was underage, so he'd let me do odd jobs in return for free admission. Of course, my parents never knew about any of this. I lied about where I was going, and my brothers and sisters helped me keep the secret because they knew how much it meant to me.

One of my jobs at the theater was to dress up like a clown during Saturday matinees and help the manager award door prizes (this was during the days when theaters still did things like that). I dressed behind the screen and used a broken mirror to apply my makeup, even though I had no idea what I was doing. I bought the wrong kind of white face makeup and lipstick, and would spend up to 45 minutes in the men's room trying to wash it off with horrible abrasive soap. I'm sure there were telltale spots of makeup on me when I went home, but my parents never noticed it.

I made my stage debut, if you can call it that, when I was in the fourth grade. I had made myself known to the gal who was directing the annual high school junior/senior class play, and she invited me to do a musical number between acts.

I sang a song called "Umbrella Man," and came out looking at the audience holding a big umbrella over my shoulder. I got to the end of the stage and turned around, but I was so nervous that I forgot to reverse the umbrella, so no one could see my face. The audience was howling, and broke into wild applause at the end. I thought my stage debut had gone great and that my career as an entertainer was off and running. Only later did my brother George tell me that the audience was laughing because all they saw was a giant umbrella with two tiny feet sticking out below it.

A genuine break came when I was 10 and won the Ford Rush Search for Talent Show. Ford Rush had been a popular country-western star and he, along with a singer named Bradley Kincaid, had opened a country-western radio station in Springfield. They hosted a talent show in the Fairbanks Theater, which, in its heyday, had been a very famous vaude-ville palace, and I won the first round, then the semi-finals and finally the Search for Talent. I sang two songs—"Little Red School House" and "Fuzzy Wuzzy," with Shirley Herman playing piano for me—and walked away with the $100 grand prize, which was a lot of money in those days.

My oldest brother Henry took me out to dinner at a local steakhouse to celebrate, then said we had to go home to tell my parents. The idea of telling my mother and father that I had won $100 by singing terrified me, because I knew how they felt about show business. But Henry insisted, so we went home and woke them up. I didn't know how to break the news to them, so I just threw the ten $10 bills on the bed. I don't think my parents had ever seen so much money at once in their lives. Their eyes just grew wider and wider.

Henry told them with great pride what I had done, and my father said that I had disgraced them. But Henry supported me, and so did my mom. My father was impressed that I had won the money merely by singing. He couldn't believe it, and kept asking, "You won this for singing just two songs?" It was a wonderful moment because my father, who spent nearly every dime he had helping the poor, was having trouble making ends meet himself, and I could finally help out.

Winning the Ford Rush Search for Talent opened a lot of doors for me. I received my own live radio show on WWSO, called Teen Talent Time, and I started getting more singing gigs, for which I got paid. Not much, but it was the beginning of my entertainment career and I couldn't have been happier. Of course, I still had to hide nearly everything from my parents. They accepted the fact that I had won the talent show and were pleased I received $100, but they continued to oppose show business as a career.

Later, with a bunch of schoolmates, I formed the Stargazers Troupe, which performed often at Wright-Patterson Air Force Base. I loved everything that went into putting on a show, from the writing and directing to the performing, and realized this really was what I wanted to do with my life. I had determined long ago that my parents were wrong. Show business wasn't evil, it was just a way of expressing myself and making others happy, and I couldn't see anything wrong with that.

If anyone deserves credit for my childhood successes as an entertainer, as well as my motivation and drive, it's a wonderful woman named Mom Cockrell. She was an entertainer and old vaudevillian, and she really listened to me when I told her I wanted to be a singer and an actor. Though religious, she differed from my parents in that she didn't think show business was evil or wrong. She understood the burning desire I felt, and helped me whenever she could. Once things started to happen for me in Springfield, I would use her house for correspondence and to make phone calls because I couldn't do it at home. She also gave me advice, found work for me at local fraternal lodges, and covered for me when I was in rehearsal so that my family wouldn't find out. My parents thought the world of her, and never suspected she was preparing me for the career I wanted. I'm certain that if it hadn't been for Mom Cockrell, any ambition I had would have been quickly snuffed out by my family.

I was terribly ambitious in my junior high school days, and wrote a musical that I titled "Get Hep, Jackson." I got the local American Legion to sponsor it and talked the principal at Keifer Junior High, where I went to school, into letting us use the auditorium. We got costumes from New York City and had a complete orchestra made up of students from the local high school. It was an extravaganza of singing, dancing and comedy. At least I thought it was. After the show my sister, Lucille, came back to congratulate me. As she hugged me, she whispered in my ear, "The show was wonderful, but the people came to be entertained—not spend the night." I hadn't realized until then that the show lasted well over four hours! It was my first big lesson in show biz regarding how less can be more.

It always makes me smile when I think back on some of the kids in my Stargazers Troupe. Many had names so unusual that I was sure they were destined to appear on a marquee, such as Neysa Wildoner, Iris Hess, Mahala Weaver, Moeita Hartwell and Dorwilda Cockrell. Other talented performers in our little group included Nanette Bohrer, Anita Goodfellow, Shirley Herman, Joan Burr, Ruth Casey, Lucille Martin, Doris Zeigler,

Jean Parrish, Eileen Dulaney, Earl Miller, Wanda Tolle (who was my fa-
vorite jitterbug partner) and two funny guys, Carl Rice and Henry Beier.
Wanda and Ed Horton were our official chaperones, along with Mom
Bohrer, who did everything.

As I grew older, the lure of Hollywood grew increasingly stronger, and
when I was 15 I ran away from home during summer break to check out
this magical fantasy land. I had saved up a little money delivering papers
and caring for a friend's horse, so I told my parents I was going to Arizona to
visit an old friend who had moved there from Springfield. I had visited him
a couple years earlier at his parents' expense so it was a solid story, but my
father was still pretty skeptical. Anyway, I took a bus from Springfield to
Indianapolis and hitchhiked the rest of the way to California.

It was a strange adventure. Outside St. Louis I was picked up by a
school teacher who was driving a hearse to Mexico. At night, he would sleep
in a hotel room and I would sack out inside the hearse because I had limited
funds. It was comfortable, but rather spooky, especially when I would suddenly awaken in the middle of the night. In the mornings, there would
often be people looking at the hearse in the parking lot, not knowing that I
was inside. I would have to lay low until they left, which wasn't easy because
I usually needed to go to the bathroom quite badly. On one occasion I just
couldn't hold it any longer. I thought everyone who had been looking at the
hearse had left. I raised up and saw an elderly man and woman peering in.
Their reaction was right out of a Mack Sennett short—they screamed and
grabbed each other and took off as if they had seen a ghost.

I was stopped by the police only once, somewhere in the middle of
nowhere Missouri. I told the cop I lived down the road, and was carrying
a suitcase because I had just returned from my grandma's. Of course, he
didn't believe me and was about to take me to the station when he received an urgent call on the radio and had to take off. Luckily, I got a ride
shortly after he left and managed to avoid more police all the way to
California.

The guys who picked me up next were three no-good hoods in a
beat-up old Ford. They always let the gas gauge go to zero before they
pulled into a gas station, which scared me to death. Somewhere in the
wilderness of Oklahoma, they made me get out of the car and took all the
money I had in my wallet. Then they got back in the car, told me "You're
stayin' here, kid!" and left me standing on a lonely, dark highway somewhere west of Oklahoma City.

However, I had fooled them; I had $40 hidden in my shoes. After an hour, which seemed like an eternity in the pitch black of night, a truck carrying new cars stopped and picked me up. We drove for several hours and were in the middle of the desert when the driver pulled over to take a nap. I couldn't sleep so, inspired by the beauty of the desert, I decided to take a walk. I had been walking about a half hour when I heard a noise that made me stop in my tracks. I heard the noise again and reached down to pick up a stick at my feet. Then I saw it—a huge rattlesnake sunning itself on a rock to my right. Without thinking, I started flailing at the snake's tail in an attempt to knock off its rattles. The snake struck at me several times, but missed. I finally beat it to death, and dragged the carcass back to the truck driver to proudly show him what I had done. I told him how I had knocked the rattle off first and so on, after which he said, "You stupid little fuck! The poison is in its mouth—not the rattles!" I had always thought it was the other way around! The truck driver also told me that if a snake that size had managed to bite me, I probably would have been dead before I reached the truck. The thought made me nauseous and I threw up my breakfast. Then we hit the road again. Not surprisingly, I never ventured far from the truck after that!

I had made friends with a woman named Kay Manno when I had visited my friend in Arizona a few years earlier, and I stayed with her in a small house when I finally reached Los Angeles. I didn't know anyone in the motion picture business, so I checked out the ads in the newspaper, not knowing that nearly all of them were screen-test scams designed solely to relieve hicks like me from our money. I made a few calls, but nothing came of them. I was in Hollywood, young and talented, but completely clueless about the industry. Kay and her friend Beatrice Phillippi, took good care of me. They lived way out in Eagle Rock, so I had to take the streetcar to downtown Los Angeles and transfer to another streetcar to get to Hollywood, a trip that took about two hours. Once in Hollywood, I would walk to the various "casting" offices that I found in the newspapers. Hollywood is a big place, It wasn't unusual for me to walk six or seven miles a day, then hop back on the streetcar for a two-hour trip back to Kay's place.

Then I got sick, and Kay broke down and called my family, who were none too pleased with my little vacation. My parents made a deal with Kay's boyfriend, Howard, to buy me a bus ticket, and a sheriff's deputy made sure I got on the bus. But I was such a physical wreck at that point that I couldn't have gotten off even if I wanted to.

My parents were absolutely furious when I finally arrived home, and I received more than one whipping for heading off to Hollywood without telling them. My father was deeply disappointed by what I had done, but he couldn't understand how desperately I wanted to see Hollywood and become a part of it. My brief taste of California only made me want it more.

My father died when I was 16. I went back to school, and got another radio show on WIZE, which was a larger station. I even had a small orchestra. By now my mother had realized that entertaining was what I wanted to do, and that I had the talent to make it work. She didn't exactly approve, but she knew there was little she could do to make me stay in Springfield.

In the meantime, I worked a variety of jobs to make money and tried to make some contacts in Hollywood. When Kay (who had married Howard) agreed to let me stay with them for a couple of weeks until I could get established, my mother finally realized everything would be okay, and she gave me her blessing.

My second trip to California almost occurred a little sooner than it did. Danny Kaye's company was holding a nationwide search for someone to play the younger him in a movie version of comedian Harry Lauder's life story. Kaye somehow found out about my local success and that I resembled him, and his people actually came to Springfield to meet me. They took a lot of pictures, shot a little test footage, then went back west. Someone from the studio (Paramount, I think) called shortly after to say I had been chosen, and arrangements were started to get me to Hollywood for a screen test.

But as with a great many things in Hollywood, my big break never materialized. Apparently Harry Lauder's family didn't like the way the fast-living comic was to be portrayed and rejected Danny Kaye's script, along with any chance it would be resurrected. The news devastated me because I adored Danny Kaye and I was really looking forward to working with him.

Years later I ran into Danny Kaye and his wife Sylvia at a restaurant in Beverly Hills. I got up the courage to go over and introduce myself, and I told him the story of how we almost worked together on "The Harry Lauder Story." Danny apologized for the whole fiasco and admitted that he had been just as disappointed as I was because he was a tremendous fan of Harry Lauder and was really looking forward to bringing his life story to the screen. The saddest thing for me is that I never had another opportunity to work with Danny Kaye again.

I vowed not to let that little disappointment stop me from achieving my childhood dream. Once I had saved some money and graduated high school,

I again took a bus to California and moved into an $8-a-week boarding house a short distance from Hollywood. My first job was washing dishes in a greasy spoon on Santa Monica Boulevard. It was owned by a big Greek guy, who insisted I use some awful detergent that was murder on my hands. After two weeks, my mitts were so cracked and bleeding that I could barely use them. The owner of the restaurant gave me rubber gloves, but they didn't help much, so I quit. I asked the owner for the money that was owed me, and he told me to come back the next day. When I did, he refused to pay me. I went nuts, but there was little I could do. The boyfriends of some girls I had met went to him on my behalf, and the bastard had the audacity to say I had never worked in his restaurant! I did everything I could think of to get my money, but I never saw a dime and no one could prove that I worked there.

That put me in a terrible fix, of course, because I needed the money to pay my rent. I became frantic as I saw my dream of becoming a Hollywood movie star going down the drain before I even had a chance to prove myself. I didn't want to return home, yet my money was running out fast and I knew I'd be evicted within days.

My savior, bless her heart, was one of the girls who had befriended me at the Greek restaurant. Realizing my plight, she called my brother George and he and my mother scraped together $20, which helped me over the hump until I could find better-paying work.

Like most aspiring actors, I held a number of odd jobs before breaking into The Big Time. I worked at Albert Allens, a restaurant on Vine Street that specialized in cheese-cake. My job? To take the cheese cakes out of their pans. It wasn't glamorous, but at least I got paid. After a couple of months on cheese cake duty I moved across town to the Carnation Building on Wilshire Boulevard, where I scooped ice cream. The place was amazingly popular; people would line up out the door waiting for ice cream. I became a scooping machine, dishing out ice cream like a robot. At the end of the day, I'd be covered in the stuff. I'd find ice cream in my shoes, in my pants, even in my hair. Ice cream quickly became my least favorite dessert!

While working at Albert Allens, I moved into a boarding house on Sweetzer Drive near the Sunset Strip—and learned just how bizarre Los Angeles could be. The house was run by a wonderful lady who used to be a notorious Hollywood madam. Every now and then she would get tipsy and bring out all these outrageous costumes and dresses that her girls used to wear when she was still in "the business." Most of the outfits looked like they sprang from the pages of a Fredrick's of Hollywood catalog, with strategically placed holes where the naughty bits would be. For a sheltered eighteen-year-old straight off the Ohio turnip truck, it was a real education.

That rooming house was like living in a B-movie. The owner was pretty odd, in a fun way, but not nearly as odd as the butler who worked for her. Every now and then he would get falling-down drunk and try to get into my room. Perhaps I should have been flattered, but I was terrified of him, so I had to keep the door to my room locked at all times to thwart his drunken advances. I'm sure he was just lonely, but he was a major aggravation. The only things that kept me in the boarding house was the low rent and the former madam's erotic fashion shows. I later moved to a more sedate rooming house.

Through all of this, I did what I could to break into the movies. I diligently read the ads in the back of the papers, still unaware that most of those advertising Hollywood screen tests were scams. The trick was to entice wannabe actors into paying big bucks for a "screen test" that usually never left the building. In fact, it was a miracle if there was film in the camera! And, sadly, a lot of young kids fell for it, visions of Hollywood stardom clouding their better judgment. My limited finances kept me out of these places, though I did visit one screen test shop on Melrose that was run by the mother of a very famous singer. She was so into the scam that she actually tried to get me to beg money from my family so she could shoot my test. Of course, my family couldn't do it so I escaped unscathed. But later, when I found out that ninety-nine percent of such businesses were cons, I was amazed that the mother of a very prominent performer would stoop so low.

Getting legitimate representation is difficult in Hollywood when you're a relative unknown. I was a big cheese in Springfield, but my credits there didn't mean much in La-La Land, so I decided to take a different route. I revised "Get Hep, Jackson," the play I had written as a teenager, retitled it "Hit the Road" and produced it in a little theater on Sunset Boulevard called the Gateway with the help of producer Joe Scott. We had a good run and later opened the show at the Music Box Theater in Hollywood. We hired Lu Leonard, a wonderful comedienne who later became a big star on Broadway, to play opposite me in the show. The front money for our second run came from a notorious San Francisco procurer, shall we say, named Jimmy Sheldon, who was the boyfriend of one of my best friends, a gal named Nunci Harlan. Nunci was a drop-dead gorgeous showgirl who happened to live in my boarding house. She had taken me under her wing, and we became like brother and sister. We had a lot of fun on the town together, and did everything we could to help the other succeed in show biz.

Nunci worked with three other gorgeous blondes in an act I helped them put together. They called themselves "The Atomic Blondes" and were booked into a club in San Francisco right across from the Downtown Theater, where Lenny Bruce frequently appeared. Nunci invited me to come up and see the show and offered to take me around San Francisco. She had come to know Sheldon, who was a very handsome guy, and he showed us the town. He also introduced us to a famous lesbian named Tommy Vasu, who owned several gay nightclubs in San Francisco. Regardless of who or what they were, Sheldon and Vasu had hearts of gold and agreed to invest several thousand dollars in my show. I never knew where the money came from, nor did I ask. "Hit the Road" received good reviews in the local papers and helped me get my first agent.

One more thing about Nunci: She was one of the first women to go to Mexico to get breast implants. I don't know if there was a connection, but she developed cancer after numerous trips to a Mexican clinic and died horribly at the very young age of 40. She was a dear friend and a wonderful person and I owe her tremendously for my success in Hollywood.

My very first on-screen acting job in Hollywood was a Stanley Donen film called "Fearless Fagan" (1952), starring Carleton Carpenter, Janet Leigh and Keenan Wynn. It was the true story of a soldier at Fort Ord who brought along his pet lion, Fagan, and hid it in the woods. Hardly Academy Award material, but I couldn't have cared less. I was finally achieving my dream of acting in a motion picture, and I was so excited that I could barely think. I played a soldier with a flashlight who is searching for Fagan in the woods. My only line—but my first in a major motion picture—was: "All clear over here, sir!" Donen instructed me to just act scared. But he didn't have to tell me—it was my first time before a movie camera (and for fabled MGM!) and I was scared to death. If you look really hard the next time "Fearless Fagan" is on the Late Late Show, you might actually see me!

Unfortunately, the four or five days I was to be on the set of "Fearless Fagan" turned into just two days, thanks to the U.S. Government...and my mother.

You see, I still retained residence in Springfield, and most of my mail went to my mother's house. When it started to pile up, she would send it to me. I received a batch of mail the day I went to wardrobe for "Fearless Fagan," but didn't open it until that evening. One letter was from the Springfield draft board telling me that I had to report for service the next day.

I freaked out and called my agent, George Ingersoll, who told me he would make some calls and get me deferred so that I could finish the film. In the meantime, I called the draft board in Ohio in an attempt to straighten things out, and talked with a very nasty woman who told me I was in big trouble for not correcting my address, and that I would have to fix things at the draft board in downtown Los Angeles. This wasn't exactly what I wanted to hear.

I went to work at MGM the next day. I was a wreck. The situation with the draft was on my mind, but I was also in a daze because this was my first time on a real movie set and I was still pretty nervous. Stanley Donen couldn't have been nicer. He treated all of the actors, even those of us with just one line, as equals, and made the job a genuine joy. George visited me during lunch and reassured me that he would have me deferred, which made me feel a little better.

The next morning I went to the draft board to try and fix all this craziness. They kept pushing me to do this and fill out that, no matter how often I tried to tell them that I was supposed to be deferred. No one had heard from George and further, they couldn't have cared less. I suddenly found myself plunging headlong toward military service and, like a character in a Kafka novel, there was nothing I could do about it. I knew George was on the way, but at that point there seemed to be little he could do. I continued wearily through the induction process.

Believing that I would be deferred and back on the set of "Fearless Fagan" within just a few hours, I hadn't thought to bring anything with me to the draft board. All I had were the clothes on my back and about $3 in my pocket. As the hours wore on, I hoped and prayed that I would be deferred and the whole nightmare would be resolved. But around 4:30 p.m. I was sworn in. Suddenly I was in the Army, and there was no turning back. I was placed on a bus for a quick ride to Union Station in Los Angeles, where a train would take us to Fort Ord—an outrageous twist of irony, since that's where "Fearless Fagan" was set!

We arrived at Ford Ord around 4 a.m. It was cold and damp and since I didn't have a sweater, I was miserable. The cold hit me hard and I ended up contracting walking pneumonia. I found myself in the base hospital that afternoon, my acting career gone before it even began. How I longed to be back at MGM looking for that lion!

For basic training, I was sent to Camp Roberts, where I met a sergeant named Maury Dexter, who had just returned from Korea. He was assigned to special services, and took an interest in me because of my show-business background. Maury was a former Hollywood actor who was close to a lot of stars, and he arranged for many of them, including Janet Leigh, Tony Curtis, Debbie Reynolds, Marge and Gower Champion, and others, to visit and entertain the troops. Maury took me under his wing and gave me advice about the Army and Hollywood. It was a friendship that would be of great benefit after I got out of the military and throughout my lifetime.

From Camp Roberts I was sent to Camp Kilmer, New Jersey, which was the holding post before transferring overseas. True to the Miller luck, my records got lost on the way from Camp Roberts, so I was put in temporary billets. I waited and waited, desperate to get out of there. After a month or so, I broke out in awful boils on my legs and other parts of my body because the hygiene there was so bad.

I couldn't get a leave to go home to see my family in Springfield, which was only about 400 miles away, so a couple of "experts" who had been at Camp Kilmer for a while suggested I just go on my own. I carefully planned my first AWOL and hitchhiked my way to Springfield. My family was devastated by my physical condition and nursed me back to health over the three days I was there. It was brutally cold when my brother Dick drove me through a blinding snowstorm to the Pennsylvania Turnpike so that I could hitchhike back to camp. Fortunately, I had little trouble catching a ride because I was wearing my uniform.

I went AWOL several more times and never got caught. I even did a TV show about the Armed Forces in New York City with Arlene Francis, even though I wasn't supposed to be off base. I was stopped several times by MPs but always managed to talk my way out of it. Perhaps they, too, realized what a hellhole we were living in and felt sorry for me.

My records finally showed up and from Camp Kilmer I was sent to Berlin. I looked forward to it because it seemed so exotic to me, a hick from Ohio. My MOS was infantry, but God smiled on me when a young lieutenant called me in and asked me to take care of entertainment for the Sixth Infantry. I was made entertainment NCO and given a room out of barracks. Later, I moved into boxer Max Baer, Sr.'s former house, which really impressed my friends!

Working as entertainment NCO was a dream come true for a stage-happy guy like me. My duties included working with people at the social clubs, where American and German entertainers performed for the troops. We put on a variety of musical shows and other productions, and arranged for visits from well-known movie stars. I was in seventh heaven!

While in Berlin I became involved with an American/German television remake of the "Flash Gordon" series, which was being filmed in an old television studio in Spandau. A stunningly beautiful gal named Tala Birell, who made a lot of spy movies over the course of her career, was entertainment director for the entire Berlin Command. She told me about the series, and I was cast as Tough-Luck Hogan, Flash Gordon's occasional sidekick. Steve Holland played Flash, a British actor named Joe Nash was cast as Dr. Zarkoff, and Irene Champlin played Dale Arden. All of the other actors were German, which was a strange experience because for the most part they couldn't speak English. American director Anthony Worsley helmed the series.

To say that this production of "Flash Gordon" was cheap would be an understatement. The studio where the series was filmed had been partially bombed during the war, and what was left was small and cramped. I never quite understood why they had chosen this location to make the series—Spain or Italy certainly had to have been better and just as cheap—but they managed to get by.

I appeared in several episodes of "Flash Gordon," and enjoyed the experience despite the low budget and difficult working conditions. Steve Holland was a stalwart actor who gave his all to his comic book role, and everyone else was great to work with. The German actors were especially interesting because they had to recite their dialog phonetically. Not surprisingly, a few had serious problems uttering the simplest of lines. "They were stunned!" for example, would come out, "They were stoooned!" Sometimes the shortest scenes would take the longest to film as director Worsley struggled to get even minimally understandable English out of his hard-working German cast.

Much of my work on "Flash Gordon" is a blur, but I recall one memorable scene that had us all rolling on the floor with laughter. I had been partying the night before, so my head was more than a little woozy, a condition made worse by the bee's wax smoke on the set. In the scene, my character had been captured and tied up by a villain named Flaggot, played by German movie star Jan Hendricks, who worked often on "Flash Gordon" to make a little extra money. Flash, Dale and Dr. Zarkoff show up and ask what happened. My line was: "Flaggot tied me up and knocked me out and took off in the spaceship!" but it didn't come out that way. Instead, I coughed and said, "Faggot knocked me up and tied me out and took off on the ship!" Everyone started laughing hysterically, and the more takes we did, the greater the laughter. We wasted an entire morning on that scene. Anthony Worsley finally ordered a new setup because it was obvious we weren't going to get a useable take. We went back to it that afternoon and put it in the can in just one or two tries.

"Flash Gordon" isn't one of my proudest achievements as an actor, but it was fun in its own way and has developed a kind of cult following among nostalgia fans over the years. At the time, I was terrified it would be a hit in the United States and ruin my chances of a Hollywood film career, but my fears proved unfounded. It had a very brief run on the Dumont Network before disappearing into television oblivion (helped, no doubt, by New York Times television critic Jack Gould, who viciously condemned the show as "a macabre and sordid half hour...wholly inexcusable reckless social behavior."). Some nostalgia video companies are offering several episodes on tape, but I don't know if any of them feature me. I have to admit, though, that I would like to see it again just for old time's sake.

It was while working on "Flash Gordon" that I had a very frightening encounter with the dreaded Berlin Wall on the German east-west border.

I had a German military driver who would pick me up and drive me to Spandau, which was very close to the border. But one day he wasn't available, so I took the subway. I couldn't read the signs very well, and suddenly found myself in East Germany by mistake, on the wrong side of the barricade. Luckily I was wearing my uniform, and after interrogating me for a couple of hours they let me back across. Nonetheless, it was a very frightening experience. The East Germans could have caused a lot of problems for me, but thankfully they were very understanding. I was more careful after that!

I hadn't really thought much about that incident until I watched the Berlin Wall come down in 1989. It was a monumental occasion that brought tears to my eyes as I thought about the people who risked their lives fleeing from Communism—and those who died in the attempt. You don't really feel the impact of something like that until you witness it first hand.

One of the most satisfying jobs I had while in Germany was helping produce shows for the refugees from East Germany. There were numerous refugee camps, and we would entertain them with German and American entertainers. Most of the refugees couldn't speak or understand English, but they absolutely loved American music.

A movie called "Night People" (1954) was being made in Berlin around this time, and several of the cast members, including Buddy Ebsen and Gregory Peck, made a few appearances at our shows during their time off. It was very generous of them, and the audiences were enthusiastic and appreciative.

The biggest show we ever produced was at an outdoor theater in Berlin called the Titania Palast. More than 12,000 refugees came to hear the big-band sounds of Stan Kenton, singer June Christy and Maurice Chevalier. Interestingly, Chevalier spoke fluent German, but refused to sing in anything but French because of the German invasion of his homeland years before.

I sang "Time After Time" during that concert and was blown away because the crowd was so appreciative. At one point during the show, everyone in the audience who had a match lit it and held it up as a sign of gratitude and love. You can't begin to imagine the beauty of almost 12,000 tiny flames against the darkness; it was one of the most moving moments I can remember.

One of the most embarrassing moments of my service in Germany was when I injured myself dancing nearly naked on a table during a large party hosted by a prominent German official. The truth is, we partied a lot back then, but this particular affair was the apex—or perhaps the na-dir—of my partying.

The room in which the party was held had a formal dining table with a huge Bavarian chandelier above it. My clothes disappeared sometime during the evening (an event no doubt alcohol-fueled) and I found myself dancing atop the table wearing nothing but a bath towel. A pretty young girl was dancing with me, but she eventually jumped to the floor, leaving me to gyrate by myself like some featured dancer on "American Bandstand." At one point I thought I was Nijinsky, leaped into the air and struck the chandelier, which broke into a million pieces. Glass went flying everywhere, my towel fell off and I ended up on the floor naked and bleeding like a stuck pig.

My fellow partiers cleaned me up as best they could and rushed me to a nearby military hospital, where I found out that despite my appear-ance the worst injury was merely a broken nose. The Army doctors sup-posedly set it, but it didn't heal properly and I ended up with a deviated septum and a honker that made me look like Jimmy Durante's younger brother. When I returned to Hollywood and started making movies again, I realized that I looked worse than I had thought (although before I was no beauty), so I went to a plastic surgeon and had my nose put back the way it was before—and perhaps a little better.

My second-most-embarrassing moment while in the military involved screen legend Elizabeth Taylor. I was on leave and decided to spend some time by myself on the island of Capri off the southern coast of Italy. I was staying at a gorgeous hotel, and had spent some time at the local plaza, which is pretty high in altitude. I had lunch there at a little restaurant and downed a bottle of red wine with my meal. Then I decided to walk down to where the boats docked, which was a bit of a jaunt.

As I left the restaurant, a roadster with two couples pulled up, and I realized it was Elizabeth Taylor and Michael Wilding with another couple. Elizabeth was apparently in Europe recuperating from recent neck surgery. We exchanged hellos and they went into the restaurant as I continued my walk.

I had met Elizabeth very briefly before entering the service while dining in the MGM commissary with my friend Judy Rose and her mother Helen, so on a whim I decided to return to the restaurant and drop by Elizabeth's table to say hello. In the restaurant I ordered some white wine to calm my nerves (it's not easy to approach a star as bright as Elizabeth Taylor). I finally went over and said, "Excuse me, Miss Taylor, you probably don't remember me." She said, "Why Kenny, of course I remember you!" That instantly put me at ease. She introduced me to the other members of her party and I was about to say something else when all the wine I had been drinking came spewing out of my mouth and nose and down the edge of the table! Fortunately, it didn't land on Elizabeth because she was on the other side of the table, but I was absolutely mortified. I had no warning at all that I was going to be sick; it just came up like a volcano. No burp, no nausea, no nothing. It was like the scene in "Animal House" where Flounder heaves all over Dean Wormer—only not as funny.

The maitre d' was there in a second. He and some other waiters helped me outside and I sat down to regain my composure. The maitre d' said things like that happened all the time because of the altitude and the type of wine, which came from a local vineyard. I went back to my hotel and I didn't see Elizabeth Taylor again until the premiere of "Raintree County" (1957). And you know what? She remembered the wine incident! She thought it was rather funny, and was very sweet about it. But I was still horribly embarrassed.

I had a great time in Germany, but I knew it wouldn't last forever. My stint with the military wound down and I suddenly found myself a civilian again. I went home to Ohio to get reacquainted with my family, then packed my bags and headed west to California for a third time, this time to stay. I had matured quite a bit in the Army. I had been provided an opportunity to hone my acting and singing skills, and I was eager to hit Hollywood and really make my mark.

My timing couldn't have been better!

Chapter 3
On Being a Juvenile Delinquent
& Other Teen Activities

After I was released from the military, I visited my mother in Springfield for a little while, then headed back to Hollywood to jump-start my abbreviated acting career. When I was inducted, I had cursed the military for yanking me off "Fearless Fagan" and crippling my chances of Hollywood stardom. But when it was over I really couldn't complain; I had made some invaluable contacts while overseas, and came home with an unexpected acting credit on my resume—"Flash Gordon." It wasn't exactly "Gone With the Wind," but it definitely gave me a leg up on all the other aspiring actors who arrived in the City of Angels every day.

I signed with my former agent, George Ingersoll, and he started submitting me for various projects. This was the early '50s and the beginning of the Teenage Renaissance in Hollywood—a terrific period for a youthful-looking actor-singer like me. Teens were in, and Hollywood was writing "open tickets," but I had to pay my dues first.

Because of my military service, I was eligible to take acting classes under the GI Bill. I looked into several schools, and finally signed up at the Hollywood School of Drama, which was run by a wonderful actor named Dan O'Herlihy. His assistants included Charles Davis, who had replaced David Wayne in the Broadway production of "Finian's Rainbow," Alan Douglas and Aaron Spelling, who went on to even greater success as a major television producer. Aaron was married at the time to actress Carolyn Jones, who used to visit our class quite often.

Sex siren Mamie Van Doren was in our class for a while. This was before she really made it big, and she was quite a character, always bubbly, enthusiastic and incredibly sexy. She definitely made going to school a lot of fun! We were mere acquaintances then, but I got to know her much better when we both worked in "Running Wild" (1955).

Money was tight during those first few years and I made do as best I could. I lived for a while in a one-room cottage, and living in the same court was a girl named Katy Styron, who was one of the greatest singing talents I've ever heard. Unfortunately, Katy was confined to a wheelchair, which really affected her career. Several nights a week Katy, John Gary, who would later have his own musical variety show on television, and I would go to the House of Ivy to perform. We would sing a few songs, and be paid with a delicious dinner. We literally sang for our supper, and were happy to do it. In between, we ate a lot of bologna and drank a lot of Pepsi because that's about all we could afford.

Shortly after I signed up, the Hollywood School of Drama acquired the Hollywood Repertoire Theater on Melrose Avenue in Hollywood, and decided to put on a production of "Finian's Rainbow"—a natural choice, considering all the Irish folk who were affiliated with the school. Charlie Davis played the leprechaun and also directed the show because he had been in both the Broadway production and the national road company. I was Charlie's understudy for the leprechaun role, but never got to play it because Charlie never missed a show! He was a workhorse, always there, always healthy. However, over the course of the run I played three other roles, which was a good educational experience.

We had classes during the day, then the students and staff would work on the production in the evening. Dan O'Herlihy was friendly with a number of very well-known actors who graciously volunteered to play extras during various performances. In one show, Marlon Brando had a walk-on as a tourist, and the audience went nuts. We never knew who might show up, a situation that made the show consistently fresh and exciting.

One of the outstanding performers in that production was Yvette Vickers, who played Susan the Silent. Yvette later achieved stardom of sorts in a handful of cult films such as "Attack of the 50-Foot Woman" (1958) and "Attack of the Giant Leeches" (1959). Far more impressive, however, was her stint as Playboy magazine's Miss July 1959. Her pictorial, photographed by big-breast aficionado Russ Meyer and titled "Beat Playmate," talks about her burgeoning acting career and the coffee house in which we all hung out. And while the pictures don't show a lot, what they do show is gorgeous. I recently ran into Yvette at a science-fiction convention in California, and she told me that particular issue of Playboy has become such a hot collector's item that she now charges $50 to autograph it. Kind of makes me wish Playgirl would give ME a call.

It was while attending the Hollywood School of Drama that I landed my first national television commercial, an ad for Vaseline Hair Tonic. Doug McClure was the guy with bright, shiny hair, and I was the guy with dull, dingy hair. It took a day to shoot, and we both received $90 for our efforts. At that time, Vaseline hair tonic sponsored three major network shows, so our little commercial played often. I had almost forgotten about it when I received a residual check for $14,000—at that time the most money I had made for a single project. I thought at first that it was a mistake, that perhaps it should have been $1,400 or maybe even $140. But I didn't say anything. I just cashed it, believing I had died and gone to heaven. That was my first big Hollywood money and it couldn't have come at a better time. I paid some bills and moved to a better apartment. My father was right—sometimes God does smile on you when you least expect it.

I met a great gal named Sandy Marx while attending the Hollywood School of Drama, and we went together for nearly two years. She was one of my first serious girlfriends while in Hollywood, and I loved her dearly. We had a lot of wonderful times together, and remained close even after we split up. Sandy later married and had children, but we're still soul mates and I try to see her whenever I'm in Hollywood. Sandy wanted to be an actress, though her career really never took off. She later worked as a television casting director, but today is completely out of the business. She chose family over Hollywood, which was probably a very wise decision.

While I was going to acting school, George Ingersoll sent me out on numerous movie auditions. The first film I made following my return from Germany was "The Human Jungle" (1954) for Allied Artists. It was the story of a typical day in a busy police station, and starred Jan Sterling, Gary Merrill and Paula Raymond. I played the head of a gang of juvenile delinquents (the first of many JD roles I would receive), and had about a week's worth of work. In one scene I get into a knock-down, drag-out fight and end up getting arrested. I never saw the whole script for that flick; just the pages containing my scenes and dialogue.

"The Human Jungle" was low-budget so it had a tight shooting schedule, about three weeks if I remember correctly, but it was a very exciting job for me because of the caliber of talent with whom I was working. Merrill was a terrific actor, and Jan Sterling, who was one of the most exciting women I've ever met, graciously took the time to work with us to improve our performances.

Jan was married to actor Paul Douglas, who used to come to the set to pick her up. I was in awe of him, but forced myself to act nonchalant when we were introduced because I didn't want to appear anything less than professional. Merrill was married to Bette Davis at the time, but she never came by the set. That was a great disappointment to many of us, because we were anxious to meet such a renowned performer. I don't recall much about Paula Raymond aside from the fact that she was stunningly attractive. Cult-movie fans probably remember her better for her roles in "The Beast From 20,000 Fathoms" (1953), "Hand of Death" (1962) (which also starred my good friend John Agar in some truly bizarre makeup) and "Blood of Dracula's Castle" (1967).

After "The Human Jungle," I left the Ingersoll Agency because they really weren't doing much for me. I didn't want to get stuck in the B-movie ghetto, so I went with the William Schuller Agency. It was the best thing I could have done at the time because they had great contacts within the industry and worked very hard on my behalf.

"The Human Jungle" was the first in a spate of movies in which I played a "troubled teen." Juvenile delinquent flicks were really big at the time—the newspapers were filled with horror stories of kids gone bad—and it turned out to be a bonanza for me.

My second JD movie was "Running Wild" (1955) for Universal. Directed by Abner Biberman, it was about a gangster (Keenan Wynn) who heads a gang of young car thieves out of his service station. William Campbell is the highway patrolman who tries to break the case, and Jan Merlin plays the leader of the youth gang. Jan was perfect casting. He looked like the ultimate Nazi, and played a lot of Nazi characters in later films. John Saxon and Chris Randall were also in our gang, along with a handful of others.

That film was great fun to make because of the cast. William Campbell was a riot to work with, as was Kathleen Case, who was also a member of our party group. I had met Kathleen through a mutual friend named Steve Rowland. The two of them were an item for a while, and attended a lot of movie functions together.

The highlight, though, was working with Mamie Van Doren. She was well on her way to achieving status as one of Hollywood's reigning sex symbols, and she proved to be one of the funniest people I have ever worked with. She could curl your hair with some of the dirtiest jokes ever to pass a woman's lips, but she was just a darling to be around. Gorgeous AND smart. She knew what she wanted, and she was doing everything she could to make it happen. Mamie and I had a little dance sequence in "Running Wild" that took forever to film. I didn't mind, though—time spent with Mamie was a little slice of paradise. But I have to admit, I danced in so many of these teen flicks over the years that I felt like a poor man's Gene Kelly.

"Running Wild" was John Saxon's first big film, and the test that would determine whether Universal would put him under contract. John is a great guy, but he was a nervous wreck during filming. He was concerned that his performance wasn't up to par, and that his acting career would be over before it started (at least he didn't have to worry about the Army dragging him away!). However, John did fine and Universal did put him under contract. Like me, his career has run hot and cold, with an interesting mixture of big films and quirky B flicks.

One other actor I had a great time with during the filming of "Running Wild" was Keenan Wynn, who played the crooked service station owner. Keenan had an outrageous sense of humor (which was often ignited by Mamie Van Doren's sensual teasing) and he would have the entire crew in stitches with just a couple of funny lines. We revered Keenan because he was one of the "senior" actors on the set. The rest of us were just punk kids, so we watched Keenan and learned. And we couldn't have had a better teacher.

Shortly after completing "Running Wild," I moved into a rental house owned by actor Pat O'Connor, who had been in films but was most famous as Humphrey Bogart's double. He really looked like Bogart, and was frequently stopped on the street by autograph seekers thrilled to meet the star of "Casablanca" (1942). Pat had also been in vaudeville and had a repertoire of dirty stories that would curl your hair. I don't think he kissed the Blarney stone, I think he was hit over the head with it! His Irish limericks and stories had the patrons of many a bar yelling for more, more, more.

Pat's long-time love was a wonderful Southern lady from Kentucky by the name of Frannie Watkins, who reminded me a lot of my mom. Frannie often worked as a housekeeper for the likes of Clifton Webb and his mother Mabel, Noel Coward, Cole Porter and Charles Laughton and Elsa Lancaster. She was also a talented cook who could whip up good old southern food and complicated gourmet dishes with equal ease. Frannie often regaled us with wild stories, but they always came out a little different when she told them. To say that Frannie was naive would be the understatement of the decade. One time she came home from Charles Laughton and Elsa Lancaster's house and related a story about another famous actress. In great confidence she said, "and do you know, she's a lesbiana!" I said, with a straight face, "She's a what?" And Frannie said, very distinctly, "She's a lesbiana." I looked at Pat and he looked at me and shook his head as if to say, "Don't say word!" We never told Frannie that the correct word was "lesbian." Truth is, I kind of like "lesbiana" better.

One day Pat, Frannie and I went shopping at Sears. In the pharmacy department, Pat whispered to me to keep Frannie occupied because he wanted to buy some K-Y Jelly and he didn't want Frannie to know. The reason was simple: Pat was a switch-hitter, and Frannie didn't have a clue. Alas, I couldn't seem to keep Frannie in one place, and she finally went looking for Pat. She found him standing in line, K-Y in hand, and innocently asked, "What's that?" Thinking quickly, Pat said, "It's K-Y Jelly. You put it on your lips when they get chapped." Not knowing any better, Frannie accepted Pat's explanation and went on with her shopping.

Another time during the Pat and Frannie days, my sister Lucille and brother-in-law Ralph Cook came to Hollywood for their first visit west. To this day, they say it was one of the most amazing vacations of their lives. On their first day in town, Pat and I had planned to drive them around Hollywood and Beverly Hills to see some of the stars' homes. Pat was working as a dialogue coach for Kirk Douglas at the time and had to pick up something at Kirk's house on the way. When we got to Beverly Hills, we pulled up to the Douglas mansion and waited for Pat while he went inside. While we were sitting there, a stretch limo arrived and Hugh O'Brian got out. Inside I could also see Dinah Shore, Hedda Hopper and some other people. I went over to the limo and said hello to Dinah, who I had met earlier, and asked if she would do me a big favor and come say hello to my sister and brother-in-law, who had just arrived from Ohio.

Not only did she come over, but she brought with her Burt Lancaster, Hugh O'Brien, Hedda Hopper and another actress who I can't remember now. Well, you can imagine my family's reaction to all of these stars standing around the car talking to them. And then, of course, out came Pat with Kirk and Ann Douglas!

After our tour we went home to get ready for a "surprise" birthday party for me that my friend Helen Thompson was hosting at her home in the Hollywood Hills. I picked up Lucille and Ralph and my date, Jackie

DeShannon, and off we went to Helen's. It was a small cocktail party and the guests included Connie Stevens and her fiancé Jim Stacey, Troy Donahue and Suzanne Pleshette, Bob and Patty Fuller, Burt Reynolds and Judy Carne, Jimmie and Colleen Rodgers, my agent Henry Wilson, and producer Maury Dexter. Lucille and Ralph were absolutely speechless.

Following the party, Helen invited Jackie and me, Maury, Lucille and Ralph for a birthday dinner at Don the Beachcomber's in Beverly Hills. After exotic drinks and many laughs, we ordered dinner. I had teriyaki steak, which was delicious—until a piece became wedged in my throat. I started to choke, but I didn't want anyone to know. However, the more I coughed, the more firmly the meat became stuck in my windpipe. Finally, in desperation, I grabbed Helen. Maury noticed that I was choking and started pounding on my back, which only drove the meat down further in my throat. The maitre d' and waiters came and everyone was yelling different things to do while everyone continued to smack me on the back. By this time, I was starting to turn blue, and I was certain I was going to die right there at my own birthday party.

Laurence Harvey was seated a couple of tables away. He jumped up, ran over and knocked everything off the table, then ordered Maury and Ralph to turn me upside down so he could grab me by the feet. He then kicked me in the back and the meat came flying out. Laurence Harvey saved my life. I didn't realize who he was until we all sat down again.

Pat and Frannie took good care of me as long as they lived. They spent their last days in Las Vegas and did finally get married. They had a wonderful life, and I was lucky to have had them in mine.

I made "Rockabilly Baby" in 1957. That was a wonderful film for me for so many reasons. Foremost, it continued my long friendship with Maury Dexter. Maury had given up acting to work behind the scenes, and "Rockabilly Baby" was one of his first projects as a producer at 20th Century-Fox. Maury told me about the movie, and I told my agency, which secured a role for me. In fact, a lot of the actors in that film were placed by my agency.

As my career started to take off, Maury took me under his wing and offered advice when I needed it the most, even though he was extremely busy himself. More importantly, he brought me into his family. I spent a lot of time with Maury and his mom, who was a delightful woman and one of the best cooks I ever met. Her name was Emma, but I affectionately called her Emmo. I ate at their house often, stuffing myself on scrumptious home-cooked meals.

As a busy bachelor, I seldom ate at home, so dinner with the Dexters was a real treat. Emmo was a constant believer and boost to me along the way.

Another great thing about "Rockabilly Baby" was that it cemented my friendship with actress Irene Ryan, who is probably best known as Granny on "The Beverly Hillbillies." I had met Irene earlier through Maury, and liked her immediately. Irene had a small role as a nosy neighbor in "Rockabilly Baby" because she was married at the time to assistant director Harold Knox. She and I spent time together on the set just sitting around and talking, and we became instant soul mates. She was a wonderful lady and a tremendous actress, and our relationship became very close.

Shortly after "Rockabilly Baby" wrapped, Irene opened a nightclub act at the Biltmore Hotel in Los Angeles. She called and insisted I be at the opening, so I invited Sandy Wirth, who was in "Rockabilly Baby" with us, to be my date.

Irene was wonderful. She wore a beautiful gown, sang her heart out (most people don't know that she had a great singing voice) and told some hilarious stories. Irene's husband Harold wasn't supposed to be there because of a filming conflict, but he managed to show up at the last minute, which really made her smile. Maury Dexter was there, too, but I was dumbfounded that few other major celebrities were in attendance. Irene knew and worked with just about everyone in Hollywood, yet only a small number showed up to applaud her, which struck me as very strange—but typically Hollywood, I suppose.

After she became wildly successful through "The Beverly Hillbillies," Irene starred in another act at the Sahara Hotel in Las Vegas, and again insisted I go. This presentation was even more grand than her earlier show and—much to my relief—a ton of celebrities turned out to offer their support, which made Irene quite happy. Those who know Irene Ryan only through "The Beverly Hillbillies" don't know what they missed—her talent far exceeded that little sit-com. And I'm not ashamed to admit that I miss her with all my heart.

Marlene Willis, who would appear with me the following year in "Attack of the Puppet People" (1958) was the star of "Rockabilly Baby." She was just a kid at the time, so she was always accompanied by her mother, who made sure she stayed out of trouble. Marlene was a darling girl and a delight to work with. And boy could she sing!

The film also starred Virginia Field and Gary Vinson (who would later appear in "McHale's Navy"). It was an amusing tale about two young teens who are driven out of town when it's revealed that their mother was a former fan dancer. It featured the music of Les Brown's band (with whom Marlene performed) so the "rockabilly" thing didn't make much sense, but no one seemed to care. It was light entertainment and did fairly well at the box office.

I had a featured role in "Rockabilly Baby," and because it was a teenage musical, I got to dance again. In fact, I danced my ass off. This time my partner was Cindy Robbins, who played my girlfriend in "I Was A Teenage Werewolf" that same year. Thankfully, I didn't have to play another juvenile delinquent. "Rockabilly Baby" was set in the Midwest, where kids were still wholesome and never got into trouble.

The most difficult aspect of that film—for me, at least—was the swimming scenes. My character is a member of the high school swim team, so we filmed a number of sequences with us in trunks and swimming caps. I'm not a particularly strong swimmer, and I almost drowned. In one scene they wanted a shot of us all swimming down the lanes, and they couldn't use an extra for me because it would be too obvious. I jumped in and started to swim, but it wasn't easy. I went under a couple of times, and they had to drag me out of the pool and let me rest because I had swallowed so much water. Maury said to me later, "Why didn't you tell us that you couldn't swim well? We could have done something!" But I wanted to be in front of the camera so badly that I was willing to risk it. And I don't regret a minute of it. In my scrapbook I have a wonderful photo of the swim team featuring me, Gary Vinson, Tony Marshall and Jimmy Murphy.

Also in 1957 I made "Dino" for Allied Artists. It was based on a "Kraft Television Theater" (or was it "The Alcoa Hour"?) drama by Reginald Rose, who adapted his teleplay for the big screen, and starred Sal Mineo as a young juvenile delinquent who is paroled after serving time for a robbery in which a man was killed. Brian Keith played Sal's social worker, and Susan Kohner was his concerned girlfriend. I had a small role as Danny, a smart-assed juvenile delinquent who hung around with the usual gang of rowdies. In one scene, we disrupt a class room in typical JD style. The guy who started it all in the film was the most typical looking juvenile delinquent you ever saw. But what an actor he was! His name was Richard Bakalyan, and Dick and I became good friends. Everyone said he looked like a young Jack Palance, and he turned out to be one of the most helpful actors I've ever worked with.

And yes, we danced. This time I wore white bucks, which seemed to get more screen time than my face. It was getting to the point where I could play these roles in my sleep, but I was just content to be working. And you couldn't beat my extremely talented co-stars.

"Dino" wasn't much of a stretch for Sal Mineo. He had played troubled, angst-filled youths in "Rebel Without A Cause" (1955) and "Crime in the Streets" (1956), as well as the television production that spawned "Dino." But Sal was a talented performer who brought a specific intensity to such roles, and it was fun watching him work. Interestingly, director Thomas Carr had to work closely with Sal because Sal had a tendency to over emote, a result of his extensive theater training. On stage you have to project to reach the audience all the way to the last row, but extreme theatrics don't work in the movies. Everything is magnified greatly on the big screen, so overacting comes across as just that. Carr managed to get Sal to tone things down without diluting the emotion, which was no small feat.

Sal was about 18 when he made "Dino." His older brother Mike was his constant shadow, always around to keep an eye on Sal and make sure he didn't get into any trouble. Mike was a hoot because he was a New Yorker right out of Central Casting, thick Bronx accent and all. He was on the set almost every day, but didn't seem particularly impressed with the Hollywood scene. His job was to make sure his younger brother be-haved himself, and that no one took advantage of him. And no one did, because Mike was a quiet but formidable presence who always had his brother's best interest at heart.

Sal and I had met very briefly during preproduction for "Rebel With-out A Cause," but we became better friends during the making of "Dino." Which is not to say we were best buddies. Sal seemed somewhat imma-ture, a bit young for his age. And he wasn't much of a partier. After a day's shooting, he might go out with us for a bite to eat, but you seldom saw him at big events with the rest of us. He was young and somewhat shy, and it just wasn't his style.

"Dino" was Susan Kohner's third film. She was very young, but ex-tremely talented. She went on to appear in a lot of major films, including the 1959 remake of "Imitation of Life" with Lana Turner and John Gavin, in which she played a black girl passing for white. Susan's father was Paul Kohner, at one time a very powerful Hollywood agent (he handled Eliza-beth Taylor, among others), so she had a wonderful entree into the indus-try. She was nominated in the Best Supporting Actress category for "Imi-tation of Life," but lost to Shelley Winters ("Diary of Anne Frank").

"Dino" was, I believe, a three-week shoot, which was pretty tight but not as bad as it could have been. Allied Artists was a small studio that churned out a lot of exploitation flicks during the '50s, and "Dino" was one of them. It was aimed at the youth audience, and delivered the goods pretty well.

In 1958, I made "Going Steady" for Columbia. This was the first and only film in which I worked with Molly Bee, who had made quite a name for herself as a singer on "The Pinkie Lee Show" and "The Tennessee Ernie Ford Show"—and who would later become my wife.

Molly and Alan Reed, Jr. (the son of the actor who voiced Fred Flintstone during the cartoon's original six-year run) were the stars of "Going Steady," along with Bill Goodwin and Irene Hervey. Susan Easter, with whom I worked in "Dino" and "Rockabilly Baby," played my girlfriend in the flick. Susan and I provided comedy relief because she was so much taller than I. We had a Mutt-and-Jeff kind of thing going that worked real well.

The story was rather simple: Molly and Alan are high school students who secretly get married. Molly's character gets pregnant, causing all sorts of confusion and problems. Although was a light comedy, they threatened to block its release in my hometown of Springfield because the blue-noses there thought it set a bad example for young people. But once you saw the movie, it quickly became apparent that it wasn't as bad as people assumed.

I received my part in "Going Steady" following an interview with Fred Sears at Columbia. At the time I had no idea that Molly was up for it, too. We were just hanging around and I told her that I was doing this film and that she would be great for the lead. She laughed like crazy and said, "I think I'm going to do it!" Because of her television success, Molly also performed the movie's title song.

Molly and I have a long history together, which I'll discuss in detail later on. We first met through a mutual friend, a make-up artist named Dodie Warren. Molly was doing a local Saturday night country show on Channel 13 called "Hometown Jamboree" from the El Monte Legion Stadium in Los Angeles, and Dodie was a make-up artist there. One evening I went with Dodie, just for something to do, and she introduced me to Molly and Molly's mother, Lou Adams. Molly and I hit it off immediately, and I kept going to the show on a regular basis with Dodie just to hang around. Molly was the sweetest thing, and absolutely adorable, which is why she was such a hit on television. TV Guide even did a photo feature on her, in which she and I are shown lounging around her house barefoot in typical Hollywood teen style. It was ridiculous, but we had fun and laughed all the way through the shoot.

Molly and I became close friends and dated quite a bit. I also met Tommy Sands around that time. He was somewhat new to the Hollywood scene, so he started hanging around with Molly and me, attending premieres and the requisite parties. Molly's mom would also have us over and cook for the whole gang. We were a tight-knit family.

Molly and I were close, but our relationship gradually evolved into more of a brother-sister thing, with me watching over her. She had led a rather sheltered life because she was a child star, so she would confide in me and I tried to help her when I could. After we cooled off, she dated Tommy Sands for a while, then a bunch of other guys. But we were always special friends. When Molly's mom was diagnosed with tuberculosis, I stayed at the house with them because someone of age had to be there to watch over things so that the insurance would be valid.

In 1958 I cut my first real record with Faro Records. Eddie L. Davis was the studio head, and he wanted me to be a big recording star. Under his guidance, I recorded a rather forgettable song called "You Are Love To Me," with backgrounds by Tony Butala, who would later head The Lettermen. The b-side was a funny song titled "Zombeeshe Blues." Eddie was really excited about the record (even though I didn't think it was that good) and wanted to hold a "world premiere" for it, something that had never been done before in the Hollywood music business. He booked the Hollywood Palladium for this event and went hog-wild. He hired a prestigious PR company to handle the party, invited every conceivable young star in Hollywood and even had a full orchestra to perform for the guests. The funniest thing, though, was the 30-foot blow-ups of me outside the Palladium, illuminated with massive klieg lights. It was one of the most outrageous parties I've ever attended—all over a tiny record that really had no business being promoted so heavily. I loved every minute of it!

My hostesses for the evening were Molly, Kathy Nolan of "The Real McCoys" and Yvonne Lime, who co-starred with Michael Landon in "I Was A Teenage Werewolf." Connie Stevens, who was and still is one of my closest friends, was also supposed to be there with me, but she had had a falling out with Eddie Davis over a recording contract dispute and he refused to let her be one of my hostesses. That broke my heart. Connie attended the premiere, but she should have been at my side because we were so close.

I arrived at the party in a Chrysler limo with Molly, Kathy and Yvonne—all looking radiant and gorgeous, of course. On top of the limo was a revolving blow-up of my record with my picture on it, and another reproduction was placed near a huge fountain in front of the Palladium. It was like a Mike Todd production—spectacular, gaudy and a huge waste of money. I ate it up.

The press and the fan magazines covered the premiere from top to bottom because every young performer in Hollywood was there, from Edd "Kookie" Byrne to Troy Donahue. When I arrived, several TV people were there, including Stan Chambers, who was a reporter for LA's largest independent station. He was interviewing Nick Adams when I pulled up, which pissed me off royally. Nick was the nemesis on my premises, and was constantly stealing my thunder. He had an uncanny knack for finding out where I would be appearing, then showing up just early enough to grab a little publicity for himself. We were all publicity hungry at the time, but it was considered poor form to upstage another performer during his or her moments of glory. Yet Nick did it all the time. Perhaps I should have been more like him.

In 1960 I made the ultimate juvenile delinquent flick, "This Rebel Breed," for Warner Brothers. It was originally titled "All God's Children," and it had one of the best scripts I ever read. Sadly, the final product didn't exactly match my expectations.

This was at the height of the JD craze, and "This Rebel Breed" had it all—hooligans of every ethnic persuasion, knife fights, dope dealing, trampy girls, frightened citizens and cops who tried to break it all up. It borrowed from every other juvenile delinquent flick through the years, and tried to push it over the top. The movie starred Mark Damon, Gerald Mohr, Rita Moreno, Jay Novello and Dyan Cannon as a black girl trying to pass for white. I was the rich kid no one liked, so I had to buy my friends. The exteriors of my house were actually Al Jolson's old home in Encino, but the interiors were a studio set.

In one big scene, my parents are away and the gang talks me into letting them come over for a party. Things get out of hand and a rumble ensues. At the time, it was one of the biggest JD fights ever filmed, larger even than "The Blackboard Jungle" (1955). Director Richard Bare (who was later staff director on "Green Acres" from 1965 to 1969), shot all the close-ups beforehand because he knew all hell was going to break loose and the set couldn't be rebuilt.

When it was time to shoot the fight scene, the stunt men and doubles were told to go for it—no holds barred—and they did! By the time Bare yelled cut, the set was a shambles. Furniture was broken, drapes torn down, the place looked like a tornado had hit it. We were genuinely impressed and horrified.

I also had a fine scene with Dyan Cannon in which we commiserate over our respective problems. She feeling sorry for herself for being black passing for white, and I being the poor little rich kid that no one can stand. It was a very intense, emotional scene, and everyone on the set applauded when we were done. Rita Moreno came up to Dyan and said, "That was delicious!" I haven't seen "This Rebel Breed" in years (I understand it was later re-released as "Three Shades of Love") but I'd really like to. It wasn't a perfect movie, but it was fun to work on and a marvelous experience.

Speaking of the lovely Rita Moreno, early in my career I played a minor role in helping her and Marlon Brando get a little "private time" together, if you get my drift. Rita was living at the Hollywood Studio Club, a boarding house of sorts for aspiring actresses. Boys were strictly forbidden, and the house had a stern den mother who made sure the rules were enforced.

One evening I took Annette Farmer, who was the comedienne in "Hit The Road," home to the Hollywood Studio Club after rehearsal, and Marlon and Rita were on the enclosed porch. Rita asked Annette and I if we would stay outside for a few minutes while she and Marlon went around to the other side for a little privacy because it was curfew time. We agreed, and chatted quietly on the porch while Rita and Marlon disappeared. A few minutes later the den mother came to the door to tell us that the girls had to be inside in ten minutes. Rita and Marlon were making so much noise necking and groping each other on the side porch that the den mother asked what was going on. Annette, thinking quickly, grabbed me and loudly kissed me to cover for Rita and Marlon, who were obviously in the throes of some serious passion. Shortly after, the two of them came back looking like teenagers who had been caught making out in the back seat of a car. Rita's hair was disheveled and Marlon looked like he had a gun in his pocket. They smiled sheepishly and thanked us, and the girls went inside.

Maury Dexter signed me for "Surf Party," which I made in 1964 for 20th Century-Fox. In fact, I was one of the first to sign on. Maury directed, and we had tons of fun. I was going with Jackie DeShannon at the time, and I pitched her strongly to Maury. They met, and Maury was impressed because Jackie had a few strong musical hits under her belt, plus she was really cute. As a result, Jackie landed the female lead opposite me, and Pat Morrow performed opposite Bobby Vinton, who played the owner of a Malibu surf shop.

Unlike the zany surf movies produced by American International Pictures, "Surf Party" tried to be an accurate representation of the California surf scene, with a lot of music thrown in. Professional surfers doubled for us during the surfing scenes, and a lot of people who were into the sport later said it was one of the best surfing movies they had ever seen.

I played a guy who wanted to be one of the top surfers, but didn't have the right stuff. My character hits a piling and breaks his shoulder while riding a wave, so I spend most of the movie in a cast. I've already admitted that I'm not the world's best swimmer, so it should come as no surprise that I did most of my "surfing" not on a surf board but on the back of a speedboat. It was better than actually climbing on a board, but not much. They didn't photograph my feet in those scenes because I was spread-legged on the back of the speedboat, trying desperately not to fall off. The cameraman and lighting guy were in front, and I was on the back with the pier in the background and the wind and spray whipping around me. I fell off about 20 times while shooting those scenes because I didn't have anything to hang on to. They put some rosin on the boat in an attempt to give me some traction, but it didn't help much. Every time the boat hit a wave, into the drink I went. But they were able to piece it together to make it look like I was actually surfing.

Repeated dunks into the Pacific ocean aside, "Surf Party" was great fun to make, and managed to spawn a couple of good songs, including "Pearly Shells," which I sang, and "Glory Wave," which Jackie sang. We did an album for 20th Century-Fox but Bobby's label, Epic, wouldn't release him to do it, so I sang Bobby's songs too. It did quite well and was even number one in Australia.

I have to laugh when looking back on the juvenile delinquents I played in many of my movies because of the sheer ludicrousness of the image. Here I was, the son of a fundamentalist preacher, playing characters that were as far from the real Kenny Miller as you could imagine. I certainly wasn't a bad kid growing up, despite what my parents might have thought from time to time. I went to church, I respected my elders (even when I was forced to lie to them), I never drank or smoked. All in all, I was the antithesis of the juvenile delinquent. Which could explain why I enjoyed playing them so much! There's something cathartic about playing a nasty character, and I found almost all of my "evil' roles great fun. They were able to behave in ways that most of us could only imagine, to really get down and dirty—and I was being paid for the privilege! Later, I would go on to play a lot of "boy next door" roles, but the juvenile delinquents will always be some of my favorites.

People often wonder whether these kinds of movies actually reflect the times in which they were made. I believe that Hollywood saw what was going on in society, and reflected it back in a sideshow mirror—much worse than it really was. After all, that's what movies do; they take reality and magnify it for entertainment value. The bad kids in most juvenile delinquent movies were really bad, but they always paid the price in the end. Some people say such movies glorify juvenile violence, but I disagree. These are morality plays, nothing more, and it's silly to read more into them than that. The gang violence we're seeing today is much, much worse than anything presented in any motion picture.

Drugs were often a big part of juvenile delinquent movies, including several that I made, and I'd be less than honest if I said I never tried drugs. The truth is, I did, especially during the late '50s and early '60s, when marijuana was considered one of society's greatest menaces. But we didn't see it as particularly harmful.

Many actors back then (and probably still today) smoked pot because it was a great way to relax after a hard day on the set, and it didn't have the lingering effects that alcohol did. If you drank, you usually felt bad the next day and it showed on your face, which wasn't good when you had to go before the camera. A hit or two helped you chill, made you sleep better— and was completely out of your system the next morning. Some saw it as the lesser of two evils. However, I knew a few people whose careers were ruined because they used too much pot. They couldn't remember their lines and developed a bad reputation, which made them persona non grata in Hollywood. Two very big stars of my acquaintance were let go by their studios because they wouldn't (or couldn't) give up dope.

Among my group of friends, the big thing was to pile into a car and smoke a couple of joints as we drove (with the air conditioner off) to

Malibu or Santa Monica. By the time we hit the beach, we were really stoned, so we'd roll around in the surf and generally goof around. Then the munchies would hit and we'd eat everything in sight. We saw it as harmless fun, and a great way to relax after a hard week of shooting. And despite what many people think, movie making is hard work.

During my "drug days," if you want to call them that, I knew a great gal named Sue, a psychologist who traveled around the world quite frequently. One time Sue returned from a Far East trip with some uniformly wrapped cigarettes that looked and smelled exactly like pot. I said, "How the hell did you get through customs with that?" She lit one up and I was positive it was marijuana. Sue explained that it was nothing but various kinds of very legal herbs, which astounded me.

That night we were going to a party at UCLA and I talked Sue into bringing several packages of her special cigarettes. After a few drinks at the party, I teased her into lighting one up, just to see what the reaction would be. It was amazing; everyone around us was going, "Oh wow! That smells like great stuff!" They asked Sue for a hit, but she was reluctant at first because she knew it wasn't real marijuana and she didn't want to get the group mad at her because she worked with them. She finally gave in, though, and everyone started puffing away, getting stoned and commenting on what great dope it was. When all the cigarettes were gone, I quietly suggested that Sue and I slip away before someone got wise to the fact that they were smoking nothing but harmless herbs. Sometimes it's ALL in the mind!

I don't smoke pot now because I gradually became allergic to it and broke out in hives whenever I would take a hit. But I don't mind if other people smoke. I favor the legalization of marijuana because prohibition just doesn't work. We've spent billions of dollars and thousands of man-hours trying to keep drugs out of this country, yet they're more popular than ever. The system is obviously ineffective and needs to be overhauled in a big way. Also, it just doesn't seem right to put someone in jail for partaking of something that's no worse than alcohol. Okay, Miller—get off the soap box!

I've also tried cocaine, but it didn't appeal to me. I tried it twice many years ago, and felt nothing. One time I was in Miami with some fellow actors and we went into an office at the swank hotel where we were staying to take a couple of snorts. One guy had a little gold spoon and we took turns using it. I had tried cocaine only once before, and that was with a straw, so the spoon thing was new to me. When it was my turn, I placed the spoon up to my nose and started to inhale— and accidentally sneezed instead, sending a cloud of white powder all over the desk! It was just like that scene in "Annie Hall" in which Woody Allen's character sneezes on a big pile of cocaine. Needless to say, I wasn't very popular at that moment.

One thing I have to be careful about is pain pills. I've had various injuries that required pain medication, and I know how easy it is to become addicted. I've been lucky, but I have several dear friends who are pain-pill junkies, and it's ruining their lives.

The one big drug I've never tried is LSD. It was popular with the Hollywood crowd back in the '60s, but I was never into it because, quite honestly, acid scares the hell out of me. A lot of people have told me they've had some really great trips on acid, but it's an unpredictable drug and I was always afraid something bad would happen. So I've left LSD alone.

I can't help but think that a person's upbringing plays a big role when it comes to excessive drug use, addiction and the misery it brings. My parents were strict disciplinarians, and went out of their way to explain why we shouldn't do drugs—and I think that was always in my subconscious. I experimented with drugs, but I knew when to stop and I would never go beyond a certain point. But most people don't have that little angel on their shoulder, and that's why they get in too deep. I was lucky.

Nancy Streebeck visits Jimmie Rodgers and me on the set of *The Little Shepherd of Kingdom Come* (20th Century Fox, 1961).

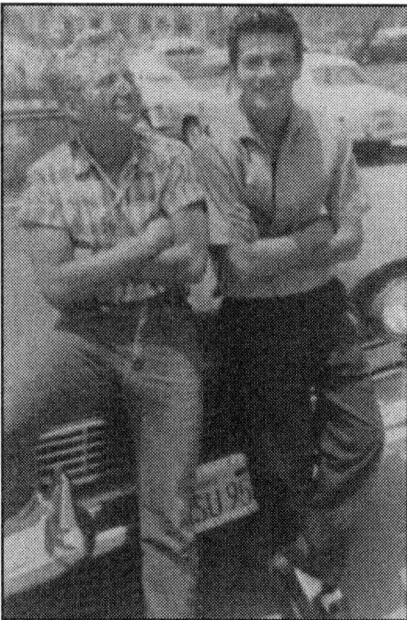

Hanging out with Tommy Sands on my new '57 Red Ford convertible.

Martha Raye embraces long time friend KM at a party in Palm Beach.

Dolly Parton & KM on the cruise ship *Eastern Star*. Dolly was guest and I was
performing on the ship.

Arriving at a gala opening at The Royal Poinciana Playhouse in Palm Beach with two
of my best friends, Danielle Basil and Allan Endries.

KM and Frankie Avalon get in a discussion about pop records at a
Hollywood party. (Photo by Jack Knox)

Connie Stevens and KM dining in Palm Beach, 1984.

KM with his miniature Schnauzer, Sassifras.

"Schmoozing" with glamorous Ann Hamilton, George's mother, in Palm Beach.

KM and George Hamilton in the dressing room we shared as guest stars of *The Palm Beach Follies*.

Ossie Davis and KM on the set of *B.L. Stryker*.

Whoopie! My name in lights—with screen legend Janet Gaynor at
The Stage Company in West Palm Beach, Florida.

KM, Jo Anne Pflug and Doug McClure on the B.L. Stryker set.

My 21st birthday party with Sandy Wirth and Molly Bee.

Colleen & Jimmie Rodgers, KM, Marianne & Mike Starkman at a Hollywood party.

Clowning on the set of B.L.
Stryker—Doug McClure
and KM.

Burt Reynolds and KM
on the set of ABC-TV's
B.L. Stryker.

KM and Connie Francis at her
opening at the Diplomat Hotel
Hollywood, Florida, 1990.

Publicity shot for 20th Century-
Fox's *Surf Party*.

Sarah O'Meara, Connie Stevens, Yvonne Lime Fedderson and KM at
a Child Help, USA benefit.

KM and movie screen legend Gloria Swanson, having lunch in Cuernavaca, Mexico.

Loni Anderson and KM at a party in Palm Beach.

Charles Nelson Reilly, Burt Reynolds, KM and Dom DeLuise backstage at the
Flatrock Playhouse, North Carolina.

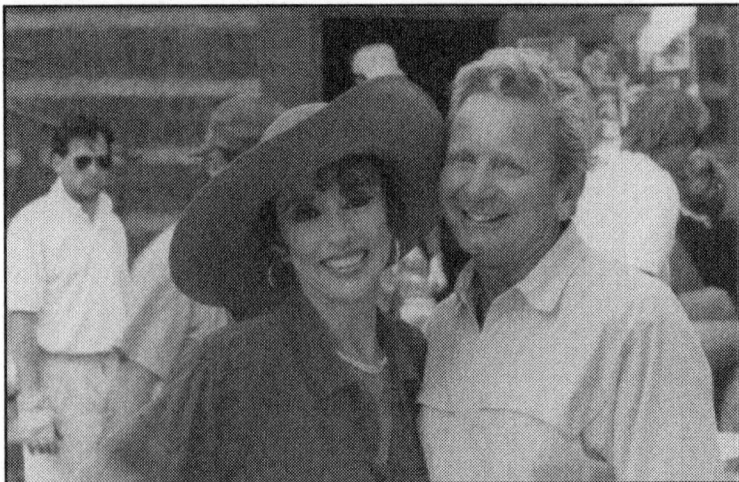

Rita Moreno and KM on the set of *B.L. Stryker*.

Muna al Hussein, former wife of King Hussein at my concert with the
U.S. Coast Guard Band in Connecticut.

KM in a publicity shot as
Kentucky in *The Buccaneer*.

Connie Stevens and me at a Hollywood
premier in the 1950s.

Valerie Harper at a party after the opening night of her play with my business
manager Ted Holden and me.

Left to right: George,
Kenny and Richard Miller
on Karr St. in Springfield,
Ohio.

Adria Firestone and I co-starred in Man of La Mancha in Florida.

KM at the Spring Break Vacation Special party in Ft. Lauderdale with Connie Stevens, Frankie Avalon, Peggy Levitz and friends.

"Carnival in Rio," 1986. I didn't know she was going to kick so high!

"Broadway Joe" Namath and KM at a PGA charity guest golf tournament in Florida.

Lynda Day George and KM backstage at a benefit show in Palm Beach.

Backstage with the dancers in A Funny Thing Happened on the Way to the Forum at the Jupiter Theater in Palm Beach.

KM and starlet Suzanne Arthur at a Hollywood opening.

Her Highness Sassifras at home by the pool in Hollywood.

KM and Maury Dexter, producer-director of Little Shepherd of Kingdom Come, Surf Party, Rockability Baby, etc.

KM, Lady Sarah Churchill, Baroness D'ogillre, Douglas Fairbanks, Jr. at a Red Cross Ball in Palm Beach.

Her Highness Sassifras getting out of our limo during the filming of The Girvia Social Club, a docu-drama for PBS, shot in Texas and Palm Beach.

KM and Burt Reynolds, Sr. at the Burt Reynolds ranch in Jupiter, Florida.

Chapter 4
Working and Playing In Hollywood

I was in the thick of Hollywood's bustling teen scene during the 1950s and '60s, thanks in part to the fan magazines that helped keep my name and face in the public eye. I worked constantly during this period, with appearances in numerous teen exploitation flicks as well as several respectable mainstream movies. And even though I wasn't a huge, huge name like Troy Donahue or Sandra Dee, I was invited to most of the important events, including movie premieres, parties and other social events. The press liked me and gave me tremendous coverage, which boosted my ego as well as my public visibility.

The motion picture industry is enormous, but it's also a collective of small, tightly knit communities made up of various crafts. Being a so-called "teen actor," I usually hung out with other young performers. There really weren't that many of us, so I saw the same faces over and over at parties, screenings and social functions. There was a friendly competition for roles, but for the most part we were all good friends who enjoyed being together.

One of the bigger names at that time, of course, was Annette Funicello. Annette first made it big as a Mouseketeer on the "Mickey Mouse Club" (and became the obsession of every red-blooded American boy as she matured and generously filled out her sweater!), and later went on to appear in a number of successful "beach party" movies with Frankie Avalon for American International Pictures. Her resume is considerably longer, but these are the things for which Annette remains best known.

The "Mickey Mouse Club" was tremendously popular during its time, and I recall meeting many of the Mouseketeers at a pre-teen Coketail publicity party. Annette was one of the show's brighter stars, but the

Mouseketeer I remember most vividly was Darlene Gillespie. She was, in my opinion, one of the most talented members of the troupe and was featured more often because of her versatility. Darlene later exited show business for a career in nursing and disappeared from the scene. But I saw her name in the press recently, and it wasn't on a happy note. Darlene and her fiancé had each been sentenced to three years' probation in Ventura, California, for stealing clothing and a food processor from a department store. The judge said the duo were professional thieves—a situation that no doubt made Walt Disney spin in his grave!

I actually met Annette through my brief affiliation with the Hollywood Christian Group, a nondenominational religious fellowship for actors that was started by Roy Rogers, Dale Evans and others. I have to admit I was rather skeptical at first because some of the members were performers who had "found religion" only after their star had taken a fatal plunge, and as a minister's son I resented that form of opportunism. Most of the members were deeply religious, but others blatantly used it as a networking forum, just as many of today's actors use Alcoholics Anonymous meetings to make contacts.

However, after several Monday night meetings at the Knickerbocker Hotel in Hollywood, I was hooked. The stars who attended were sincere, devout Christians of all denominations, and included Rhonda Fleming, Jane Russell, Jane Withers, David Brian and his wife Adrian Booth, Jimmy Dodds and many others. There was also a wonderful group of non-celebrities, such as the Eiler family, who had a ranch in the valley that looked after the needy and troubled. They hosted several wonderful fellowship barbecues for all of us.

I met Shelley Fabares through the Hollywood Christian Group. Her family was really wonderful, and Shelley and I got to be very good friends because she was one of the most unaffected girls I ever met in Hollywood. We hung around together, did some photo shoots for the fan magazines, and also participated in a religious youth organization established by actor Bob Turnbull that helped juvenile delinquents and other young people by showing them that not all actors were drug addicts and alcoholics.

Shelley was Annette's best friend, and one day she said to me, "I'm going to Annette's house. Want to come?" I said yes, and that was how I met Annette Funicello and her family. Annette and I hit it off, but didn't really date that much because she wasn't old enough for me. I took her to the Ice Capades, which was a big thing at the time, and we attended a lavish Hawaiian luau together—a huge publicity event that ended up in several motion picture magazines, including "Teen Magazine."

Annette and I were not a romance, though the fan magazines tried desperately to put us together. "Teen Hop" magazine had the two of us together on its cover with the headline "Annette's New Romance!" The photos inside suggested much more than what our relationship really was. In truth, Annette had a crush on Paul Anka, and they ended up dating for a while.

Annette and Paul officially became a couple at a special party for "American Bandstand," which I helped put together. Connie DeNave—who was one of the nation's top PR women at the time with clients like Frankie Avalon, Fabian, Dion and Andy Williams—called to tell me that Dick Clark wanted me to set up and co-host a special West Coast edition of the show. Marge and Clem Poor, who I've always been devoted to, suggested we do it at the ranch of "Rin Tin Tin" star Jim Brown. It was a perfect setting for the show, and Jim loved the idea. The guest list was very select and impressive. Annette arrived with Paul Anka and it was quite obvious they were in love. They both tried to apologize to me, and I let them know in a white hot second that it wasn't necessary because I loved them both, and thought they were a good match.

That special episode of "American Bandstand" was a lot of fun. Dick wanted to pepper the show with interviews with various west coast celebrities, one of whom was George Hamilton. George agreed, but asked that we interview him at a friend's house in Beverly Hills because it looked nicer than his own home. I arrived at the house about a half hour before the film crew—and I couldn't get George up and going. He finally got up, but said he couldn't do the interview because he didn't think he looked good. "Get yourself together!" I told him. "We'll shoot it by the pool!" We did, and it went wonderfully. George looked terrific with his trademark California tan, and the interview was a hoot.

Though there was nothing romantic between us, I adored being with Annette. She was a cuddly, loving person who was as genuinely sweet in real life as she appeared on TV and in her movies. But there were no sparks between us. We enjoyed being together, and we were in the same business, but it wouldn't have worked if we had tried to go further. Annette is currently married to a man who worships her. She's been through hell of late battling multiple sclerosis, and even though we haven't seen each other for a few years, I think of her always. She was one of the highlights of my early days in Hollywood.

Speaking of Annette, I would have loved to have been in one of the beach movies with her and Frankie Avalon, but the timing was never right. I knew Frankie and he would tell me about upcoming movies, but I never got a role. It was disappointing because there were so many characters in those films that I would have been perfect for, but I was always doing something else. To this day, people swear they saw me in an AIP beach movie, but I'll set the record straight right here—it never happened.

Annette Funicello was a very good friend, but Connie Stevens was—and still is—one of the my best and dearest friends. I met Connie during a period when we were all struggling for as much work we could get. Her agent, Byron Griffin, really wanted her to succeed, and he worked hard on her behalf. I loved Connie the minute I met her, and that love has only grown stronger over the years. She's one of the dearest things in the world to me.

Connie was in the chorus of our production of "Finian's Rainbow" at the Hollywood School of Drama. She wasn't a student there, but joined the cast because they were hiring. She received only minimum pay, but she really wanted to work on the production. We became good friends during that period, and started doing things together. One of our favorite after-hours spots was a wonderful coffee house on Fairfax Avenue owned by Terera Lea call The Garret. It became quite popular because all of us young Hollywood types used to hang out there. Terera sang and played the guitar, and she was wonderful. It was a very creative atmosphere. Connie and I and a lot of our friends would sing and perform there just for the hell of it. There were a lot of coffee houses in Hollywood, but the most famous was The Garret.

I love reminding Connie about the infamous Hamburger Incident. My brother George came out to Hollywood for a visit, and Connie decided we should have a cook out at Zuma Beach because that was one of the few public places where we could legally light a picnic fire. So we stoked up the coals, put the burgers on the grill and went off to play. We returned a few minutes later to discover that the burgers had fallen through the grill into the ashes because Connie had neglected to bring aluminum foil. (Okay, none of us thought of it, either.)

Which is not to say that Connie couldn't cook. She could—and well. Because we didn't have that much money, Connie, who's Italian through and through, made A LOT of pasta when she and I moved into a house together with her father, musician Teddy Stevens, and a friend of Connie's named Marianne Gaba. Marianne was a beauty contestant (Miss Illinois) and, later, a Playboy centerfold (Miss September 1959). She appeared in "The Adventures of Ozzie and Harriet," and had good roles in "How To Stuff A Wild Bikini" (1965) and "GI Blues" (1960) with Elvis Presley. Marianne went out on one date with Elvis (who, she says, was a very good kisser), but ended up marrying a businessman named Mike Starkman. Connie, not surprisingly, was Marianne's maid of honor when Marianne got married.

Marianne and Mike had a huge wedding in Las Vegas. Connie, Gary Clark and I were members of the wedding party. We all had suites at the Desert Inn and lived high on the hog. I remember the first morning after we arrived, Connie called Gary and me and said to come to her suite because she had ordered breakfast. When they rolled it in—a long white table cloth, silver, china and crystal—I thought we were a part of an MGM extravaganza! The wedding was sensational, and afterwards there was a sit-down dinner in the main showroom where Colonel Parker (yes, THAT Colonel Parker) and his wife joined us, and Patti Page sang for us.

One of the funniest—and most embarrassing—moments Connie and I shared together was the premiere party for "Sayonara" (1957) on the Warner Brothers back lot. Connie had just done "Young and Dangerous" (1957) and had signed to co-star with Jerry Lewis in "Rock-A-Bye Baby" (1958), and I had done a few things that made me one of the fan mags' fave, so we decided to play it up big. Tommy Sands wanted to go, too, so I fixed him up with Barbara Parkins, and we all went together. We saw the movie in a small screening room, and there was to be a party afterward. The whole Warner's back lot had been transformed into Chinatown for the occasion.

Connie wore a small stole of white rabbit, which she had rented just for the premiere. She looked darling, but the screening room was hotter than hell, and that, combined with our body heat, caused the fur to shed. When the lights went up, Sara Miles, who had been sitting in front of us, looked at us and started laughing hysterically because there was fur all over my tuxedo where I had put my arm around Connie. I took off my jacket and tried to shake it out, then I went to the men's room, where a guy with a brush tried to clean me up. But it was a lost cause. Nothing short of dry cleaning was going to fix the problem. We finally said to hell with it and went out to face the press looking as if a bunny had exploded on my jacket. No one mentioned the fur, however, and we managed to get a lot of good media coverage because Connie was so darling and had just signed with Paramount.

When Connie and I moved in together (more for financial reasons than anything else), the fan magazines had a field day. I remember one story titled "Too Poor to Marry—But I Lived With Connie Anyway!" We dated for a long time, but our relationship gradually turned into a friendly family kind of thing. Eventually Connie started dating Gary Clark and others.

Connie and I really enjoyed performing together, and as a lark she created a group called Connie Stevens and the Apollos, with me, Tony Butala, Gary Clark and Jim Blaine. I could sing lead, but I couldn't do harmony for shit. We played a number of gigs, though, including a Catholic school benefit in San Francisco. We looked better than we sounded (though Connie always had a great voice), but it was fun.

While we were in San Francisco, the father at the Catholic rectory where we stayed asked us where we wanted to go after the show, and we all said Finochio's, an outrageous drag club that was all the rage at the time. We were looking for something new and different, and that certainly fit the bill; Finochio's defined avant-garde. We watched the review of female impersonators, then went backstage to meet the guys (gals?) who worked there. Connie had a wonderful time, trying on all their clothes and discussing fashion tips. That was my first drag show, and it was an interesting experience to say the least. Everyone who worked there was wonderful because they all wanted to be movie stars. The spectacle was amazing, and they all adored Connie.

In the early '60s, Connie, Anne Jeffreys and I were cast in a Broadway show titled "Take Me Along." The producers set up auditions at the Chateau Marmot in Hollywood, and the three of us were accepted. I immediately signed up with voice coach Harriet Lee because I knew we would be doing eight shows or more a week, and my voice just wasn't that strong. But shortly after, producer David Merrick fired the show's first director and brought in George Roy Hill, who immediately changed all the leads. So Connie, Anne and I were out just as quickly as we were in. Ironically, I was replaced by Robert Morse, who became somewhat of a Broadway legend with shows that included "How to Succeed in Business Without Really Trying."

Connie and I never appeared in a movie together, but we were always very supportive of each other's success. Connie's first big movie for Paramount was "Rock-a-Bye Baby," which starred Jerry Lewis. Jerry was not the easiest person to work with at that time, but the studio made up for the aggravation by sending Connie to New York for a whirlwind promotional tour. I was in New York at the same time doing fan magazine interviews, so we were able to pal around together.

Connie was staying at the Essex House, and was given a limousine for her personal use. So we went down to Fifth Avenue and had the limo follow us as we went in and out of some of the ritziest stores on earth. It was such a Hollywood thing to do, and we had a blast. We were two young actors playing at the real thing. Most people had no idea who we were, but several people recognized us from this or that, and asked for our autographs, which made both of us feel important. Connie was on an expense account, so she bought gifts for friends and family and put them in the limo as we walked down the street.

That afternoon, we went to Brooklyn to see Connie's mother and stepfather. On the way, she stopped by a perfume store and presented me with a silver bottle of men's cologne called Zizanie. It was really expensive—about $40 for a tiny bottle. That was something I'll always remember. Connie's generosity is one of her most endearing attributes. For years after, I would get another holiday bottle of Zizanie from her as a reminder of our New York adventure. That's why I've always loved her.

Burt Reynolds was another friend during those early days in Hollywood. I got to know Burt well at a party to welcome Connie Francis to Hollywood. This was a couple of years before "Where The Boys Are" (1960) was released, and the studio had high hopes for her. The party was arranged by public relations honchess Connie DeNave, who handled Connie Francis at the time, and was held at the Crescendo on the Sunset Strip. I went with Kathy Nolan of "The Real McCoys," and every young performer was there. It was definitely the event to see and be seen.

Burt crashed the party with Robert Fuller. I had met Burt a couple of times in the past, but we never really talked much. He seldom went to events like this because he felt it didn't fit his macho image. However, this particular party was just too important to pass up if you were an aspiring young actor.

After the party, Marcia Rogers and Beverly Noga (whose mother Helen managed Johnny Mathis) decided to invite a few people back to Beverly's house for a quiet get-together. Burt was attracted to Marcia, and he and Robert Fuller begged me to get them invited. I talked to Marcia and Beverly and they agreed. Also invited were George Chakiris, Nan Morris and Fabian.

Burt had developed a reputation in Hollywood as a hot-head with a chip on his shoulder, and he didn't do much to change that. He got in fights and was well-known as a trouble-maker. He also refused to play the Hollywood publicity game. He once told me that he turned down opportunities to appear in the fan magazines because all they showed were young performers sitting around barefoot eating potato chips. He was partly right, but that was what you had to do to keep your face and name in the public eye. It WAS goofy, but most of us understood it was just part of the biz.

Burt and Robert set the tone for the party the moment they arrived. They pulled up just as Fabian was walking toward the front door, so they grabbed him, threw him in the trunk and took off down the road! They drove about a block, turned around and came back. It was a pretty funny stunt, but it really upset Beverly and Marcia, who were horrified and ready to call the police.

Thankfully, everything turned out fine. We all had a few drinks, the girls made pasta and we sat around talking well into the night. We discussed our work a little bit, but mostly we talked about our families and our lives. Burt got to know Marcia better, and their friendship quickly blossomed into a long-term romance. But more importantly, Burt realized we weren't just a bunch of publicity-hungry phonies. He got to know us as real people—and we got to witness the quiet, introspective side of him that the press and fans seldom saw. It was a revelation for everyone, and Burt and I became very good friends as a result of that evening.

Burt and I, as it turned out, had more in common than we ever thought. We came from similar, middle-class backgrounds—and we both had strict parents. My father was a minister, and Burt's dad was a police chief in Florida. His parents were always wonderful to me, and they became my surrogate family when my own parents passed away. Years later, when I returned from Europe sick as a dog following an accident in Frankfurt, Germany, Burt and his parents insisted that I come to Florida, put me up and took care of me until I was well again.

In Hollywood, I was sort of the "social secretary" of our group of friends, arranging parties and notifying people of what was going on. We were a bit spoiled because we got invited to everything. Of course, we were invited only because we were "movie stars" and our hosts knew our attendance would result in coverage in the various magazines and newspapers, but we didn't mind. It was a giddy ride and something many of us felt we were entitled to. All in all, it was harmless and a great ego boost.

The whole fan/publicity thing was a big part of my life from the late '50s to the late '60s. I was a popular "newcomer" to the Hollywood scene, and in 1958 "TV Star Parade" magazine asked me to do a regular column for them called "The Young Set." Because of that column and my growing popularity among young movie fans, my agents later decided I should have a nightclub act. I got together with a very talented writer/arranger named Al Anthony, a terrific musician who wrote some special material for me and basically put the whole thing together.

Al was a true bon vivant with a white Cadillac convertible for daytime driving and a black Caddie convertible for night trips, plus a Beverly Hills home right out of the pages of "Town and Country." He was also one hell of a party host. His typical guest list looked like a Who's Who in Movies and TV, and he always made sure to invite a lot of celebrities who sang. It was great fun just to sit and listen to Sue Raney, Connie Stevens, Dorothy Provine, Rona Barrett doing her impersonation of Ethel Merman, Jack Jones, Jack Jones and more Jack Jones. Once Jack got singing, you needed a crowbar to shut him up!

Everyone loved singing with Al because he was a perfect accompanist. At one party I introduced Suzanne Pleshette. We all coaxed her to sing—including her date, Troy Donahue—and she just wowed the place. Martha Raye, one of my favorite entertainers in the world, would always show up at Al's parties a bit late. After a few cocktails, Martha would become a little melancholy and belt out some incredibly passionate torch songs.

Al wrote several pieces of special material for my first night club act, including a humorous little ditty titled "The Name Dropper," which mentioned just about every young actor in Hollywood. It was a smash. I also sang a song titled "Strange Love," written by a young actor named Chad Everett. I was really impressed with the tune and was happy to incorporate it into my show. Chad was very excited when he heard me sing it for the first time. Afterward he said to me, "I'll keep writing them and you keep singing them, and we'll both be famous!" However, that was the only song Chad ever gave me. His acting career really took off shortly after and he had to put his music on the back burner.

I premiered my act on September 13, 1960, at a tiny club in Beverly Hills called Marshall Edson's Ye Little Club, which more than lived up to its name. But the place had developed a reputation because a lot of name stars often broke in their acts there, so my agent got me a two-week booking. On opening night, the place was packed. I mean wall-to-wall people. Everyone who was anyone was there. In fact, Army Archerd noted in "Daily Variety" that if a bomb had gone off that evening, Hollywood would have had to shut down. There were so many people in attendance that I couldn't reach the stage, so Burt, Doug McClure, Chad Everett and James Franciscus literally lifted me over their heads and carried me to the stage. To make things even more interesting, the air conditioner went on the fritz, so the place was hotter than Hades. But the show went on, and came off without a hitch.

The club didn't have a dressing room, so I was forced to change my clothes for the second show in the kitchen. While I was changing, I heard a ruckus outside, but I wasn't able to see anything. Evidently some yahoo standing beside Burt, Marcia Rogers and Georgianna Montalban (Ricardo Montalban, her husband, was absent because he had an early call the next morning) was using very foul language and refused to stop when Burt asked him to. The guy kept swearing so Burt hauled off and cold-cocked him. Burt hit the guy so hard that the poor sap knocked over three tables, at which point the bouncers grabbed the troublemaker and hustled him outside. It was later reported in the press that the fight occurred during my act, but that isn't true.

Burt joined me in the kitchen and apologized profusely. He said he didn't mean to ruin everything, and was sorry for losing his temper—even though he had every right to. Burt had tremendous respect for the people he was with, especially the ladies, but you could push him only so far. I reassured him that everything was fine (and truth be known, the incident only garnered me more publicity, which was great) but he insisted on following me after the show to make sure I got home because he was worried that the jerk he decked might be waiting somewhere outside to get even with us. That's the kind of friend he was.

Burt and I had some outrageous times together, especially during the early days. We partied our asses off and it's a wonder we didn't end up in jail. Or the hospital.

I remember one party for Connie DeNave at the home of agent John Vestal, who handled a lot of the people in our inner circle. John and his family lived on the second story of a house, and you had to go up a lot of wooden steps to get to his place. There were a lot of young players there, including Robert Fuller, Doug McClure and others. We were all drinking a concoction we called apple sauce, which was made with shaved ice, vodka, orange juice and brandy. It had a subtle kick, and you could get plastered on it pretty quick.

Sometime during the party, Burt and Robert Fuller, who were both former stuntmen, said they could toss me down the stairs without me getting hurt. (Yes, it was stupid. But we were drunk.) When I started to protest, they picked me up and swung me back and forth. Neither intended to let me go, but suddenly I was flying through the air. I landed on my ass near the bottom of the stairs. I couldn't move at first, and they thought I had broken my back. Luckily, all I had were a few bruises, which is amazing when I think back on it. I was sore, but relatively unbroken. The only thing I can think of is that the alcohol saved my life. If I hadn't been plastered, I might have tensed up more when I hit the ground and suffered some serious damage. Burt never threw me down the stairs again!

Kathy Nolan was another good pal and constant companion, and we had some good times together. One of our funniest adventures was an evening out with Jack Jones and Will Hutchins, who was doing "Sugarfoot" at the time. Kathy and I had been to a party celebrating the wedding of singers Randy Sparks and Jackie Miller at Dimitri Tiomkin's house, and that's where we picked up Jack and Will. We were hungry, so we stopped by a restaurant called The Beachcomber for something to eat. We ordered some wonderful and very potent exotic drinks and a bunch of hors d'oeuvres and dipping sauces, and proceeded to eat, drink and have a great time.

Well into the evening, Kathy noticed that the president of Sylvania, which was one of biggest sponsors of Kathy's show, "The Real McCoys," was sitting across the room with his wife and kids. He was in town for a big Sylvania convention, and just happened to be there the same time we were. Kathy panicked and begged us to be on our best behavior when they came over to say hello so she'd look good and not cast a negative shadow on the series. Because we loved her, we were all little angels when the guy came over, smiling and shmoozing like pros.

We went home shortly after and crashed at Kathy's place. When we woke up the next morning, we noticed for the first time that our clothes— including Kathy's gown—were splattered with all sorts of dipping sauces. We were a drunken mess and looked like we had slept on the condiment counter at a Chinese restaurant. Kathy started to freak out, terrified at what the president of Sylvania must have thought. She was certain the show would be canceled and she would be held responsible. Of course, nothing happened, but Kathy was a wreck for a couple of days. The moral, if there is one, is don't get drunk and order messy finger food when there's a chance you'll run into your boss.

I later took Kathy to the premiere of one of my favorite films in which I appeared, "The Buccaneer" (1958). She looked gorgeous as she finished getting dressed in the limousine on the way to the Wiltern Theater. The formal dinner that followed the premiere was at Perino's, one of LA's most prestigious restaurants. We got to sit at the table with my director, Anthony Quinn, his wife Katherine DeMille, Charlton and Lydia Heston, Cecil B. DeMille and Henry Wilcoxon. Kathy was quite impressed.

One of the nicest things Kathy ever did was invite me to have dinner with her, Linda Darnell and Linda's husband, Merle Robertson. Linda was more beautiful than I ever imagined, and we got to chat intimately while Kathy and Merle talked business. We had after-dinner drinks in front of the restaurant's roaring fireplace, and Linda gave me tremendous encouragement over the course of that short evening. It haunts me when I think of that roaring fireplace and then Linda's horrible death as she tried to save her former secretary's teenage daughter in a raging fire.

By the way, my fun-loving, hardworking Kathy became Kathleen Nolan, the first woman president of the Screen Actors Guild!

Rock Hudson—real name Roy Fitzgerald—lived next door to me on Fredonia Drive in the Valley, a few minutes from Universal Studios. Our houses shared a 110-step stairway and a patio, and you could practically jump from one to the other. Rock was staying with his publicist and the guy's wife at the time, having just become a contract player at Universal.

Rock was never a particularly sociable person. He was friendly, but he didn't attend parties and barbecues with the rest of us, preferring instead to concentrate on his work. I thought at first that he was just egotistical and stuck on himself, but the better I got to know him, the more I came to realize that he was insecure and in awe of the fact that he actually had a contract with Universal. He worked extremely hard, attending acting classes and taking voice lessons. Our bedrooms were fairly close together, and I could hear him doing his diction exercises every goddamn evening. It about drove me crazy. He was an obsessed workaholic. He had been given a tremendous opportunity and he didn't want to mess it up.

Every now and then Rock would come over and ask me to go over lines with him, which was beneficial for both of us. This was around the time I got my nose fixed, so for a while I was doing lines sounding like Elmer Fudd. It made it hard to concentrate because both of us kept cracking up. It isn't easy being dramatic with a nose full of cotton!

Rock was one of the most caring people I had ever known. Kay and Otto Boe, from whom I was renting, had a Siamese cat that often left "gifts" for us, such as dead birds and other small animals. One day Rock came out of the house and stepped on a freshly killed bird. He was really pissed off, and they could probably hear his ranting all over Hollywood Hills. I'm sure he would have flung the cat down the stairs had he been able to catch it. He loved animals and just couldn't understand why one living thing would kill another. The whole thing revolted him; he thought it was absolutely terrible.

It's now common knowledge that Rock Hudson was gay, but it was a closely kept secret back then. There was nothing "swishy" about Rock; he was as macho as the next guy. It was important that he maintain that image because in the 1950s, even a rumor of homosexuality could end an actor's career. These days, coming out as gay is no big deal in Hollywood. In fact, for many it's actually a smart career move. But back then, magazines like "Confidential" lived to out supposedly gay actors, and the studios spent big money and effort assuring the public that their biggest stars were straight— even the ones who weren't. Rock may have been gay, but he understood the necessity of keeping it a secret, and succeeded very well. He even married Phyllis Gates to throw off anyone who might suspect otherwise.

The only time Rock let his guard down even somewhat in the early days was when the couple he stayed with would go out of town for the weekend. It was then that I noticed the steady stream of very good-looking guys who were constantly dropping by Rock's place. Naive as I was, I thought at first that they were fellow actors who were helping Rock with his lines. But later, I wondered how could they go over lines with the lights off?

It dawned on me that Rock was probably gay, or at least bisexual, but it really didn't matter. He was a very nice guy and a very talented actor, and what he did in privacy was his own business. An individual's sexual preference has never been an issue with me. What's most important is what they're like as a person. And Rock Hudson was genuinely kind and caring. That's how I remember him.

In 1960, I participated in a USO show for American troops in the Far East. Veteran actor Charlie Watts was the MC and sort of the manager of our troupe. We were sent over as an addition to the Bob Hope Christmas show to play places that Bob's troupe didn't have time to visit. It was a very talented and lively group that included Irish McCalla (Sheena, Queen of the Jungle herself!); Robert Mitchum's sister Carol, who sang wonderfully and played cocktail drums; dancer Marian Collier, who was also a regular on "Mr. Novak;" impressionist Elizabeth Talbot Martin, and accordionist Donna Reaser.

We flew by commercial jet from Los Angeles to Honolulu, where we joined Johnny Grant's Christmas Tour. From there we flew by military plane to Tokyo, touching down in such glamorous spots as Guam and several obscure islands in the Pacific. The flight took 32 hours.

We were in Tokyo for one night with Bob Hope's troupe, and then we took off for our own destinations. We ended up on Christmas Eve at Clark Air Force Base in Manila. Everything was closed, including the PX, but we decided to get into the Christmas spirit regardless. We cut down a small tree outside the cottages where we were staying and the girls decorated it with jewelry, knickknacks and their underwear. It was quite a unique tree! Thankfully, there were refreshments and champagne in our cottages, and we celebrated by doing a show just for ourselves.

Christmas Day we went back to entertaining the troops, and on the following day we were bused to a small village outside Manila. While walking through the town, we saw a huge banner connected to the local movie house. Irish McCalla said, "Kenny, that looks just like you!" As we got closer, we realized that it was an advertisement for "Battle Flame," a movie I had done a little while before. In that area of the Philippines, they are very partial to blonds because there aren't that many of us, so the movie distributor blew up a color photo of me life-size to publicize the film. I was suddenly a big star in the Philippines—all because of my blond hair.

Another destination during the tour was Taiwan. The night we arrived on the island I was coming down with the flu. Fortunately, we were billeted in the beautiful and only Grand Hotel there. During dinner, it was suggested by our military liaison that I should go to bed and they would send up a local massage therapist—the kind who walk on your back in their bare feet. I was game for anything, as we had a lot of shows left to do. So I went to my room, got in bed and waited. I expected a beautiful young, Nancy Kwan lookalike to come to my door any minute. What arrived was a 70-year-old, shriveled native woman, which shattered my fantasies. However, she gave me a wonderful massage and got rid of my cold completely.

At that time, Taiwan was the base for Chiang Kai-Shek, and they were expecting war to break out with mainland China at any instant. The place was littered with foxholes filled with Taiwanese soldiers, all facing mainland China. A few days after my massage, we went by bus to entertain some troops stationed outside Taipei. We did a great show and started back. After an hour or so, I really had to take a whiz. I held it and held it, trying to explain to the driver, who spoke little English, that I wanted him to stop.

He kept saying, "No! No! No!" but I didn't know why. Irish McCalla came up and said that she had to pee, too. The driver finally stopped after everyone on the bus yelled at him. He kept saying, "No! No! No!" We ignored him, and I went down the side of a hill and started to pee into the darkness. Oriental screams greeted me immediately, but I couldn't stop peeing. All of a sudden, out of the darkness, came four Taiwanese soldiers with their rifles in front of them—madder than hell. Fortunately, the driver was there in a New York second and tried to explain through all the yelling and screaming. Unknown to me, I had peed on four soldiers in their foxhole. They were going to knock me silly with their rifle butts but stopped short when Irish rose out of the darkness like a great white goddess. They became like stone in her presence. In fact, everywhere we went in the Far East, people would follow Irish around in awe, looking up at her because she was so beautiful and so tall. They had never seen anything like her.

One of the highlights of the trip was having lunch with Madam Chiang Kai-Shek. She asked us to do a show for a group of Taiwanese soldiers, and we readily agreed. But it was a very bizarre experience because in the Far East, they clap only if they DON'T like you. If they're having a good time, you don't hear a peep. We knew the troops didn't speak English, so we cut out all the comedy and skits and just gave them the music. And there wasn't a sound through the entire performance. Not a laugh, not a clap—nothing. They sat there like statues, which we knew was a good sign, though it was a little hard to get used to. At the end of the show, the entire audience of five hundred or more soldiers stood up in unison and bowed. It was then that we knew we had really entertained them, and that they were appreciative of our efforts. Thank God American audiences aren't like that, though. Entertainers crave applause. That's what we do it for.

Chapter 5
I Was Friends With a Teenage Werewolf

Of all the teen movies I made in the 1950s and '60s, very few have experienced the continual popularity of "I Was A Teenage Werewolf" (1957). It's a movie that nearly everyone is familiar with, and any mention of its title invariably results in a wide grin of recognition. Countless people have come up to me over the years and told me that "Teenage Werewolf" is one of their favorite guilty pleasures, an admission that always makes me laugh.

At the time, "I Was A Teenage Werewolf" was just another small picture to add to my burgeoning resume. The late '50s was one of the most productive periods in my acting career, and that film was little more than a two-week gig that I hoped would lead to bigger and better things. In retrospect, I have to admit that I never thought it would amount to much, and I certainly never thought it would achieve the astounding cult status it has today.

"I Was A Teenage Werewolf" was, for various reasons, a movie that I disliked greatly at first, but later grew to love (with a couple of reservations).

I became involved with the project through the efforts of my agent, a wonderful, ambitious woman named Polly Jacobson, who was with the William Schuller Agency. When Polly got wind that producer Herman Cohen was going to make "I Was A Teenage Werewolf," she immediately recommended me. I have to admit, however, that in the beginning I wasn't sure I wanted to be in the film because everyone in the industry was making fun of the title. Teenage werewolf? What the hell was that all about?

When Polly and I dropped by Herman's office to discuss the film, he informed us that they were fine-tuning the script and he wanted to wait until it was finalized before deciding which part I would play. He then asked me to do a cold read for him, which I did. It was awkward and difficult (as unrehearsed auditions usually are) but Herman apparently liked what he saw. Polly kept after him on my behalf, and Herman eventually offered me the role of Vic, one of the male leads. Vic was an integral part of the group that Michael Landon's lead character, Tony, hung around with, and it meant I would be involved in some fun—and key—scenes.

For those of you who have never seen "I Was A Teenage Werewolf," it's a modern take on the traditional werewolf myth. Only instead of a full moon, it's hypnosis that transforms Tony into a rampaging monster in a letterman jacket.

Tony is a hot-headed kid who keeps getting into trouble because he can't control his violent temper. His girlfriend Arlene (Yvonne Lime) is worried about him, her parents don't like him, his friends are afraid of him and the cops say he's one fight away from reform school. At a Halloween party with friends, Tony explodes after a practical joke and beats the hell out of Vic, much to the horror of all of his friends.

Realizing that he needs help, Tony finally visits Dr. Alfred Brandon (Whit Bissell), a psychiatrist who supposedly is experimenting with hypnosis as a way of controlling violent behavior. However, Dr. Brandon is more than a little mad—he's actually using hypnosis and a special serum to regress the human race back to its primitive past, to "unleash the savage instincts that lie within." Oddly, the good doctor believes that such regression will somehow save the human race from what he perceives as its imminent extinction.

Dr. Brandon finds the perfect guinea pig in the anger-filled Tony, and he begins regressing the boy on a regular basis, taking him further and further back. Shortly after the sessions begin, Tony has a run-in with a friend, who later is viciously mauled to death while walking home through some woods.

The police are baffled by the boy's death, but not the police station janitor, who conveniently is from the Carpathian Mountains (home, apparently, to many a monster). After seeing photos of the dead teen, the janitor immediately deduces that it was the work of a werewolf!

Meanwhile, Dr. Brandon is continuing his demented experiment on Tony, who senses something is wrong but can't quite put his finger on it.

Tony's teachers, however, have noticed a marked improvement in his de-meanor, and Tony is told by the principal that he'll get a coveted college recommendation after all.

As Tony is leaving school, he stops by the gymnasium to watch a pretty girl named Theresa (Dawn Richard) practice on the parallel bars. A class bell rings right next to Tony's head, causing him to transform into a werewolf. He chases Theresa through the gymnasium and kills her as the principal and others watch in horror. Cornered, Tony the werewolf turns tail and runs away, leaving his friends to wonder what the hell is going on.

Tony, still a werewolf, hides in some nearby woods while the police put together a posse. They search the woods, but Tony eludes them and later transforms back into a hot-headed teen. He makes his way into town and finally ends up at Dr. Brandon's office. Brandon decides it's times to photograph his bizarre experiment and sets up a movie camera while trans-forming Tony into a werewolf yet again. But he fails to restrain the boy and Tony attacks the doctor and his assistant, killing them both. Just then, the police arrive and fill Tony full of lead. In death, he transforms back into human form. Concludes the philosophical cop who did the shoot-ing: "It's not for man to interfere in the ways of God."

"I Was A Teenage Werewolf" was a fun but grueling shoot and I was there for almost every moment of it. We were scheduled for 11 shooting days, but came in at 10, primarily because of the stellar cast and crew. We were all very enthusiastic despite the film's low budget (which was ru-mored to be only $125,000) and we worked long, hard hours to bring the film in on schedule.

A great deal of the film's success must be attributed to director Gene Fowler, Jr., who was a genuine pleasure to work with. He was what we call an "actor's director," but he also had a wonderful eye for the technical side of movies. Gene's background was in film editing, and that's how he ap-proached filmmaking. He saw a movie as a connected series of scenes, and edited it in his head as he went along. As a result, nearly all of the scenes in "Teenage Werewolf" were staged quickly and efficiently. There was a mini-mum of retakes and shooting progressed at a pretty good pace. Gene was perfect for a project like this because he knew how to make optimum use of limited time and money. To quote the old cliche, he "shot the budget."

We all became close on the set of "Teenage Werewolf" because, with a few exceptions, we were always there, waiting to be called. We never knew when a retake might be required, or if weather would cause a change in the shooting schedule, so we just hung around until needed. Despite its apparent glamour, movie-making is often a pretty boring process, but the time you spend waiting on a set can bloom into some long-lasting friendships. And that's the way it was with our cast.

It's common knowledge that "Teenage Werewolf" was Michael Landon's first movie. I think he had done a little live television before that, but he was relatively new to Hollywood and quite eager to make a good impression, even if his first film was a low-budget teenage horror flick. I once heard a rumor that Michael won the role of Tony by biting Herman Cohen on the leg. I doubt if that's true (though it does make a good story), but it illustrates the kind of unbridled enthusiasm Michael brought to the project.

And the critics noticed. While many dismissed "Teenage Werewolf" as little more than youth-oriented fluff, the majority made special mention of the explosive angst and intensity Michael brought to the role of Tony. Two years later, Michael was cast as Little Joe on "Bonanza," and worked steadily in television until his untimely death from cancer in 1991 at age 54.

Michael and I didn't see a lot of each other after "Teenage Werewolf," which is something I've always regretted. Michael wasn't into the Hollywood party scene, preferring to spend his time at home with his family, so we seldom socialized. For example, I recall that Michael's then wife, Dodi, came with gossip columnist Rona Barrett to the opening of my night club act at Ye Little Club in Beverly Hills. Nearly all of Hollywood's young stars were there, except for Michael; he was a no-show. Dodie told me he sent his best, but he had an early call. He wasn't being rude or snobby; he just wasn't part of that scene. Nonetheless, working with him was a genuine pleasure and something I'll always remember with fond memories.

Filming "Teenage Werewolf" was difficult on all of us, but it was especially demanding for Michael because of the werewolf makeup he had to wear. Most people assume it was a rubber mask that could be put on or taken off as needed, but in truth it was a series of uncomfortable facial prosthetics that took make-up designer Philip Scheer as long as two hours to apply and about 30 minutes to remove—a situation that usually required Michael to be on the set long before anyone else.

Michael was one of the most outgoing people I've ever worked with and a real trouper when it came to being the film's requisite teenage werewolf. However, I did see his temper flare on a couple of occasions when, after already being in and out of makeup for a day's shooting, he was told to don the fur once again for some pick-up scenes. Of course, this meant that the rest of the cast and crew had to wait around while Michael was made up. During those down periods we played cards and talked about the glitz and glamour of Hollywood. Then we would watch a now unrecognizable Michael Landon drool and growl as he worked himself into a full werewolf frenzy.

My biggest scene was the party sequence, in which Tony, Vic and the gang get together at a local hangout for some Halloween fun. Most people remember it as the scene in which Michael knocks the crap out of me after I blow a horn in his ear. It's an intense moment that clearly illustrates Tony's deep-seated rage, but despite the pathos, I had a hard time keeping a straight face as we went through it.

The problem was Michael's ears, which at the time were almost as big as Clark Gable's (he later had them fixed). Because they stuck out like car doors, Philip Scheer spent a lot of time and effort trying to pin Michael's ears against his head with spirit gum and other gunk. All of this was hidden from the camera but plain as day to anyone who was standing behind him. After Michael punched me and sent me flying into the couch, he turned his back to me—and all I could see were the wads of stuff behind his ears. The image stuck me as very funny, and it was all I could do to keep a straight face until Gene Fowler finally yelled "Cut!"

Another thing I vividly remember about the party scene was being clobbered on the chin by Michael during the very first take of our fight. Tony Marshall, who played Jimmy in the movie, was also a stunt man and he choreographed the fight scene between Michael and me. Michael was so much into character that he got carried away and really clobbered me.. The blow sent me reeling, and I had to sit down for a bit while ice was applied to my throbbing jaw. Michael was beside himself, apologizing over and over. He felt terrible, even though the whole incident was an accident. I reassured him that I was okay, and after a brief moment of recovery I started laughing hysterically because one of his ears had come loose from the goop holding them, and boy did he look silly—one ear pinned back and one ear sticking out. It took a few minutes before I could compose myself and continue with the scene. Michael was much more careful with his punches after that, and we managed to get through the whole thing without further injury to either of us.

It was also during the party sequence that a practical joke was played on my character Vic—and on me. Vic is told to check something in a closet, and when he does, a bucket of water is dumped on his head. During rehearsals the bucket was filled with confetti, and I thought confetti would also be used during actual filming. But it wasn't—the confetti was replaced by water. Very cold water. During the first take, I was so surprised (and angry as hell) at being doused that I turned around and cussed a blue streak, making the scene unusable. So the next time you watch the movie, remember that I'm not acting during that sequence. I really was pissed off, and it shows.

Of all the talented people involved in "Teenage Werewolf," Michael Landon probably received the greatest celebrity over the course of his career. But everyone was terrific in their own way, and many of us managed to go on to far greater things in front of the camera and off.

Yvonne Lime, for example, later formed an organization called Child Help USA with her good friend Sarah Buchner O'Meara, who was also an actress. They visited Korea, Vietnam and other locations in an effort to bring home orphans fathered by American military personnel.

I had known Yvonne long before we appeared together in "Teenage Werewolf." In fact, we dated for a while. She was the typical, sweet, girl-next-door from Burbank, and "Teenage Werewolf" was just one of her many teen-movie credits. With her youthful looks and bubbly personality, she was perfect for such roles. When Yvonne grew tired of the Hollywood scene, she married a very well-known producer named Don Fedderson and raised a wonderful family.

Cindy Robbins, who played my girlfriend Pearl, was also a very talented gal with whom I worked on several occasions, including "Rockabilly Baby" and "Dino." Cindy appeared in numerous other movies and television shows, as well as on Broadway. She later married a popular singer named Tommy Leonetti. Cindy was a doll and we had great times together working and otherwise.

Dawn Richard, who played the upside down gal in the gymnasium who is attacked by Tony when he turns into a werewolf, was an absolutely beautiful girl. She became very close to Cindy and Yvonne, and they all hung around together during the filming. Dawn's part was supposed to be much larger and she filmed several additional scenes, but they were cut out of the final print. I always thought that the photography during the gym scene, in which we see Tony as werewolf from her upside down perspective, is one of the movie's finer moments. It evokes some genuine horror, which is accented by Dawn's blood-curdling screams as she runs for her life.

Filming that scene was actually rather funny. At one point Dawn was hanging from the parallel bars, which were pretty high off the ground, when the entire crew was suddenly called outside to film a quick scene because the light was right. A minute later we heard a scream and a stream of obscenities from Dawn, who was stuck upside down on the parallel bars, unable to get off. A couple of grips rushed inside and helped her while we just fell about laughing. Dawn, poor thing, failed to see the humor in the situation, but we thought it was hilarious!

Whit Bissell, who played our "mad doctor," was a consummate performer who always gave his all no matter how ridiculous the scene or concept. He played a similar role in "I Was A Teenage Frankenstein," which was considered a sequel of sorts to "Teenage Werewolf," and his dramatic performances in both films almost make you believe their outrageous story lines.

I was around during Whit's scenes, which were filmed in sequence over three days, but I didn't get to know him very well. I wish I had, though, because fans constantly ask me about him. He has a tremendous following because of his work in numerous other cult movies and television shows, including "The Lost Continent," "Airport," "The Creature From the Black Lagoon" and Irwin Allen's "Time Tunnel." All I can say from the brief time we were together is that he was a sweet man who knew his craft and did his homework.

"I Was A Teenage Werewolf" was a movie with a lot of firsts. It was one of the first exploitation movies to use the "I Was A Teenage..." concept, it was one of the first low-budget flicks aimed directly at the teen market— and it has the distinction of being the first movie in which I sing.

When I signed on for the project, the script contained no song-and-dance sequence. But a fellow named Jerry Blaine, who has done a few horror movies since, had written a song titled "Eeny, Meeny, Miney Mo" and taken it to Herman Cohen, who decided to put it in "I Was A Teenage Werewolf." Jerry was originally slated to sing the song in the movie, but when my agent found out, she called Herman and begged him to let me sing it. I went to Herman's office and did a song for him, and he quickly approved me. Jerry Blaine wasn't too happy about that. He wanted the screen time, and I don't blame him. But as it turns out, that song became Jerry's Revenge.

Normally, when a movie contains a musical number, the song is first performed on a sound stage and then you sing it to a playback during filming. But as I mentioned earlier, "I Was A Teenage Werewolf" was an incredibly low-budget film, even for that period. I sang the song to almost no musical accompaniment with the understanding that it would be scored when they scored the movie. In that scene, perhaps you'll recall, I do a little dance with Cindy Robbins. But because there was no music, we had to count to the song in our heads. It was very difficult and required several takes before we got it right.

But when we premiered the movie, I almost died of embarrassment because the whole song was two measures out of synch! We had a little Coketail party for the opening and the last four rows of the theater were filled with my contemporaries, many of whom were professional singers. When my song came on, I literally wanted to crawl out of the theater because of that glaring error. The kids in the audience loved the movie and applauded wildly after my song, but I'm sure the lousy synchronization was painfully obvious to the pros. Gratefully, no one said anything.

Herman Cohen promised me that the problem would be fixed before "I Was A Teenage Werewolf" went into general release. But he never came through, even though it would have cost just a few hundred dollars to fix. And I still wince every time I see it because to me the problem is so apparent.

A couple of years after "I Was A Teenage Werewolf" was released in the United States, I was working in Paris and came across a small art house near the Champs Elysees that had been playing the movie for an entire year. Apparently "Teenage Werewolf" really struck a cord with the movie-loving French, who are renowned for their long-standing fascination with anything related to horror or science fiction.

Being dubbed in French was hilarious. My voice was sort of bizarre and froggy, but the funniest was the guy who dubbed Michael Landon's lines. He was probably a very good actor, but his voice was just a little too high, making Michael sound more like Don Knotts than the rage-filled, masculine antihero he was. Whoever brought in the French actors to dub the film either didn't have the money to do the job right, or didn't study the characters very closely. But it was an interesting experience, and my friends and I were on the floor laughing.

Unfortunately, they didn't dub "Eeny, Meeny, Miney Mo"—and the song was still two measures out of synch! Even in Europe, that song continued to haunt me.

Another disappointment for me was not being able to actually play the bongos. Vic was supposed to be an expert bongo player and a guy came in to show me how it was done. But because of the musicians union and other factors, I couldn't actually hit them—so I just rapped on the rim. Jack Costanza, one of the nation's top bongo players, was supposed to come in and dub my bongo playing when the movie was scored, but again the movie's paltry budget raised its ugly head and it never happened. So you never really hear me play bongos in the film, which is a shame because I think it would have been neat. What makes this really embarrassing is that there's a line of dialogue about what a great bongo player I am, but if you listen closely all you can hear is me smacking the rims very, very faintly. Wow!

Interestingly, because "I Was A Teenage Werewolf" did huge box office wherever it played, there was talk of releasing "Eeny, Meeny, Miney Mo" as a single with another Jerry Blaine song I had recorded for the B side. But it never happened, which was a great let-down because I think it would have done quite well. Everyone was talking about the movie, and anything related to it was a sure seller. Herman Cohen considered the song my bonus so he didn't give me any extra money for performing it. And I guess he was right—everyone seems to remember it. Even today, more than 30 years after the film's release, fans come up to me and start singing that goofy little ditty.

An amusing side note: "I Was A Teenage Werewolf" was mentioned during the 1957 presentation of the Academy Awards. The person announcing that year's five nominated songs commented: "It saddens me that 'Eeny, Meeny, Miney Mo' was not nominated." The audience went nuts with laughter, proving just how popular that silly little film had become.

"I Was A Teenage Werewolf" was a tremendous success, despite its low budget and relatively unknown cast. I heard that it grossed nearly $9 million its first year—a figure almost unheard of for a film of that type. In fact, I've been told that the profits from "I Was A Teenage Werewolf" allowed producers Samuel Arkoff and James Nicholson to expand the output of their company, the now legendary American International Pictures.

But because they had no production studio of their own prior to that, most of the interiors of "I Was A Teenage Werewolf" were shot at the old ZIV television studios. I knew the place well because that was where I did some of my very first television work, including the old "Cisco Kid" series with Duncan Renaldo and Leo Carrillo. Most of the exterior scenes, such as those in the park and the high school, were shot at various locations around Hollywood. Three decades later, it's difficult for me to remember exactly where, but I'm amused at the thought of school kids today playing on the location sets once terrorized by Michael Landon's legendary teenage lycanthrope.

"I Was A Teenage Werewolf" did so well nationwide on a double bill with "Invasion of the Saucermen" that we didn't have to do much promotion for it. There was some talk of sending Michael, me, Yvonne and Cindy on a promotional tour, but that was eventually deemed unnecessary because of all of the hype the movie was generating on its own. We made a few public appearances on behalf of the movie in California and elsewhere, and we were interviewed by several of the fan magazines, but that was about it. I thought it would have been cool to travel the country promoting such a campy flick, but the higher-ups didn't want to spend the money and didn't need to.

Believe it or not, one of the movie's greatest fans was Elvis Presley. I met Elvis for the first time on the Paramount lot in 1958. I was there to make "The Buccaneer" with Charlton Heston while Elvis was making "King Creole" (for which, I understand, he received a two-month military deferment before being drafted). I was walking by the commissary one day when I noticed a big crowd. Someone called out "Kenny! Hey, Kenny!" and when I turned around, there was Elvis, big as life and twice as cool.

Elvis invited me to join him and his friends for lunch, and I quickly agreed. We ate in the commissary with the regular studio workers because Elvis' entourage wasn't allowed in the Green Room, which is where most of the big celebrities ate. I remember Elvis had mashed potatoes with sauerkraut on it. He gave me a bite, and I've loved it ever since. He later arranged for me to have a small role in "King Creole," but I couldn't do it because "The Buccaneer" went two weeks over schedule and they had to cast someone else.

When Elvis and I got a chance to talk, he told me that he had screened "I Was A Teenage Werewolf" several times at Graceland. I was a little skeptical when he told me how much he loved that movie, but then I figured it had to be true because that's how he recognized me—he remembered me as Vic.

Elvis was staying at the Beverly Wilshire Hotel in Beverly Hills, along with his entourage, during the filming of "King Creole," and he invited me up to join them one evening. He was in his room when I arrived, so I had a drink and chatted with the guys. There was always booze and stuff around, but I never saw Elvis take a drink. He couldn't go anywhere because his fans had practically surrounded the hotel, so he was forced to entertain himself in-house. That evening he and the guys called down to a drug store in the hotel and requested several huge tubs of ice cream in a variety of flavors. They also brought up a wild assortment of toppings, including hot fudge, butterscotch, whipped cream and nuts—anything you could put on ice cream. The entertainment that night was to see who could make the most outrageous banana split and eat it all! I didn't participate, but it was hilarious watching these good ol' boys stuff themselves with ice cream until they could barely move. There were toppings and ice cream everywhere; it made me feel very sorry for the maid. It seemed to last forever. These guys could really put away the ice cream. It's amazing the outrageous things you think up just to escape the boredom when you can't go outside, which was the curse of Elvis' popularity.

Elvis later rented a home in Bel Air, and I was invited up there one night for a party. I can't remember if I took Jackie DeShannon or Molly Bee, but we had an interesting time. The whole Memphis Mafia was there, along with Elvis' cooks and other aides. It was great fun because all we did was sit around, play the guitar and sing. You would never imagine that being with Elvis Presley was just like being at home, hanging with friends and singing. It was a very home-spun evening—in a Bel Air mansion!

Sometimes on Sunday mornings, there would be a touch-football game down in a small park at the bottom of Coldwater Canyon. I'm sure the people driving by would have wrecked their cars if they had known that some of the biggest stars in Hollywood, including Elvis Presley, were playing touch football just a few yards away. Some of the guys wanted to play tackle football, but that was pretty much out of the question. No one wanted to hurt themselves because we all had to be at the studio the next day. Plus, we were all too egotistical to let anyone get that close to our faces!

A few years ago, I visited Graceland while attending the annual Memphis Film Festival, and I had the great pleasure of meeting Allan Crough, who was Elvis' personal pilot. Allan confirmed that "I Was A Teenage Werewolf" was one of Elvis' favorite films (he even had a copy on the plane) and that Elvis knew all the words to "Eeny, Meeny, Miney Mo," which made me cringe. But I'll bet that if Elvis had cut that song, it wouldn't have been out of synch!

Elvis once invited my friend Connie Stevens to visit him in Palm Springs. She went down and had her own suite, as did he. Elvis' entourage was there, too. All the time. Connie and Elvis were almost never alone, and during those brief periods when they were, Elvis acted so shy that nothing romantic ever happened. She called me and whispered, "How do I get out of here? There's nothing going on and I'm really bored!" She wanted me to come down and join the party, but I didn't think that was a good idea. I told her I couldn't just call Elvis and invite myself over. Instead, I suggested that Connie tell him that she had to leave suddenly because the studio had called her, which I believe is how she got out of it. It was sort of sad because she was hoping for some kind of excitement with The King and without his entourage.

A similar situation happened in Las Vegas when a good friend of mine, singer Joanie Sommers, was invited to join Elvis in his hotel suite. She found herself in the same situation—Elvis was seldom alone, and was painfully shy when they were. The next time I saw her, Joannie asked my advice because she wanted to see Elvis again, but she couldn't stand all the people around him. I told her she was on her own!

Rock singer Jo-Ann Campbell, whom I adored, often appeared in Las Vegas. She did a great impersonation of Elvis in her nightclub act, and Elvis heard about it. One evening he called her and invited her over for dinner after their individual shows, but it also turned out to be with the whole group. It was as if Elvis never had a moment to himself! She did her impersonation for him, and Elvis just fell on the floor. He really loved it. But Jo-Ann was hoping it would be just for him, not the entire Memphis group.

Interestingly, Yvonne Lime was one of the first women to be invited to Graceland as Elvis' guest after he moved there. She told me that he was very charming and that she had a wonderful time. I guess he became smitten with her after seeing her in "Teenage Werewolf," though apparently nothing romantic happened between them. However, they remained good friends.

"I Was A Teenage Werewolf" did so well nationwide that the other studios couldn't help but notice. The result was an overnight "I Was A Teenage..." craze that would include "I Was A Teenage Frankenstein," "I Was A Teenage Caveman," "Teenagers From Outer Space" and many others. Teens were hot in Hollywood!

But if anyone should receive credit for making "I Was A Teenage Werewolf" the success it was, it's the young people who flocked to the theaters and drive-ins to see it when it was first released.

Until then, I believe, there really hadn't been a specific genre of film that spoke directly to young audiences. The '30s and '40s had Andy Hardy and films of that nature, but mostly they presented teenagers as adults wanted to see them—wholesome, studious and respectful of their elders. Kids in the 1950s demanded movies that showed teenage life a tad more realistically (not that "I Was A Teenage Werewolf" was realistic in any sense of the word, but it did portray teens as more mature and worldly). I think young people liked having a movie that featured rough and tumble teens, rock and roll, a scary monster and a slight disrespect for anyone over 30. Remember—if it hadn't been for Dr. Brandon's mad scheme, Tony never would have turned into a werewolf. When you think about it, adults are to blame for the whole sordid mess!

Another reason "I Was A Teenage Werewolf" was such a runaway hit, I think, is that it made a great date movie. It was frightening (in a silly kind of way), and young people found it a terrific flick to see with their friends—groups that no doubt mirrored in many ways the group Tony hung around with. They could identify, and as a result many went back to see the movie again and again.

Herman Cohen was brilliant in deciding to make "I Was A Teenage Werewolf." He analyzed the market and gave the audience exactly what it wanted. I'm sure he knew the studio would get its money back many times over, but like me, he probably never thought the movie would become an international cult classic. You just can't predict these things. A cult following develops on its own; it can't be created.

With "I Was A Teenage Werewolf," we all got very lucky.

Chapter 6
Attack of the Puppet People

"I Was A Teenage Werewolf" resulted in a few embarrassing moments for me—but at least it wasn't hazardous to my health, which is more than I can say for "Attack of the Puppet People" (1958). That movie almost killed me!

"Puppet People" was one of a multitude of teen-oriented sci-fi flicks churned out on the heels of "Teenage Werewolf" and other early successes. Producers quickly realized the teen market was practically a license to print money, and they went hog wild in the latter years of the 1950s, filling theaters with an astonishing array of movies aimed at the youth market. Science fiction and horror seemed to be the most successful formulas and those are the genres that a lot of producers concentrated on, including the legendary Bert I. Gordon.

Bert is a man who likes extremes. Some of his most famous cult movies include "The Beginning of the End" (1957), in which giant grasshoppers invade Chicago; "The Amazing Colossal Man" (1957) in which a guy grows to a height of 60 feet after being hit by an atomic blast; its sequel, "War of the Colossal Beast" (1958) and "Village of the Giants" (1965), a movie ostensibly based on H.G. Wells' "Food of the Gods" in which a bunch of teenagers grow to be giants after ingesting a special serum. "Attack of the Puppet People" was the other end of the spectrum. Instead of making really big people, Bert decided that doll-sized people could be interesting, too.

The movie is about a lonely dollmaker named Mr. Franz (John Hoyt) who shrinks everyone he likes so he can keep them around for company. He hires a new receptionist named Sally Reynolds (June Kenny), who falls in love with salesman Bob Wesley (John Agar). When Bob proposes to Sally and it looks like Sally will be leaving, Mr. Franz shrinks them both, much to their chagrin.

The other victims of Dr. Franz' shrinking device (which, it's explained, changes people into energy by breaking down their molecular structure with high-frequency vibrations) include a Marine named Mac (Scott Peters), a pretty young singer named Laurie (Marlene Willis), a brassy gal named Georgia (Laurie Mitchell) and a handsome young man named Stan (yours truly).

The others have adjusted pretty well to being doll-sized, but Bob and Sally have trouble making the transition and they encourage their tiny pals to try to escape. During a party sequence in which Mr. Franz is kept busy by an unexpected visitor, Bob and Mac try to use the shrinking device to make Mac large again while Stan scales the door and keeps watch through the keyhole. But Mr. Franz returns before they can succeed.

The police become suspicious at the number of people who have disappeared around Mr. Franz' shop, so the old guy decides to kill himself and take his tiny friends with him. But before they go, he treats them to a private puppet show at a local theater. The play is "Dr. Jekyll and Mr. Hyde," and Mr. Franz places Bob and Sally on the tiny puppet stage and forces them to interact with the two-faced marionette. Sally freaks out and Bob flies into a rage, tearing the Jekyll/Hyde puppet to pieces.

Just then a stagehand interrupts Mr. Franz, allowing his tiny creations to make a break for it. Sally and Bob make it outside and head for Mr. Franz' lab while the others apparently take refuge in the theater. Along the way Bob and Sally are attacked by a rat and a dog, but manage to make it to the lab and reverse the shrinking process just before Mr. Franz arrives. They glare at the aging doll maker and leave to summon the police while a pathetic Mr. Franz pleads, "Don't leave me. I'll be all alone." It's assumed (but never shown) that the other puppet people are also returned to normal size.

The circumstances under which I became involved with "Attack of the Puppet People" are very similar to how I came to make "I Was A Teenage Werewolf." My agent, Polly Jacobson, submitted me to Bert Gordon when she found out that "Puppet People" was going into production. I was very youthful looking and had received quite a bit of publicity in the fan magazines at that time, so Bert thought I'd appeal to the audience for whom the flick was intended—teenagers. The character of Stan didn't have a lot of dialogue, but he was integral to some key scenes and I thought the whole thing would be a kick.

The shooting schedule for "Puppet People" was about two weeks, and we managed to come in right on schedule, despite the fact that this was an effects-heavy film. It was also a low-budget movie (I don't know the exact shooting budget, though I'd be surprised if it were more than "I Was A Teenage Werewolf") but you'd never know it from the special effects, which I believe still hold up pretty well 30 years later. It was all special props and in-camera effects, but it works. Well, most of the time.

Arriving on the set for the first time was awe-inspiring because the oversized props were unlike anything I had ever seen before. The place was packed with giant cups, boxes, pencils, cans, scissors and dozens of other objects. In our miniature state we were supposed to be about 12 inches tall, so everything had to be to scale.

Bert Gordon has developed a reputation over the years for cheesy special effects (the see-through grasshoppers in "The Beginning of the End" is a perfect example) but he tried to do things right with "Puppet People." A great deal of time and effort went into making all of the props the appropriate size, and it was quite effective. I'll never forget seeing the huge telephone for the first time because it was larger than any of us. Even the telephone cord that John Agar and I shimmy down was exactly the way it would be on a regular telephone. Bert insisted that everything be as close to scale as possible (within budget).

The movie was filmed on two large sound stages at the old ZIV television studios, which is where we also shot the interiors for "I Was A Teenage Werewolf." The two sound stages were necessary so that the camera could be positioned at a great distance to give the illusion in certain scenes that we really were 12 inches tall.

Bert, who also produced the picture, was a pleasant man but not really a people-oriented director. He was more concerned with the technical side of the film, and tended to give us actors a minimum of direction. I guess he just trusted us to take what we had and make the best of it.

This is not to say that Bert completely ignored the actors. His primary concerns were with the special effects and making sure the movie came in on time and on budget; he had only a certain amount of money to spend and he wanted to get every nickel's worth. But when necessary, Bert could be quite manipulative when it came to getting the most out of his talent. John Agar, for example, noted in a recent magazine interview that he climbed down the telephone cord and up a giant dresser during the party escape scene primarily because Bert said he didn't think John could do it. John's a proud guy, and refuses to let others do what he can do himself. So all Bert had to do was push the right buttons to get John motivated. And that's what a good director does—he motivates his actors so that they give the very best performances they're capable of.

It should be noted that Bert wasn't above a little nepotism in his movies. In "Puppet People," for example, the little girl who almost exposes Mr. Franz' activities to the police was played by Bert's young daughter, Susan. And she did a pretty good job, too.

The star of the movie was John Hoyt, a veteran character actor with a string of eclectic films to his credit, including "Blackboard Jungle," Casanova's Big Night," "The Conqueror" and even "Flesh Gordon," a soft-core porno cult classic.

John was a wonderful man and terrific actor. He had to be, because whenever he had to talk to his miniature creations, he was forced to talk to a blank wall! He knew basically where we would be during any given scene, but our reactions were added later in post-production. It was a tough role for John, but he pulled it off effortlessly.

If "Puppet People" were made today, computer technology would make it fairly easy to composite John with his living dolls. But our budget was small, so as a cost-cutting move, a lot of our interaction consisted of a shot of John talking, then a cut to our reactions. I think the few scenes in which we are together—creator and puppet people—look pretty good.

"Puppet People" was the only film in which I worked with John Agar, who ably played the film's stalwart hero. John was a great guy, and I really enjoyed working with him. I think he was a man who was thrown into a business he really didn't know—acting—but he found it so lucrative that he decided to stick with it. He quickly learned his craft, and while he may not have been the greatest actor in the world, he held his own as a solid, dependable B-movie personality.

John appeared in more than two dozen motion pictures over the years, some better than others. Several of his movies were westerns—I believe he got his big break starring with John Wayne in the John Ford classic "Fort Apache" (1948)—and science-fiction flicks. Of the latter genre, some of John's better efforts include "The Brain From Planet Arous" (1958), "Revenge of the Creature" (1955), "Journey to the Seventh Planet" (1962),

"Tarantula" (1955) and "The Mole People" (1956).

Working with John was like working with the guy-next-door. He had no temperament whatsoever. He'd do anything he was told to do, and he never balked at requested retakes. He was very conscientious and always a gentleman, and it's a pleasure to know him.

Marlene Willis, who plays my girlfriend of sorts in "Puppet People," was already a very good friend because we had worked together the year before in "Rockabilly Baby." She was fairly young when she broke into acting, but her voice, which really carried her career, was wonderful. Marlene's background was country, but she could sing practically anything so it came as no surprise that she continued her singing career long after she stopped making movies. We stayed in touch for several years after making "Puppet People." The last time I saw her was in Las Vegas, where she was performing.

June Kenney didn't really belong in Hollywood because she was such a sweet, laid-back kid. We knew each other through some mutual friends, and when we first met, she was working as a secretary. But she really wanted to be an actress, and she took acting lessons to help her toward that goal. I can't remember anything she was in after "Puppet People." She did a wonderful job and was a true professional, but it takes an aggressive attitude to succeed in this business, and June always appeared to me to be too sweet. I felt protective of her—I think we all did—and I didn't want her to get hurt or taken advantage of.

Laurie Mitchell was as brassy off screen as she was on. She was a mother figure of sorts on the set because she had been in the business for ages, and she took Marlene and June under her protective wing. In fact, she sort of took care of all of us. If Bert Gordon or someone else on the production tried to push us too hard, or didn't to give us our required breaks, Laurie would say something—nicely but with just the right amount of attitude. And everyone listened. She was definitely a force to be reckoned with.

The cast became a tightknit family over the movie's two-week production because we worked so closely together. We all did our own stunts because we didn't have any stunt doubles; in fact, we didn't even have stand-ins, which was unusual. So we found ourselves spending 12 or 14 hours a day on the set, working or sitting around waiting to work. Luckily, we all got along great together and the experience was relatively pleasant for everyone. We knew this was a small B-movie, but each one of us strived to do a good job.

"Attack of the Puppet People" was a very physical film for all of us—but especially me. In fact, one scene almost killed me!

It was the party scene, in which we puppet people try to get to the shrinking device in a desperate attempt to reverse the process and escape. This scene required John Agar and Scott Peters to climb down the phone cord and climb up a table while I scaled the door to keep watch through the keyhole.

This scene put me in tremendous jeopardy—more than any scene in any other movie I've made—and in retrospect I should have demanded a stunt double. But I was young and cocky and thought I could pull it off without a problem.

The scene called for me to climb a flexible rope about 30 feet up the giant door to the doorknob. Because the rope was actually made of rubber, it would stretch a little each time I placed one hand above the other, so climbing it was extremely difficult. Making matter worse, my pants were so tight that they felt as if they had been painted on, and they split up the crotch shortly after I started the climb! Because we weren't running sound, I yelled, "My pants are splitting!" To which Bert yelled back, "Don't worry, it won't show on film! Keep going!" So I did, one agonizing foot after another. But all I could think of was that the whole world was going to see my ass!

I finally reached the top, peered through the keyhole like I was supposed to, then started down. That's when things really started to go wrong. As I slowly made my way down the giant prop door, the doorknob to which the rope was attached started to come loose. My panic button started to scream because I had nothing to save me if it came off—no net, no support wires, no nothing. It was just me and the rope.

Again, I yelled, "The goddamn doorknob is coming loose!" And again Bert replied, "It'll be okay! Keep going! It looks great, baby!"

But it wasn't okay, and when I was about fifteen feet from the floor, the doorknob gave way completely, sending me plummeting. Luckily there were a couple of grips waiting below to break my fall, otherwise I would have gone splat on the floor. It was a frightening experience and one of the more difficult things I've ever done in a movie. The whole scene was completed in a single take (with one small pick-up of me climbing down to the floor), which was good because there was absolutely no way I was going to climb that damned rope again! There comes a time when common sense takes over, no matter how wonderful a scene may appear.

That stunt was so physically difficult that my entire body ached to the point where I could barely move. The producers were forced to bring in a physical therapist for a deep massage so I wouldn't miss the next day's filming.

Apparently John Agar felt the physical effects of his stunts, too— especially the scene where he climbs off the table using the telephone cord and then climbs up the giant dresser. He wasn't nearly as high off the ground as I was for my scene, but it was still a difficult stunt and he really hurt afterwards. John and I caught up with each other at a recent auto- graph convention and we reminisced about "Puppet People." "Kenny, I'll never forget the pain," John told me. "I used muscles that I didn't even know I had!"

The door-climbing scene was for me the most physically grueling aspect of making "Puppet People." Mentally, though, the most difficult scene was being sung to by Marlene. The song was "You're My Living Doll" by Albert Glasser and Don Ferris and it embarrassed me tremen- dously. I literally begged Bert Gordon not to do it, but he felt the movie needed a song and nothing I said could change his mind.

For me to react to something like that was difficult because the whole situation was so damned silly and the song was so gratuitous. There was absolutely no reason for it, and it brought the action of the movie to a grinding halt. I think Marlene thought so too, but she was stuck with it. I tried to react without looking weird, but I was very uncomfortable and I think it shows. Although I have ego, it's certainly not enough for a beau- tiful young girl to sing directly to me about being a living doll! How the hell do you react to that? With embarrassment, that's how. I hated every second of that scene.

However, Marlene was lucky—unlike my disastrous experience with "Eeny, Meeny, Miney, Mo" in "I Was A Teenage Werewolf," she got to prerecord her song in a studio with live musicians. The song was sweet- ened when they scored the movie, and it sounds fine, but to this day I still don't think it works very well. We had to dance a little to that song just as we had to dance to "Eeny, Meeny, Miney, Mo," but at least this time we had music to follow so it wasn't that difficult.

The oversized props in "Puppet People" are probably the movie's most impressive special effect, but there are some other cool things as well. The tiny cylinders that housed us in suspended animation, for ex- ample, actually contained cut-out photographs of us on heavy cardboard.

That's how they were able to produce a whole bunch of John Agar dolls. The photos were curved slightly to give them a three-dimensional look, and I always thought it was a nice effect.

The giant cylinders that housed us during the live-action scenes were made of plastic and they were extremely difficult to get in and out of without messing up our clothes. The easiest thing would have been to use a crane to lower the tubes over us, but apparently a crane wasn't in the budget so we would crawl inside the tubes and then a couple of grips would right them. And once we were in, that was it. Neither wardrobe nor makeup could reach us, so we had to be careful not to muss anything. The shots of us in the tubes were done fairly quickly, but it was still kind of claustrophobic. I felt like a lizard in a glass jar!

The scenes of John Hoyt and us together were done using either split-screen or rear-screen projection, which is how Bert accomplished a lot of the special effects in his movies. Split screen requires careful camera placement, but is relatively easy to do, and it looks good when filmed properly. The most important thing is to have the two actors—who are filmed separately and then composited together—act and react in synch so that the scene blends smoothly. Movie special effects have evolved tremendously since "Puppet People" was made, but many of these old effects techniques still work. When I watch "Puppet People" today, I'm still impressed, especially when I think about the tiny budget we had.

Fans often ask me which movie I'm most fond of—"I Was A Teenage Werewolf" or "Attack of the Puppet People." It's a difficult question for me to answer because they both had their pluses and minuses, so I usually answer that I like them both equally.

But upon closer analysis, I have to say that "Teenage Werewolf" had considerably more meat to the script than "Puppet People." It was a solid tale that builds quickly and provides quite a bit of character development, especially for Michael Landon's character, Tony. There really wasn't that much development of my character in "Werewolf," but I had a lot to say and do, and that made up for it. "Werewolf" was Michael's vehicle, and everyone understood that.

The story in "Puppet People" is quite a bit thinner, in my opinion. It's a simple tale of fear and escape, and there was little development of any of the characters. The special effects were the real stars, and the actors were there to support them. We all knew that going into the project. But "Puppet People" just doesn't seem to have the drive or the strength that "Teenage

Werewolf" does. You wonder if the puppet people will get out of their predicament, but your heart isn't with them the way it is with Tony.

One of the biggest problems with "Attack of the Puppet People," I believe, is the ending. Nothing is really resolved. Sally Reynolds and Bob Wesley manage to return to their normal size, they briefly confront Mr. Franz, then they leave to contact the police. But what about the rest of us? Our fate is never explained, and the audience is left wondering.

Ah, there's a reason for that—Bert Gordon was really hoping for a sequel. He apparently had made arrangements with American International Pictures for a continuation of the story, but "Attack of the Puppet People" (which was also released under the title "The Fantastic Puppet People") was only moderately successful upon its initial release and the option for a sequel was never picked up. Too bad, because I'd give anything to have my character, Stan, returned to normal size! To the movie-going public, I'm still a 12-inch munchkin running around somewhere.

I can't complain about "Puppet People" too much, though. In all honesty, I was just happy to be working. And both "Teenage Werewolf" and "Puppet People" were happy experiences fun to make (my death-defying fall in the latter not withstanding). I went on to make more prestigious films, but to many fans, these are two of my most memorable movies. And I guess the fact that they're both still in popular release and rent well on videocassette proves that.

Ah, the good ol' days.

Burt Reynolds, KM and Charles Engel, now a head executive for
MCA/Universal Television.

KM and Kathy Nolan (The Real McCoys) at the International Grand Masque in Hollywood.

KM and Molly Bee at the premier of Raintree County. I got to dance with Elizabeth Taylor!

Marianne Gaba and KM on a photo shoot for a fan magazine.

Singing in Gilda Dahlberg's villa in Cuernavaca, Mexico.

In between scenes of Cecil B. DeMille's The Buccaneer.

Molly Bee, KM and Burt Reynolds.

Connie de Nave, KM and Marcia Rogers.

With my good friend Roxanne Pulitzer at a press party in Florida.

KM in A Funny Thing Happened on the Way to the Forum in Palm Beach.

Sassifras and KM as Grand Marshals in the South Florida State Fair parade.

KM with my niece Kimla Davis, Donald O'Connor and George Murphy
partying it up!

KM with Morgan Fairchild.

My forever friend and
press agent/writer Nancy
Streebeck in Palm Beach.

George Hamilton and KM backstage at a benefit.

On the cover of *Movie Life* magazine.

Ricardo Montalban and KM on B.L. Stryker.

KM, Burt Reynolds, internationally renowned America-Indian sculptor Bruce Lafountain and his daughter Eve.

Model/actress Carol Alt and
KM on set.

Mary Woolworth Donohue, KM, Lynda Day George, George Hamilton and Ethel
Smith in Palm Beach Follies.

Lady Sarah Churchill and KM at the International Red Cross Ball at Breakers Hotel in Palm Beach.

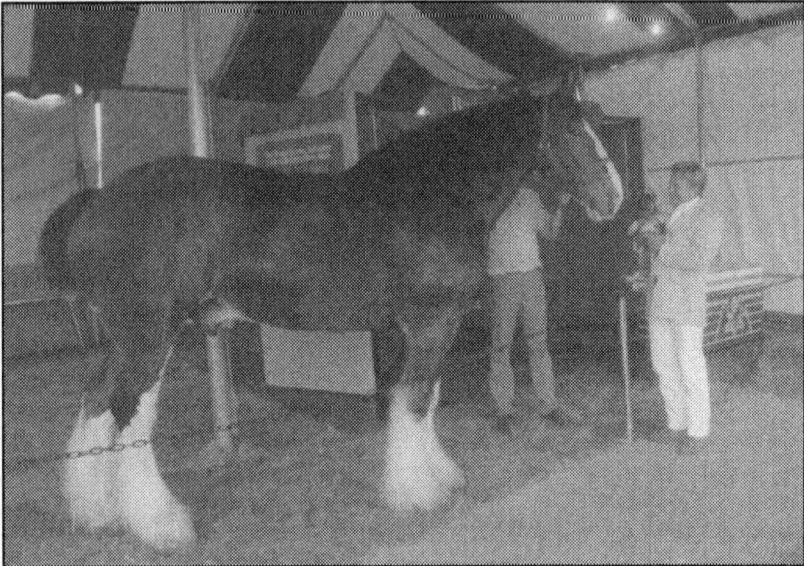

Sassi being kissed by a Clydesdale!

KM in *Battle Flame*.

KM in *This Rebel Breed*, 1958, Warner Bros.

Ike Carpenter, KM and Gerald Mohr in *This Rebel Breed*.

This Rebel Breed.

A publicity shot for *This Rebel Breed.* Left to right: Sharon Wiley, KM, Jennifer Adams and Paula Lane.

Chris Randall, Jan Merlin, unknown actor and KM in *Running Wild*, Universal-International, 1955.

The Human Jungle, Allied Artists. Next to me (right) is Steve Stevens who much later became my agent.

KM as Private Jon Schmidt in *Rat Patrol*, shot in Almeria, Spain.

Dead in *Bloodstalkers*, United Artists.

Bloodstalkers.

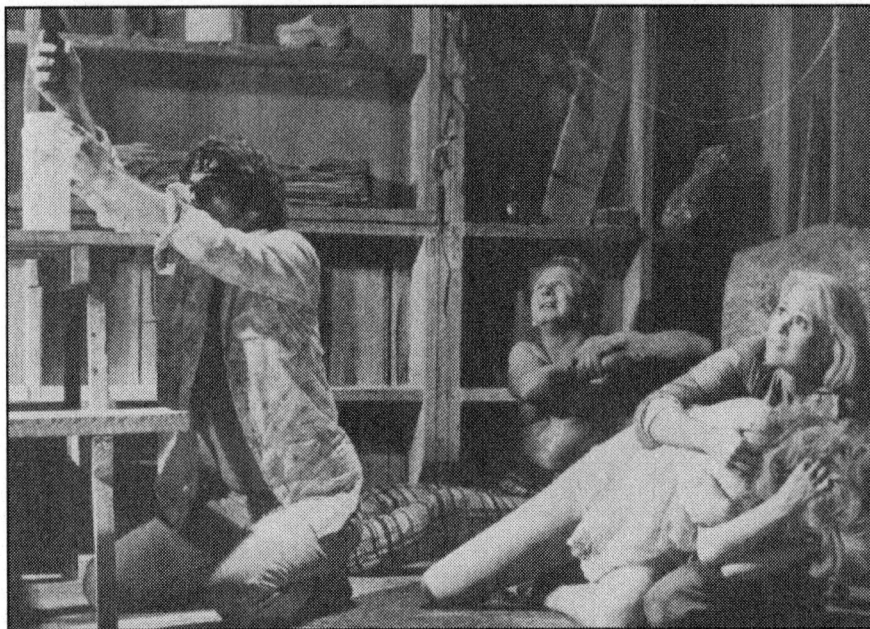

The Night Daniel Died was changed to *Bloodstalkers* for the home video market.
It starred KM, Celea-Ann Cole, Jerry Albert and Toni Crabtree and had the
most miserable location shooting with 100-degree temperatures and
mosquitoes and deer flies by the zillions.

Going over the script to *The Night Daniel Died*: Robert Morgan (writer/director),
KM, Herb Goldstein and David Legge.

KM listens to director Anthony Qunn on the set of *The Buccaneer*, 1958.

Dancin' Miller in a big party scene in *The Buccaneer* filmed at Inger Steven's mansion.

KM and Charlton Heston in *The Buccaneer*.

Marlene Willis, Scott Peters, June Kenney, Laurie Mitchell, KM and John Agar as the Puppet People.

ALL DWARFS versus the CRUSHING GIANT BEASTS!

ATTACK OF THE **PUPPET PEOPLE**

starring JOHN AGAR · JOHN HOYT · JUNE KENNEY · Produced and Directed by BERT I. GORDON

the CRUSHING GIANT BEASTS!

ATTACK OF THE **PUPPET PEOPLE**

starring JOHN AGAR · JOHN HOYT · JUNE KENNEY · Produced and Directed by BERT I. GORDON

Michael Landon, Yvonne Lime and Cindy Robbins look on as I pretend to play the bongos in *I Was a Teenage Werewolf,* American International, 1957.

Michael Landon, Yvonne Lime, Cindy Robbins & Kenny Miller in "I Was A Teenage Werewolf" - American International Pictures

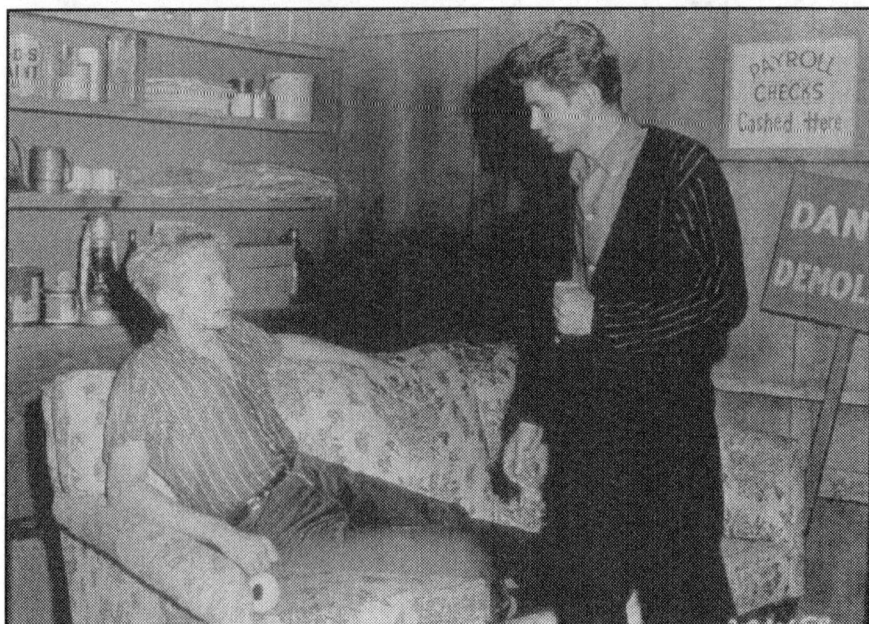

KM and Michael Landon in *I Was a Teenage Werewolf.*

The cast and crew of *I Was a Teenage Werewolf* on the last day of shooting.

"Everybody Ought to Have a Maid" sings (left to right) me, Michael O. Smith and Avery Schreiber at the Burt Reynolds Dinner Theater production of A Funny Thing Happened on the Way to the Forum, 1990.

With Avery Schreiber in Forum.

The Odd Couple by Neil Simon at Burt Reynold's Dinner Theater in Jupiter, Florida with Charles Nelson Reilly and Darryl Hickman. Directed by Nancy Walker. 1989. The first play ever to be filmed in its entirety for Showtime TV.

KM, Joseph Petrullo and New York City opera star Adria Firestone break up during dress rehearsal for Man of La Mancha.

A tense moment in the Broadway play Tribute with Iris Acker and KM.

Singing up a storm at The Fountainbleau Hotel in Miami Beach's Club Gigi. The supper club is like an MGM musical set—fantastic!

Burt Reynolds and KM washing Burt's car.

Broadway star Larry Kert, Kitty Franciscus, KM and Jim Franciscus.

A parade in Mirot, South Dakota with Judy Harriett and Sherry Jackson.

Jackie DeShannon and KM
layout for a fan magazine

Shelley Fabares and KM in another photo layout for a fan magazine.

KM, Sharon Wiley, Paula Lane and Jennifer Adams in a publicity shot for
This Rebel Breed.

These lovelies (l. to r. Kathy Nolan, Yvonne Lime and Molly Bee) cohosted the
premiere of my first recording and my first appearance at the Hollywood Palladium.

Chapter 7

Learning From the Masters
"Touch of Evil" & "The Buccaneer"

Two of the movies of which I'm proudest—and on which I learned the most when it came to the art and business of filmmaking—are Orson Welles' "Touch of Evil" (1958) and Anthony Quinn's "The Buccaneer" (1958). These were two of the biggest-budgeted films on which I worked, and their casts read like a Who's Who of Hollywood. For a small-town kid like me, this was heaven.

I did "Touch of Evil" first (though released in 1958, it was made a few years earlier). My agent sent me over to Universal because the producers were looking for certain types of people to appear in Orson Welles' next film, originally titled "Badge of Evil." I read for the casting director, did some test footage and sat for a few still photos, which I was told would be sent to Mr. Welles. I was called back a few days later and told to go to a specific cottage on the lot. When I got there, I was handed a few pages of dialogue and asked to do a cold reading. I thought it was odd because the scene involved Welles' character, Hank Quinlan, and Marlene Dietrich's character. I couldn't see what it had to do with me, but being a professional—and too nervous to say no—I went along.

To say I was anxious about meeting Orson Welles would be a huge understatement. He was one of the biggest names in Hollywood, a living legend. As I sat in the outer office talking with assistant director Chico Day, I could hear Welles' booming voice and laughter from beyond the door. I was literally shaking in my shoes. This was big, and I knew it!

After a few minutes I was ushered into Welles' office, where he sat in a jumpsuit like King Farouk with a huge cigar in his hand. He was a big man, though not nearly as big as he would get in later years. Still, he was quite imposing—in both size and reputation.

Noticing my nervousness, Welles did what he could to put me at ease. We chatted about this and that, then he asked me to go over a scene. I had the female part, and I remember Welles laughing loudly at one line because it was so funny. After a few more lines he stopped me and said, "That's wonderful." Then we chatted some more, mostly about my family and background. I never had a producer or director who was as friendly as Orson Welles was that morning. When I thought about it later, it seemed that he was a lonely man who wanted to become a part of someone else. I think he craved company, and enjoyed talking with people.

As I left, Welles proclaimed in his booming voice, "We'll be seeing you soon!," and I felt confident that I would be working on "Touch of Evil." I had no idea what the role would be, but I knew that Welles liked me and would use me. Considering the female lines I had been asked to read, I just hoped it wasn't something in drag!

That afternoon, my agent received a call from Welles' people saying the great director wanted to see me again the next morning. I went to his bungalow about 11 or 11:30 a.m. and it was apparent he had forgotten I was scheduled to drop by. He asked if I wanted to join him and Chico Day for lunch, then promptly called the commissary and ordered me a club sandwich. After we ate, he brought up the movie and the part he wanted me to play—a member of the Mexican gang that was a fixture of the corrupt border town where "Touch of Evil" was set. He asked, "Would you mind if I sent you down to make-up and had your hair curled?" It never crossed my mind to say no. This was, after all, Orson Welles. He could have had me shaved bald and I wouldn't have said anything. I was still in awe of the man and the fact that I was going to be in his movie.

"The rest of the gang has dark hair," Welles continued, "but since you'll be the gang leader, I thought it would be better if you had curly blond hair combed in a DA (duck's ass). That would add a lot to your character." I just nodded. Whatever you say, Mr. Welles!

The casting people talked to my agent and gave me a "run of the picture" contract, which meant I would work on the film—and be paid— from beginning to end. My part didn't call for many days of work, but Welles decided he wanted me around for the entire production. For some reason, he really took to me, and liked having me around as his sidekick. Sometimes before shooting, he would invite me over for a drink. We'd go over to his bungalow, have a cool one, and talk about the script or whatever was in the news that day. I was honored to get to know Orson Welles on such familiar terms. And better yet, my salary started the second time I had lunch with him!

Two days after that lunch, I got a call to go to makeup and hair. I met with Bud Westmore and was told that Welles specifically asked for lots of curls. "We have to give you a permanent," Westmore said, "and then we'll cut out what we don't need."

The perm took a long time, and we finally broke for lunch. I didn't want to go to the commissary looking like the illegitimate son of Harpo Marx, so one of Bud's assistants went to wardrobe and came back with an old golf hat. I felt like something from outer space, but it was still better than going outside with a headful of tight curls.

After lunch, Bud started to take the perm out and it looked absolutely horrible. He put some kind of oil on my head to relax the curls, but it didn't help at all. I looked like a bad imitation of Gorgeous George the wrestler. Bud assured me it would look okay after a couple days, but I wasn't so certain.

I went home that night and my roommates laughed hysterically. "Don't worry," I said. "It'll come out okay." To which they replied, "What the hell—you're working with Orson Welles!"

Bud worked on me again the next day, and I later went over to show Welles how things were progressing. He took one look at me and burst into gales of laughter. "What the fuck are they doing to you!" he exclaimed. He called Bud Westmore and told him to come over, then he laughed at me some more, his whole body shaking. All I could do was smile because I knew how ridiculous I looked.

The problem was that Bud had gone to extremes with my perm because he was afraid of not giving Welles what he wanted. Welles said he didn't want me to look so nice; he wanted me to look like an American pachuco, the kids who ran around in gangs. So Bud worked me over some more, and it felt like torture. He and his assistants did everything they could to loosen the curls and straighten my hair, but it was a time-consuming process. I had to go to a hairdresser four days in a row before it even started to look natural. On the fifth day, Welles said he wanted to see my head again. It looked better, but still not perfect. In frustration, Welles called Bud and said, "Don't cut off any more of his hair! I want Kenny to have a DA!"

The next day, Welles invited me to join him and Chico Day for a drive to east Los Angeles to pick out some extras for the movie. He wanted authentic Chicanos, and felt that the streets of the barrio would be the best place to find them. So we piled into a stretch limousine and cruised some of the worst areas in the City of Angels.

I wish I could have videotaped that experience, because it was genuinely surreal. We would drive up to a group of Mexicans on the sidewalk and Welles would roll down the window and yell "Hey!" in his trademark booming voice. Inevitably they would give him a hard time, cursing him in Spanish and English. Chico spoke fluent Spanish, so he would translate, telling the men that Orson Welles wanted them to appear as extras in his new movie. They didn't believe him until he gave them a card from the casting department at Universal Studios with the name of the person they should call. It was absolutely hilarious in a "gee, I hope we don't get killed" kind of way. We drove around like that for nearly two hours, looking for extras and getting cursed at.

Welles wanted to have lunch down there, but Chico put a quick stop to that. To do so would have placed us in real jeopardy. It was obvious we weren't from around there, and we would have been eaten alive. So we drove back to Hollywood and ate at the Brown Derby, which was one of my favorite restaurants. There was a phone jack at every booth so Hollywood's elite (and not so elite) could take phone calls. Many stars had their press agents page them at the Brown Derby just so their names would be heard as it was announced.

Not surprisingly, the extras Welles hired were a rough bunch. But God, they sure fit the part! We had to have extra security to protect us from the less savory members of the group the week they were filming. However, they were exactly what Welles was looking for, and he told makeup not to touch them because they looked so authentic in their street clothes.

One of Orson Welles' fetishes was his high director's chair. Only he could sit in it—no one else. Most of the young men hired as extras had never been on a movie set and were unfamiliar with the etiquette, and one day a young kid plopped down in Welles' chair while Welles was directing a scene. Welles was calm and gentle most of the time, but when he lost his temper it was like an earthquake. He yelled at the kid so loudly that the kid probably wet his pants. Then Welles turned to Chico Day and told him to tell everyone in Spanish that NO ONE was to sit in his chair! And no one ever did, because no one wanted to face the wrath of Orson Welles more than once.

Welles also expected everyone to do their homework, to know their lines and to behave as professionals. He was directing a scene with a little old lady who must have been around 90, and she couldn't remember her lines. She was very nervous, and blew take after take. Welles wasn't feeling well that day so his temper was shorter than usual, and after four blown takes he exploded, "You haven't done your homework!" and threatened to fire the actress on the spot, which immediately reduced her to tears. Welles walked over to Chico and some others, and they managed to calm him down. Regaining his composure, Welles said, "Let's go on to another scene and we'll come back."

The dialogue coach worked with the actress, and when they came back to do the scene, Welles put his arm around the woman and explained, "I'm sorry, but we're working here and have to keep going. We don't have time to waste." Then they tried the problem scene one more time—and it went perfectly. Welles praised the actress highly, and the rest of the day went wonderfully. I had heard that Orson Welles was temperamental, and that incident certainly proved it. I guess genius has that obligation.

But Welles also had a very generous side—as I found out myself. Before shooting started on "Touch of Evil," I was sent to wardrobe to find a leather jacket. I chose a plain one without a collar, and when I tried it on, it fit perfectly. It was as if I were born to wear this jacket. The wardrobe guy said, "Okay, that one is yours," then asked if I knew who it had once belonged to. I shook my head and he showed me a name on the inside of one pocket—Audie Murphy! I was wearing the great Audie Murphy's jacket, which was a big thing to me. When I told Welles, he went on and on about it, even though I'm sure he really didn't give a rat's ass.

I wore that jacket through the whole movie, and toward the end told Chico Day that I would really like to have it. He said no, that it belonged to the studio. It was an expensive jacket, and they just couldn't give it away. Welles heard about my request and asked Chico to talk to wardrobe on my behalf, but their answer was still no. They couldn't part with it because it was handmade and rather expensive.

We had a wrap party at the end of the movie, and as I was leaving, Welles gave me a box and said, "Don't open this until you get home!" When I got back to my apartment, I ripped it open—and there was the jacket! Welles had either stolen it for me, or paid off the wardrobe guy so that I could have it. I never knew which, because Welles and I didn't see each other again for a long time. I loved that jacket and wore it everywhere for years and years. When it started to get a little tight around the middle, I gave it to my nephew Jimmy, who, alas, didn't know who either Audie Murphy or Orson Welles was.

It was important to Welles that every actor feel comfortable with his or her character, because that way they would give their very best performance. One day Dennis Weaver, who played the manager of the hotel where my gang rapes Janet Leigh's character, approached Welles and asked for direction on how to play the role. Welles thought for a moment and suggested Dennis give the character some depth and personality by playing him with a limp. Dennis followed the suggestion, even though it's not very noticeable in the movie. A few years later, Dennis landed the role of Chester on "Gunsmoke" and made the character memorable by playing him with a pronounced limp as well. You just can't argue with success!

As shooting on "Touch of Evil" progressed, I got to meet all of the stars that Welles had collected for what was assumed to be his next masterpiece. One of the first was Charlton Heston, who I would work with again in "The Buccaneer." He's a wonderful man, and had the composure of Moses when I was introduced to him. He played a Mexican and they had to dye his hair black and put him in dark makeup. All at once he became that character, and Moses disappeared. I was in awe of Charlton Heston, but we became quite good friends.

The rest of the cast included some of the biggest names in Hollywood. Janet Leigh. Akim Tamiroff. Marlene Dietrich. The list goes on and on. Welles also liked to surround himself with the astoundingly talented actors he had nurtured during his Mercury Theater days, such as Joseph Cotten, E.G. Marshall and Mercedes McCambridge. He was very loyal to his friends, and I got the feeling that they made him feel lucky. As a result, you never knew who would walk onto the set from one day to the next. They were never on the call sheet; they would just show up and do a scene, often just a cameo.

One day I was on the set but not working. Welles was shooting a scene in a dingy bar (the stripper dancing on the bar, by the way, was Zsa Zsa Gabor) and the rest of the sound stage was dark. I got some sand in my eye, and Janet Leigh told me to drop by her trailer because she had some eye drops. She helped me get the cinder out, but the drops left my vision a little blurry. I left the sound stage to go somewhere, and as I opened the massive doors, a woman wearing a white suit came in. Through my blurred vision I thought she was my good friend Jan Sterling, so I grabbed her and yelled "Jan!" The woman just smiled and said, "Darling, thank you very much!" That's when I realized it wasn't Jan Sterling, but Marlene Dietrich! My face grew beet-red with embarrassment, but she took the whole thing in good humor. I walked her onto the set so she could see Welles, and they had a friendly reunion. Later, I explained to Ms. Dietrich that I had hugged her because I thought she was Jan Sterling, to which she replied: "Oh darling! If only I were as young!" Later, hanging around the set, I heard Marlene Dietrich tell some of the funniest stories in the world—almost all of them dirty.

The scene in which my gang rapes Janet Leigh, who played Charlton Heston's wife, was one of the most controversial aspects of "Touch of Evil." The day we shot the sequence, Mercedes McCambridge came on the set looking like a bull dyke in a leather jacket, pants and boots. She also had her hair slicked down, which made her look even more masculine. In fact, she looked so different that I didn't recognize her at first. We had created a lot of subplots that didn't make it into the movie, and Mercedes' character was one of them. It wasn't actually shown, but in our gang was a blond fem who was supposed to be Mercedes' girlfriend.

The rape scene as shot was absolutely brutal. I was on top of Janet, who was screaming, and Mercedes was on the side egging everyone on. It was so ugly and vicious that the studio ended up editing a lot of it out, which didn't make Welles very happy. They also edited down the gang rumble, which meant much of my footage ended up on the cutting room floor.

It's no secret that the studio hated Welles' edited version of "Touch of Evil." They put it on the shelf for a couple of years because they thought it was so disjointed and unfathomable that they couldn't release it, and there was a clause in Welles' contract that prevented them from tinkering with it without his approval. When the clause finally expired, the studio edited it without Welles' permission or assistance, which really pissed him off. He poured his heart and soul into that movie, and it enraged him to watch the studio hack it to pieces. Now, of course, it's considered a classic, and is widely discussed in college film classes as one of the finest examples of motion-picture storytelling.

I watched "Touch of Evil" again recently, and couldn't believe how boring it was! The movie I saw on television was NOT the movie I remember making. The studio really did butcher it in editing, which is a damned shame because Welles knew what he was doing, and the studio should have trusted his instincts. In its edited form, I found the story difficult to follow, and some of the best scenes were just ruined. They could have phoned in the rape scene; it was absolutely ludicrous. But that's Hollywood for you. Genius frequently gets ripped apart by businessmen in suits.

Still, for me, to work with the likes of Orson Welles, Charlton Heston and Marlene Dietrich was one of the most exceptional learning experiences of my life. I didn't have that much to do, but Welles was gracious enough to put me under contract for the whole film, so I was there to witness its creation from beginning to end. And I tried not to miss a minute of it, because actors don't get the opportunity to work with performers of that caliber very often.

It's unfortunate what happened to Orson Welles later in his life. Even though he was one of the true greats of American cinema, he didn't make very many movies after "Touch of Evil." He eventually moved to Europe, and we ran into each other years later in Rome. He invited me to join him and some friends for dinner, which was a great treat because Orson Welles was an exceptional chef. Unfortunately, it started to show after a while. His size ballooned grotesquely, but he didn't let it bother him much. For example, after dinner, we all played a spirited game of charades, which was Welles' favorite after-dinner activity. And he moved around the room like a man half his size! It was a pleasure knowing him, and I miss him greatly.

"The Buccaneer" was my second big-budget, major-studio film— and I made a great first impression in the role of the young sentry, Kentucky, because I choked on a biscuit!

That character, who is featured in the film's opening scene, was one of the most coveted roles in Hollywood. Nearly everyone wanted in on this sweeping retelling of how pirate Jean Lafitte (Yul Brynner) helped Andrew Jackson (Charlton Heston) defeat the British at the Battle of New Orleans because Cecil B. DeMille was producing and Anthony Quinn was directing.

Paramount had been testing actors for the part for months without success when I was instructed by my agent to drop by the Paramount lot for an interview. At that time, I didn't know that they were still looking for someone to play the sentry. I had heard that Edd Byrnes had landed the role.

I arrived at the studio with a handful of other hopefuls and found out that they were reading actors on the sound stage. We cooled our heels for a while, then the casting girl gave me a couple of pages to read. I thought I would be reading for some low-level producer, but all of the big guns were there, including DeMille, producer Henry Wilcoxon, Anthony

Quinn and Charlton Heston. I'm sure they all didn't have to be there, but they hung around to see what I could do.

As I was about to read, Charlton Heston said to Anthony Quinn, "Tony, I know Kenny well. We did a film together called 'Touch of Evil.' I'd like to read with him." Usually the dialogue coach reads with you, but having Chuck there really put me at ease. I had the first line, then he had one, then me again. And that's all we read! Anthony Quinn turned to Mr. DeMille and said, "Isn't it amazing? A good actor can read one line and you know he's right for the part. He's perfect for the role!"

I was immediately rushed into makeup. They slicked back my hair, applied some freckles, and told me to put on the top of my uniform and my military hat. I was then rushed back to the sound stage to shoot close-ups for the scene in which Iron Eyes Cody, myself and a few others watch through a mansion window as Inger Stevens sings. My first scene, and it still wasn't noon!

Anthony Quinn gave me a biscuit and told me how to play the scene. As we were filming, I took a bite of the biscuit, then another—and started to choke! I tried desperately to hold it in because I didn't want to ruin the scene and look like an amateur my first day of shooting. Tears started to run down my cheeks. Tony finally yelled "cut!" and grabbed me. He exclaimed, "That was absolutely beautiful, Kenny!" Then the assistant director came over and told me how great I had been. But I hadn't been emoting—I was merely trying not to choke on a stale biscuit! Sometimes inspiration comes from the darndest places.

At lunchtime, I called my agent, William Schuller, and gave him the good news. I told him we could ask for anything we wanted because I already had a scene in the can. That shouldn't have happened, but if you're Cecil B. DeMille, I guess they don't mind bending the rules. I told Bill to ask for a substantial amount because I felt they would be adding additional scenes involving my character. But Bill was a rather conservative man who was afraid to take chances, and he ended up asking for less than he probably could have gotten. Nonetheless, I was well compensated and my role was extended through the whole movie. My big scene with Chuck Heston, which is the first scene in the movie, was the last to be shot.

After lunch, I went back to wardrobe to be fitted for a uniform. Anthony Quinn and Cecil DeMille came over and told me how happy they were to have me on the film, and that they were going to add more scenes for me. I was in clover, astounded by my good fortune. I worked on "The Buccaneer" for 17 weeks. Yul Brynner, whom I loved even though he could be a pompous ass, made the movie run over by two weeks. As a result, I lost a role in "King Creole" which had been offered to me by Elvis himself, because both movies were shooting at the same time.

Speaking of Elvis, he asked if he could drop by the set of "The Buccaneer" to meet Yul Brynner and the rest of the cast. I mentioned it to Anthony Quinn, who thought it would be a good idea because DeMille loved having dignitaries and other important people visit him. I assumed he'd be happy to meet Elvis Presley, but he quickly nixed the idea, telling Quinn that if Elvis came on the set, it would cause such mayhem that they would lose at least a half-day of shooting. I explained that to Elvis and he said that he understood, though I could tell that he didn't really think his presence would cause that much commotion.

The first version of "The Buccaneer," which DeMille had made in 1938 with Frederic March, was shot at Paramount studios and on Catalina Island. At least, that's where the battle of New Orleans was staged. For some reason they decided to shoot the battle scene for the remake on two huge sound stages on the Paramount lot. The water shots were filmed on a big tank on the Paramount back lot. This reduced the budget, but made a look of authenticity more difficult. But it worked, especially the scenes on the pirate ship.

I was in the battle scenes in which the British advance on the weakened American forces, led by Andrew Jackson. There were probably 100 extras dressed in British military uniforms, and they had to give the appearance of more than a thousand. So as they came to the cameras, the extras disbursed, ran to the back of the line, and advanced yet again. The sound stage was huge so they had a bit of a run, but it looked pretty good.

Yul Brynner was the star of the film, and I always thought he was perfect as Jean Lafitte. I was star-struck in the beginning, and I couldn't help but think that he was always playing the King of Siam, appropriately grand and very sartorial. He loved being a movie star, and never missed an opportunity to live the role to the hilt.

One day I dropped by the set to watch a scene with Lorne Green and E.G. Marshall. Suddenly the doors opened wide and in walks this phenomenon—a figure dressed in a skintight black leather suit that left nothing to the imagination, and a huge hat. He looked at me and said, "Kenny, would you like to touch it?" I must have looked puzzled because he quickly added: "I meant the leather!" It was just Yul, playing movie star for the benefit of DeMille's visitors. The suit had been a gift from Marlene Dietrich.

Always the star, Yul had a valet on the set whose sole job was to carry a napkin-covered goblet filled with special water. Whenever he wanted a drink, Yul would just lift his hand and his valet would come running.

Despite his affectations, Yul was a terrific actor—and a very talented photographer. He was allowed to mount his camera on the cinematographer's camera and take still photographs while we were filming. The last week of shooting, there was a display of life-size photos shot by Yul mounted in the Paramount commissary. He had taken two pictures of me, one with me and Charlton Heston during the Battle of New Orleans and another of me standing by the camera with Anthony Quinn and Inger Stevens. He always promised I'd get copies of those photos, but someone told me it wouldn't happen—and they were right. Despite repeated requests on my part and repeated promises by Yul, I never received any prints.

Anthony Quinn was a terrific director because he was primarily an actor. He spent a lot of time with me, helping me perfect my role. When we were getting ready to shoot the first scenes of the prologue, he whispered to me, "Just imagine you've got the biggest cock in the world and you can conquer anything—including Andrew Jackson!" He always said something like that to put me at ease and make me feel comfortable with the scene.

At the end of filming, Tony put his arm around me and said to me, "Kenny, thank you for your wonderful contribution to 'The Buccaneer.' I'm going to put you in every movie I direct!" And he was true to his word, because "The Buccaneer" was the only movie Anthony Quinn ever directed!

Inger Stevens was a beautiful, wonderful actress, but she could be unpredictable to work with because she had wild mood swings. Sometimes she was really nice, and other times she was a terror. You never knew what her mood would be, or what would set her off.

One time I brought Tommy Sands on the lot and we went to see Elvis, then back to the set of "The Buccaneer." It was after lunch and Inger was sitting outside her trailer talking to her wardrobe assistant. I politely introduced Tommy to Inger, and she was very sweet. But after Tommy left, she called me back to her trailer and hissed, "Don't you EVER interrupt me when I'm talking to someone again!" I was dumbfounded by her sudden change because she had always been very nice to me. Later that afternoon, she was pleasant again.

As filming progressed, Inger became infatuated with Anthony Quinn. He had to be very careful about these things because at the time he was married to DeMille's daughter Katherine, and his extracurricular activities were being closely watched. One day he asked me if I knew an out-of-the-way place where we could go to talk about scenes. It finally dawned on me that he was looking for a place where he could meet with Inger, and he wanted me along for appearances' sake. I suggested a place called Eddie Cano's El Torito, which was low-key and had very good food.

I always arrived first. Then Tony would arrive, followed by Inger. I had told Eddie Cano that Tony didn't want to be disturbed by gawkers and fans, so he placed them in the back room, where they carried on their doings while I stayed up front at the bar drinking margaritas and eating nachos. When they were through "discussing scenes," they would come out and have a drink with me. This happened two or three times. Tony would ask me if I wanted to join him at the El Torito for a drink, and I knew immediately what he meant. I didn't mind playing the beard in their relationship because I liked them both, especially Inger despite her unpredictable moods. She eventually acknowledged that she had fallen in love with Tony, who later divorced Katherine. Inger probably thought that once he was free, Tony would marry her, but of course he didn't.

Claire Bloom, whose character Bonnie Brown was part of Lafitte's gang of gallant pirates, was a wonderful gal, but it was like she was invisible. I saw very little of her because all of her scenes were with the pirates. And when she wasn't working, she preferred to stay in her dressing room reading. She was a dedicated actress, but she was very much a loner.

When it came time to shoot the final scene, all that was left was me, my dog, Charlton Heston and the production crew. The other big names had finished their parts and disappeared. I was really ticked because I had to back out of "King Creole," but there wasn't anything I could do about it, so I gritted my teeth and tried to be professional.

Elmer Bernstein, who scored the film, had written a special musical theme for me at the request of Cecil B. DeMille and Tony Quinn. I spent hours learning the melody so that I could whistle it as I came over the hill at the beginning of the movie—a difficult task because I'm not a very good whistler. Thankfully, we finally prerecorded it so I wouldn't have to whistle it on the set. It was a pain in the ass, but I couldn't really complain. I was working on a Cecil B. DeMille spectacular—and I had my own theme, which was quite a distinction.

Since this chapter features more than its share of movie legends, it's probably the most appropriate place to discuss my encounters with the late James Dean. I worked on both "East of Eden" (1955) and "Rebel

Without A Cause" (1955), though I don't consider myself in either one and I don't list them on my credits.

I came into "East of Eden" after being sent to Warner Brothers by my agent. The casting agent then sent several of us out somewhere in the Valley, near a school that was being used as background. It was a cattle call and I was one of 60 or 70 young actors being considered for a role in the film's prologue, and possibly other scenes. We hung around for nearly two hours before director Elia Kazan finally honored us with his presence. He didn't make us read. Instead, he just went down the line of actors and picked this one and that one. I was one of the chosen.

The casting people called shortly after and told me I would have to go to wardrobe because the movie was a period piece set just before World War II. I went to wardrobe, was fitted for my costume, and then waited at home to be called. They started shooting, but had some delays so a couple of weeks passed before I was finally summoned. This was nerve-wracking because the whole production seemed very unorganized. It was an important film but the set was uncomfortable because Kazan was extremely moody and rude. The kids working as background and extras were treated as little more than cattle, but I was an actor on day rate so I was treated almost like a human being.

Filming seemed to go at a snail's pace. In fact, we didn't do anything my first day on the set because they just didn't get around to us. Every morning Kazan would huddle in the back of his car with a typewriter on his knees writing dialogue for that day. Then he would give it to his secretary, who would photocopy it. But inevitably, Kazan would change the dialogue again, which was his prerogative.

My big scene in "East of Eden" wasn't very big at all. It was the prologue (which is seldom seen anymore), and had to do with kids talking about a submarine off Monterey Bay. Richard Davalos and Julie Harris were leaving school, and I ran up and walked along with them making small talk. I don't even remember what I said. After a few lines, I broke away and told them I would see them the next day. Then James Dean came into the scene. That was it. Now you know why I seldom list the movie on my credits.

I had met Jimmy a couple of times prior to that. He had been in Hollywood a few years before making it big with "East of Eden," but nothing happened so he went back to New York, where he sharpened his acting skills in theater. That's where he met Kazan, who became his acting coach and mentor.

There was a lot of hullabaloo even before "East of Eden" started filming. Kazan put Jimmy under contract while he was in New York, and tutored him for more than a year before bringing Jimmy back to Hollywood. It was a bit of a sticky point with a couple of actors because very few performers get the opportunity to be coached for a role an entire year before filming begins.

That tutoring obviously paid off, of course. Jimmy was a dynamic actor, capable of deep emotion and subtle subtext. But he wasn't a very nice person. During that period, I was going to the Hollywood School of Drama while trying to get my acting career off the ground. My friends and I used to hang out at a place called Googie's, a restaurant that was situated at the top of the Sunset Strip, and Jimmy would drop by occasionally with his friends, including actress Maila Nurmi. She played Vampira on a late-night horror show, but is probably best known for her role as Bela Lugosi's undead wife in Ed Wood's "Plan Nine From Outer Space." Maila was a very strange gal, but she fit perfectly into Jimmy's scene. He also used to hang out with a friend from New York, an obnoxious guy who worked with Jimmy in the background. I was never certain what their relationship was.

Sometimes I would drop by Googie's and Jimmy would invite me to sit with him. Other times he would completely ignore me and those I was with. He was an extremely moody guy, which made him rather difficult to be around. You just never knew where you stood with him. I don't expect everyone to be happy and smiling all the time, but I do expect to be recognized and treated like a person. Jimmy wasn't that way.

About a year after my stint on "East of Eden," my friend Judy Rose, the daughter of designer Helen Rose, invited me to go to the Academy Awards with her and her mom. At that time, the Academy Awards ceremony was held at the Pantages Theater in Hollywood. As it turned out, Jo Van Fleet was up as Best Supporting Actress for "East of Eden," and Helen Rose had been nominated for her wardrobe design work in Susan Hayward's "I'll Cry Tomorrow."

Jo Van Fleet went to the ceremony with us in our limo because her husband was ill in New York and couldn't attend. It was a very exciting evening for all of us, and both Jo and Helen won their respective awards. There was a barrage of press as we left the theater, and Helen asked me to hold her Oscar while her husband went to find our driver. A few minutes later, Jo asked me to hold her Oscar, too, so there I was in front of the theater clutching two Academy Awards! Some of my fans, who always managed to find me no matter where I was, went nuts at the sight of me with double Oscars. After everyone had their photos taken a zillion times, we piled into the limo and went to Romanoff's for an awards party. That was my only association with Oscar. So far.

It should be noted that Jo Van Fleet had some wonderful scenes in "East of Eden" with a actress named Bette Treadville. Bette was a big, outrageous singer/actress who lived with a dancer named Gene Fontaine, who had appeared with me in "Finian's Rainbow." I used to go over to Gene and Bette's place a lot because Bette was a fantastic cook who loved to whip up all the Southern foods I had come to love.

Bette was cast in "East of Eden" the day after I was, so I went over to her place for a big celebration dinner. Bette played a mulatto with blond hair who sat on the porch of Jo's whorehouse as James Dean went by. She was absolutely wonderful, and stole the scenes in which she appeared.

I also worked with Jimmy that same year in what remains his best-known film, "Rebel Without A Cause." Again, my role was rather small (I played a gang member again) and little of me remained in the final version, so I seldom list it on my credits. Still, I'm proud to have participated in what has become a genuine cult phenomenon.

Most people don't know this, but some dramatic changes were made in the story before it started shooting. The film was originally to take place around a drive-in theater, and all of the members of the gang had names. But I think Jimmy's representatives—and Jimmy, too—felt that the setting would take away from his character. Jayne Mansfield was going to be a carhop because she was under contract to Warner Brothers at the time. But then they changed the location to the planetarium and Jayne was out. So was I, pretty much.

Jimmy's accidental death in 1955 shook Hollywood to its core. Jimmy was proving himself a multifaceted, extremely talented actor with a tremendous future when he managed to wrap his new Porche around a telephone pole. I shudder when I think about it, because Jimmy invited me to take a drive with him the day before he was killed. He drove the car onto the sound stage where we were doing some screen tests, and took a few of us for a quick ride. He loved that car and was so damned proud of it. He decided to take a long drive the next day and asked if I'd like to join him, but I had class and couldn't get away. I found out later that he had asked several other cast members to drive with him, but they, too, were unable to go. The whole incident is still difficult for me to think about.

I was in Hollywood not too long ago for a charity benefit for Child Help USA, which was chaired by my good friends Yvonne Lime and Sarah Buchner. On my way to the benefit, I had my picture taken by a fan photographer named Jon Virzi, who told me that he had seen me on film at the Egyptian Theater the night before—they were showing "East of Eden" and "Rebel Without A Cause" as a tribute to Jimmy on the anniversary of his death. The distributors had put together some screen tests from "Rebel" and "Eden" and was showing them between the movies. I had always wanted to get a copy of those tests, but Warner Brothers would never release them.

I called the manager of the Egyptian Theater to find out about show times. He remembered me and said I could drop by any time. There were several different sets of screen tests, and I was in a couple of them—looking younger than I ever remembered. There were also tests of Kathy Grant and Pat Morrow, who were trying out for the role that eventually went to Natalie Wood. I remember that director Nicholas Ray had asked me to read off-camera with them.

There was another test where we were just sitting around talking with Ray. It was a wardrobe test, but mainly he just wanted to get us together to see how we looked as a group. At one point I looked away from the screen and when I looked back, I saw Sal Mineo, Nick Adams, Natalie Wood, James Dean and me. The emotion hit me like a ton of bricks and I started crying right there in the theater. As soon as I could control myself, I left.

Of that group, I was the only one who was still alive.

Chapter 8
Mainstream Movie Madness

Certainly, not all of my movies have been huge mega-classics. Most have been simple mainstream films that entertained their audiences— nothing more, nothing less. But as an actor I learned something important from each and made a lot of terrific friends along the way.

"The Search For Bridey Murphy" (1956) was an adaptation of a very popular nonfiction book by Morey Bernstein, which dealt with a woman's reincarnation back to 19th century Ireland while under hypnosis. Director Noel Langley was into reincarnation and the supernatural in a big way, and he convinced Paramount to make the film. However, it didn't do as well as the studio hoped, possibly because it was released too late to really capitalize on the popularity of the book.

Teresa Wright and Louis Hayward were the stars, and the film also featured Nancy Gates, Kenneth Tobey and Richard Anderson. I didn't appear with either Teresa or Louis, though I got to know them on the set. Teresa was wonderful, a terrific gal and a great actress, but Louis was a bit stand-offish. He would speak to you, but he was a bit of a snob which turned off many people. I played Duncan Murphy, Bridey's brother when she was reincarnated in Ireland. I've played a few Irish characters over the years and most people think I'm of Irish decent, but in truth I'm English and German. However, nationality means nothing to an actor. You're whatever the script says you are, and in "Bridey Murphy" I was Irish.

Eileen Jansen played Bridey during the reincarnation sequences. Brad Jackson, who had been under contract to Universal, also had a good-sized role and was viewed as an up-and-coming young star. Brad was perfect for this flick because he was really into the occult and the supernatural; he believed in just about all of that stuff. He was a bit of a loner, but we became friends during the shoot. He used to drop by my apartment on Beachwood Drive now and then and we would have deep, serious talks about the occult. He even hypnotized me a couple of times, which was rather interesting. Hypnosis was a big fad in Hollywood at the time, and no party was complete without a hypnotist. I always seemed to get picked because I was the most susceptible. One day Brad just disappeared. I never did find out what happened to him.

To get us in the right mind-set during filming, Bernstein hypnotized a few members of the cast, including Eileen and Brad. It was fascinating to watch, though I don't think it helped the picture very much.

I worked on "Bridey Murphy" for about two and a half weeks. It was a lucky break for me because Ted Taylor, who was head of public relations at Paramount then, was a good friend of mine. He and his wife Gwen lived below me when I was going to the Hollywood School of Drama and I shared a duplex with fellow actors Jon Zollan and Cole Christian. It was Ted's job to publicize the movie, and I appeared in more than my share of publicity shots. I was even called back for two extra days of work to sit for a studio portrait for the film. The resulting picture, my face eerily lit by a candle, is one of my all-time favorite film photos.

Even though much of the film was set in Ireland, few of us have an Irish accent. We tried to affect a proper brogue early on, then decided against it. It worked out okay, though, because there was little dialogue in our scenes. Eileen had the most to say, and luckily she was able to properly affect a perfect Irish accent.

"The Search for Bridey Murphy" was a very pleasant experience, and it really got me interested in the occult. One day my good friend Nan Morris (who was Troy Donahue's long-time girlfriend before Suzanne Pleshette) invited me to join her and Tuesday Weld on a trip to Santa Monica to visit a legendary clairvoyant named Dareos. He had a huge reputation and many of Hollywood's biggest stars, including Mae West, Greta Garbo and Mary Pickford, consulted him before making important life and career decisions.

Dareos supposedly knew we were coming, but no one answered the door when we arrived at his house. We knocked and hollered for several minutes before he finally let us in. Then we knew what had taken so long—the guy was ancient! It must have taken him 20 minutes just to walk from his chair to the locked gate.

First he did a tarot reading for some of us, then we had a seance in which he went into a trance and talked to each of us individually. He concluded our session with a palm reading. We were supposed to be there only one hour, but ended up staying for nearly five. I'll never forget what the aging psychic had to say to me: "Kenny, you're going to be successful. You'll have a lot of ups and downs, and will be known for some things more than others. But after you reach 60 years old, you're going to be more famous than Bing Crosby!" The clock is ticking.

I had another spooky encounter with the supernatural in the late '50s while staying at Rudolph Valentino's magnificent house, which was known as Falcon's Lair. Film producer Juan Romero was handling the estate, which was up for sale, and he asked me to stay there for a few days while he went to Europe on business. Falcon's Lair was considerably nicer than my apartment at the time, so I readily agreed. But I quickly found out that things weren't as they seemed.

In short, the house was haunted. I heard weird noises my first night there, which I attributed to my imagination. But I had some friends over the following evening, and they heard things, too. I thought perhaps it was tree branches brushing against the windows, but the caretaker said that the trees had been recently trimmed and couldn't possibly be touching the house.

I went out for dinner on the third evening, and returned to find the gas jets in the fireplace burning at full throttle, even though I hadn't been anywhere near the fireplace that day. I thought that perhaps a visiting real estate agent had accidentally left them on, though we had agreed that no one would drop by without notifying me first.

Then things really started to get creepy. That night, while dozing in the master bedroom, I distinctly heard people talking downstairs. I went down to check, but there was no one there. I attributed it to the wind, but turned on all the lights because I was starting to get more than a little scared.

Mysterious happenings occurred every evening I was there. I heard voices and unexplainable sounds. The fireplace would mysteriously turn on. Doors would slam shut, even though there was no wind or air conditioning to move them. A mysterious breeze would brush my face while I watched television in the living room. I would go to bed with the lights off, and wake up in the middle of the night to find them on. I finally cornered the real estate gal in charge of selling Falcon's Lair, and she confessed that I wasn't the first person to witness these bizarre events. Juan and others were convinced that a poltergeist or ghost was haunting that house, but the real estate people were keeping it mum because they didn't want to frighten prospective clients.

After a few more days of this, I was a wreck. I was supposed to stay a little more than a week, but bailed two days early because I just couldn't take it any more. I didn't feel that my safety was in jeopardy—the ghost never did anything that could harm me—but my nerves were so shot that I simply couldn't stay there any longer. It wasn't a healthy place to be. I gave the keys to the real estate saleswoman and happily returned to my small but unhaunted apartment.

"The Young Guns" (1956) was my only western. This Allied Artists teen feature starred Russ Tamblyn, Perry Lopez and a bunch of wonderful character actors, including Myron Healy, who made scores of westerns over the course of his career. Gloria Talbot was the love interest and Scott Marlowe was the heavy.

The story, from what I can remember (it's been a while since I've seen this movie), concerns the efforts of the sons of several infamous outlaws to clear their names. I can't recall who my character was, aside from the fact that he was the son of someone famous, but I do remember that this was a fun movie to make. The director was Alfredo Antonini, better known as Albert Band. This was his first movie, but he went on to make several others, including "I Bury the Living" (1958) and "Face of Fire" (1959). Contemporary movie buffs probably know him best as the co-founder, with his son, Charles, of Full Moon Video, which has produced a number of entertaining horror and science-fiction flicks over the years.

We shot "The Young Guns" on location in the San Fernando Valley. We would go to the studio in the morning then be taken to location by bus. Since this was a western, it was essential that we knew how to ride a horse. I learned as a kid in Springfield while earning money caring for a friend's horse, and Molly Bee, Yvonne Lime and I used to go horseback riding at a stable in Griffith Park, so it was second nature to me. But it wasn't to Scott Marlowe, who apparently lied during casting when asked if he had experience with horses. He was fine actor, but a lousy horseman.

For one scene in which we're chasing the bad buy, the cameras were mounted at the bottom of a hill and we were directed to ride at full gallop right in front of them. We started out together, but Antonini wanted each of us to come by the camera individually with the dust flying and the whole western bit. It was a great shot as conceived—but Scott, who was essentially a New York actor, had never ridden a horse before. He got one of the wranglers to show him to how to mount the horse, and received a quick five-minute riding lesson before being called to the mark.

Let's just say things didn't go well. Scott lost the reins almost immediately and was forced to wrap his arms around the horse's neck. He came down the hill screaming like crazy, his feet out of the stirrups—and then he fell on his ass because he didn't know how to get the horse to stop. Myron Healy tried repeatedly to teach Scott how to ride, but finally gave up in disgust. Scott just wasn't meant to be a horseman. They finally ended up showing him starting out on the horse, but used a stunt double in the shots of him coming down the hill. In fact, any scene of Scott actually riding a horse was a stunt double because he just couldn't do it. Horses made him look like a wimp, even though he wasn't, and the wranglers gave him a hard time for the rest of the shoot.

I can't remember if my character lives or dies in "The Young Guns," but I do recall that I was featured prominently on the poster. I always had agents who never thought billing was important, so they seldom negotiated that perk for me. As a result, I made many a movie in which I felt I should have gotten star or co-star billing plus be in the ads, but I didn't and I wasn't. They usually used my picture, though, because my face was familiar to young, fan magazine-reading movie goers. On "Going Steady," for example, the poster featured three pictures of me—but not my name! "The Young Guns" was pretty much the same—my face big, my name tiny.

A funny coincidence: I sang the title song for "Young Guns of Texas" (1962)—not to be confused with "The Young Guns." "The Young Guns of Texas" was directed by my friend Maury Dexter, and featured the offspring of many big stars, including Alana Ladd and Jody McCrea. 20th Century-Fox released the song as a single.

"Rally 'Round the Flag, Boys!" (1958) was based on the wonderful book by humorist Max Schulman about a small town's reaction to the construction of a new missile base. The impressive cast included Paul Newman, Joanne Woodward, Tuesday Weld, Joan Collins, Jack Carson, Gale Gordon and Dwayne Hickman of "Dobie Gillis" TV fame.

I was cast as one of the soldiers at the camp, and I had a terrific scene with Tuesday Weld in a record store. This was Tuesday's second movie, and she was darling to work with.

I also played a pilgrim during the movie's Thanksgiving pageant scene, which involved just about everyone from the community and the new military base. Joan Collins, who played what can only be described as the town slut, portrayed an Indian maiden decked out in full headdress and an amazingly short costume. Thoughtfully she wore pantyhose because Joan liked to sit in a director's chair with one leg up on the arm. Her costume was just long enough to cover her crotch, but it was an inspiring image we all tried to catch! I didn't get to know Joan very well, but she was a fun person on the set. She always spoke with a British accent—except when she was filming. Then she managed a very convincing American accent.

One of my scenes was with Jack Carson. I had admired him as an actor for years, but by the end of the shoot I was extremely disappointed by his unprofessional behavior. Jack would forget a line or otherwise mess up a scene, then blame someone else. He would say a grip moved a light and distracted him, or someone was talking. Everyone messes up—it's part of the game. But Jack refused to admit that he was the problem. Everything that went wrong was someone else's fault. Some people said he was ill while making "Rally 'Round the Flag, Boys!," but that doesn't excuse his lack of professionalism.

It was because of my involvement with "Rally" that I also got to meet—very fleetingly—the stunning Marilyn Monroe. I was late for my call one day because of car trouble, and as I was running by some dressing room trailers outside a nearby sound stage a woman came out and asked me the time. Standing next to her, looking somewhat dazed and confused, was Marilyn with a glass of champagne in her hand. It was only 10:30 in the morning, and she was downing champagne, which seemed almost appropriate. I looked at my watch, told the woman the time, smiled at Marilyn and ran on. That was the first and only time I ever had contact with America's reigning sex symbol. I'll never forget it.

I did see Marilyn once again a few years later, but not to talk to. I had an apartment for a while on Sunset Boulevard that overlooked a popular restaurant called the Marquis. One night I heard a huge ruckus, and when I looked down at the parking lot below there was Marilyn Monroe and Joe DiMaggio sitting in their red Mercedes convertible having a domestic battle. They never touched each other, but they were screaming obscenities like drunken Marines, calling each other "motherfucker" and other vicious names. Marilyn started to go into the restaurant, but Joe made her come out. Then he threw her in the car and they drove away. It was a very uncomfortable scene for all who witnessed it. Definitely not the way you want to remember the sexiest woman in the world and America's great baseball legend.

"Rally" was one of many films in which I played a soldier, but at least my character didn't die this time. It was nice to finish a film without having to take a bullet.

I wasn't so lucky in "Battle Flame" (1959), an Allied Artists flick about the Korean War. The movie starred Scott Brady, Elaine Edwards, Robert Blake, Richard Harrison and me. Scott was a gas to work with. He had done so many films at that point that he didn't take anything very seriously any more. I met him at an actors' hangout on Sunset Boulevard called the Saratoga a few days before filming was to start. I had gone there to meet someone else and saw Scott at the bar, so I went up and introduced myself. He put his arm around me and bought me a drink and we became good pals on the spot.

Robert Blake, unfortunately, didn't share Scott's carefree attitude. He must have been going through his James Dean phase because he wasn't the friendliest guy on the set, though he was okay to work with. It was kind of awkward, though, because while Robert sat there brooding, the rest of us were just having a blast—Scott most of all.

I also became good friends with Richard Harrison, a bodybuilder with a great physique who later became a big star in Europe after appearing in some Italian sand-'n-sandal epics. He ended up living in a mansion next door to Sophia Loren. Unfortunately, few of his films made it over to the United States.

I played Orlando, the company cook, in "Battle Flame," which always makes me laugh. I may look like a lot of things, but with my blond hair and blue eyes I never thought Orlando was one of them! I had a couple of funny scenes because I was always giving the dishes I prepared fancy names. Not surprisingly, I get shot, but it's been a while since I've seen "Battle Flame" and I can't remember if I die or not. You'd think I'd remember something like that, but after a while my death scenes sort of meld into one giant melodrama.

In 1959, I made "The Little Shepherd of Kingdom Come" (released in 1961) for 20th Century-Fox. I was cast by my good friend Maury Dexter, who was the executive producer. Andrew McLaglen was the director. We filmed on location in Big Bear, California.

Maury had come to me for suggestions on some popular male performers to star in the film. I gave him a couple of names, including singer Jimmie Rodgers, who I really hoped would be chosen. Jimmie's career was really hot then, but both Maury and Andy were a little concerned because Jimmie had never acted before. However, they had him read and finally decided he was perfect for the part.

The other members of the cast included Luana Patten, Robert Dix, Chill Wills and a newcomer named George Kennedy, who played the villain. This was George's first film, and he was great. He chewed the scenery and spit it out. George told me on the set that he was determined to be a big star, and under the circumstances of the heavy he was playing, I thought, "oh yeah - sure!" But by golly, he proved me wrong—and I'm glad.

Jimmie Rodgers was hired because of his singing success, and the producers took advantage of that. During one scene, we're sitting around our simple home talking, and Jimmy casually picks up a guitar and starts singing. But I don't believe they left the scene in. The last time I saw "Little Shepherd," Jimmie's impromptu singing scene was missing.

Hal Needam was the stunt coordinator and head stuntman on the movie. There were numerous battle scenes, so they needed a lot of stunts. In one battle sequence there was a scene with guys on a tall lookout tower. Hal was on top of the tower and he was supposed to jump into a safety net when they blew the tower up. But Hal is such a fearless stuntman that when they blew the tower off its supports, he actually rode it to the ground! He was knocked unconscious, and it was feared that he had broken his back. Hal was rushed by ambulance to a hospital in San Bernardino, which was the town closest to where we were filming. Thankfully, he hadn't broken his back, but he was pretty battered up. The doctors said he had pulled all the muscles in his back, torn some cartilage and broken a few ribs. But the next day, he was back on the set! I'm certain that Hal has broken as many bones as Evel Knievel over the course of his career. As I said, the guy is fearless.

A couple of weeks before the end of production, I got a call from my brother Dick and his wife Katie wanting to know how much longer I was going to be working. At first they wouldn't tell me why they needed to know, but it turned out my mother was gravely ill and had been placed in a tuberculosis sanitarium. They told me not to worry and to come home as soon as I could after the film was completed. Two days before the film was done, my brother George called and wanted to know how close we were to finishing. We had a couple days to go, but all my scenes had been shot and I was just hanging around in case they needed me for pick-ups. I told George that, and he said he thought it would be best if I came home immediately. I went to Maury Dexter and he said without hesitation that he would get me a flight out of Los Angeles the next day. He had a driver take me home to LA so I could get my stuff and then take me to the airport. My mother lived four more weeks, so I got to spend some time with her before she passed away. She had finally accepted that show business wasn't as bad as she and my father had believed. One reason was that Jimmie Rodgers and his wife Colleen dropped by one time to see her in Springfield, and brought her a beautiful plant. And another time, Molly Bee was appearing at the Ohio State Fair, and she stopped over and visited my mother. Plus other entertainers were friendly with her, so she came to realize that Hollywood wasn't Sodom and Gomorrah after all.

"The Nun and the Sergeant" (1962) was another military vehicle also set in Korea. I landed a role in that flick because I was being managed at the time by the renowned Henry Wilson, who handled Rock Hudson, Natalie Wood and a lot of other heavy hitters. Henry was a good friend of producer Eugene Franke, who was married to Anna Sten, a Greta Garbo replacement who did a lot of excellent work over the years. Eugene made a deal with Warner Brothers to make "The Nun and the Sergeant" as a comeback vehicle for Anna, and Henry got to pick many of the stars from his personal stable. Hence my involvement.

Robert Webber, who had been a leading man on Broadway, was the star, and he was even zanier than Scott Brady! We played Marine prisoners who are put on detail in Korea. We come across a busload of young Korean girls and a nun, and become their protectors.

Robert was a big, good-looking guy, but whenever we weren't doing serious scenes, he would pretend to be a big swish. He wasn't gay—in fact, he got married shortly after making "The Nun and the Sergeant"—but he liked to goof around and see what kind of reaction he would get.

One time he invited me to join him for dinner at a restaurant someone had recommended to him. He didn't know too many people in Hollywood at the time and he was lonely for company. We had a couple of drinks at the bar, then sat down for dinner. After a few minutes, something dawned on us...there were NO women present. It was a gay joint! Without missing a beat, Robert went into his swish routine, putting his hand on mine and doing all the little things that a man and woman would do together. I almost died from embarrassment, and Robert enjoyed every minute of it. I had parked in front of the restaurant and he had parked down the street, so as we parted ways, he grabbed me and kissed me right there on the street! I growled, "You motherfucker!" and Robert said, "See you tomorrow on the set!" It was really quite funny, and we laughed about the whole thing for days.

I still have photographs of Linda Wong, the actress who played my character's Korean girlfriend in the movie. I was in my trailer one day when we were on location, and she came over and asked me to join her for a snack. She brought out what looked like a big snowball wrapped in paper. It was a rice ball containing fish heads, seaweed, onions and soy sauce. It smelled absolutely horrible, but I knew I would have to taste it or risk insulting her. So I took a bite, which I managed to keep down. But the second bite made me lost my stomach. I quickly excused myself, ran out of the room and puked my guts out. I never told her because I didn't want to hurt her feelings. Korean fish balls are definitely an acquired taste which I never managed to acquire, but Linda would bring me one almost every morning. I would graciously accept it and tell her I would eat it later in the day. Then, when no one was looking, I would throw it away.

A lot of people thought that "The Nun and the Sergeant" was made in Korea, but it was really filmed in the Valley, outside of Los Angeles. It was the perfect location because the terrain looks just like Korea. Part of the movie was also filmed at the Iverson Ranch, where a lot of westerns have been made.

My character in "The Nun and the Sergeant" was Donnie. It was a good featured role. Not a starring role, but I had many minutes of screen time, and I was under contract from beginning to end (as I was for "Battle Flame). And yes, I get shot again. This time I take a bullet during an ambush as we're going up a hill. I was shot so many times in so many movies that after a while I felt entitled to some kind of medal!

"Little Laura and Big John" (1973) was an interesting little movie about John Ashley, Laura Upthegrove and Hanford Mobley, a gang of real-life turn-of-the-century Florida outlaws whose exploits resembled those of Bonnie and Clyde. They had a hideout in the Everglades, and terrorized the southern part of the state for several years before being gunned down by area lawmen. Theirs was a fascinating story that would have made an outstanding motion picture if it had been done properly.

I had just returned from Europe and was living in Florida when the movie was conceived. I attended a play at the Parker Playhouse in Miami with a writer friend named Bob Freund, and after the play Bob introduced me to Lou Wiethe and his wife Judy, who told me they thought I'd be great for a movie they were producing. The next day, I got a call from Luke Moberly, who owned a small film studio in Davie, Florida. He told me about the movie and I went to the studio a few days later to read for him. They hadn't cast anyone yet because Luke and Lou were going to California to talk to agents for the lead role of John Ashley. I left the reading without them saying yes or no regarding my casting.

My agent at the time, Beverly McDermott, told me they wanted me for the movie, but they weren't willing to pay very much. I ran into Lou and Judy Wiethe at a society event a few days later, and they told me they didn't have the money in the budget to pay me what Beverly was asking, which was $2,500 a week. After a few days of negotiating, they agreed to pay me $2,000 a week to play Ashley's cohort, Hanford Mobley.

Lou and Luke then went to Hollywood to cast the part of John Ashley. They talked with Bruce Dern and Christopher George, both of whom would have been great, but finally signed Fabian, who was looking for a comeback film. I was happy with that decision because I had known Fabian for years. They also signed Karen Black for the part of Laura Upthegrove, John Ashley's notorious "queen of the Everglades."

Much of "Little Laura and Big John" was shot in and around Stuart, Florida, the site of many of the Ashley gang's real-life robberies. The city and the area residents were wonderful to us, redoing streets so that they would look more turn-of-the-century and really going out of their way to help make the film look authentic. A woman named Janet Hutchinson became one of the film's technical directors because she ran the local Elliot Museum, which contained a lot of memorabilia from that era, including vintage automobiles. While in Stuart, we stayed at the Pelican Hotel, which had been a high-priced brothel years before.

Despite a lot of good intentions, making the movie was anything but easy. The actors were dedicated, but performers are only as good as their director, and Luke Moberly had never directed a motion picture before. He didn't have a filmmaker's background so he had little understanding of cinematic story-telling. We would be sitting around a campfire in the Everglades, for example, but there would be no establishing shot and no explanation of where we were or why. It was all in Luke's mind, but he never bothered to put it on film. He was enamored with the glamour of moviemaking—the parties and the recognition—but he had no experience on the technical end and the picture suffered greatly because of that.

We were on location in Stuart for several weeks, then we moved to the studio in Davie for the more rustic scenes, such as those in the Everglades. Luke wanted me to do a scene in which I'm walking through the swamp, trip on a root and get bitten on the face by a rattlesnake—all in one take. A Native-American on the crew who thought he knew everything about snakes said the stunt would be safe because he could milk all the venom out of the snake before we shot, and all I'd get was a small scratch on my face.

The stunt sounded harmless as proposed, and I trusted Luke and his technical advisors. Besides, it would look great if we were able to capture it all in a single, seamless take. But Karen and others on the crew begged me not to do it. They didn't trust Luke and they didn't want me to risk my health unnecessarily just for a good shot.

As we were getting into makeup, a guy from the Florida Game and Freshwater Fish Commission came by the set to check on the animals we were using. When he found out about the snakebite scene, he went nuts. "That's the most ridiculous thing I've ever heard!" he said. "There's no way to milk all the venom out of a rattlesnake! If Kenny gets bitten on the face, he would definitely get sick, and possibly die!"

I was so mad at Luke that I almost punched him in the face. "You dumb son of a bitch!" I spat. "You were willing to put my life on the line for a scene with a snake!" Lou Wiethe, the producer, became sick at the thought of what could have happened if we had proceeded as planned. We still did the scene, but the bite—this time on the leg, not the face—was done as an insert. And it wasn't MY leg being bitten! I didn't want to have anything to do with the snake, even if it had been milked and I was wearing safety padding.

In another scene, they wanted John Ashley (Fabian) rowing down a river in a canoe when he spots a snake in a tree and shoots it, causing it to fall into the water. Of course, no snakes indigenous to Florida hang around in trees, so they scouted some nearby zoos and found a python or boa constrictor that was on its last legs, so to speak. The poor thing was nearly dead, so they had to secure it to the tree and then yank it into the water with a wire after Fabian shoots it. The whole thing was done half-assed and it looks it, but they left the scene in the film. I laugh every time I see it, because everyone knows boa constrictors are not native to Florida. But to the producers, a snake was a snake, and they figured no one would know the difference.

One of the sequences most fun for me was my death scene. I die gloriously, and I'm very proud of the way it came out. In a nutshell, the gang is ambushed by Martin County Sheriff Bob Baker, who is believed to have been in cahoots with John Ashley and then turned on him. John gets shot before I do, and I'm running toward the camera as I get hit by shotgun blasts. They wanted me to leap in the air and throw myself back from the impact. I don't know if it was the adrenalin or what, but as I was running and they shot me, I leaped into the air and literally threw my body backward! Then I crawled along the grass and died and died. I mean, I milked it for all it was worth. It was a dramatic scene, and fortunately they got the whole thing on film in the first take because I don't think I could have done it again. After the scene, I could barely move. Every muscle in my body ached. But it was definitely worth it. That was an Oscar-caliber death scene!

The production became increasingly chaotic as we progressed, and was in shambles and over-budget by the end. Karen and Fabian were anxious to finish because they had other commitments, and we were all getting tired of the rustic sets. The producers were so tapped out by the end of production that they asked me to take a pay cut. I refused, though we all did the last couple of days for scale.

They finally stopped production, but the film wasn't quite finished yet. Karen and Fabian returned to Hollywood, and I stayed in Florida. Sometime later, I was performing at a local nightclub when Lou and Judy asked if I could do some pick-up scenes in an attempt to make the movie a little more coherent. Luke had tried to edit the film, and only made it worse. He scored it with the wrong kinds of music, and it was so bad they couldn't get a distributor.

So they replaced Luke with director Bob Woodburn, and gave my character a real sexpot girlfriend named Jacksonville, played by Terri Justin. They also added a bit more humor. For example, in one scene I'm on top of a lighthouse with binoculars when I first spot Jacksonville. I scramble down to where she's standing to introduce myself, and run into her boyfriend, a 6-foot-4 muscle man. But I make points with her later on. In another scene, I enter a room where Jacksonville is waiting for me in bed, covered only by a blanket. Bob directed me to look at her, react, then pull the blanket off of her so she could rise up to meet me. What he didn't tell me was that Terri was completely naked under the blanket! They wanted reactions, and they go them. This supposedly was for the European version, but it somehow stayed in the American release, too.

The story would be restructured so that it was told from Laura's point of view. The character of Laura's mother was added, and she narrates the first part of the tale, offering Laura's childhood poverty as an explanation of why she turned to a life of crime. The restructuring worked pretty well and Lou and Judy were able to get the movie distributed through Crown International.

"Bloodstalkers" (1975) was another Florida-produced motion picture. Originally titled "The Night Daniel Died," it was written by Robert Morgan especially for me. It had a great script; I just wish the final product had come out a little better.

The story is a nice little horror tale about two couples who stumble on an alligator poaching operation in the Everglades while checking out a supposed resort that one of the characters has inherited. The poachers try to frighten the couples away by telling them about monsters— bloodstalkers—who live in the region. But when they refuse to leave, the poachers start killing the innocents one by one. It borrows from a lot of other movies, including "Texas Chainsaw Massacre" (1974) and has more than its share of gory effects.

This was one of the most difficult productions I've ever been involved with because we shot most of the movie at an abandoned fishing camp in the middle of the Everglades. It was, quite simply, hell. We shot in the middle of July, so the mosquitoes were so thick you could practically wipe them off your arm. They were everywhere. Toni Crabtree and Celea-Ann Cole, the two female leads, had the luxury of mobile homes, but the rest of us stayed inside the camp, using a makeshift shower. It was a very remote area. There was a little bar/restaurant nearby where most of the locals picked up their weekly rations of beer. You had to be either stoned or drunk to live in the area because there was nothing but mosquitoes and alligators. Hollywood, it wasn't.

No one was able to sleep very well under these conditions, so we were tired all of the time and tempers frequently flared. Bob Morgan was a talented director, but this was his first feature and a lot of things were forced to the wayside in order to stay on time and on budget. We usually had to finish shooting before the sun went down because that's when the mosquitos and deer flies really came out. You couldn't see through the camera because of the mosquitoes. During closeups, we had to have someone just off-camera with a fly swatter so we wouldn't be covered. And if we weren't swatting mosquitoes, we were dodging alligators. Ironically, there isn't an alligator in the entire movie, even though we were in the middle of alligator country.

Toni Crabtree, bless her heart, bravely agreed to do a nude skinnydipping scene with Jerry Albert so that the movie would have greater appeal overseas. It was filmed at night and the mosquitoes practically ate her, Jerry and the crew alive. The wrong lens was placed over the camera, so the scene came out really dark. It was a waste of time because you can barely see her. A butt shot here, a breast there. The makeup people spent a lot of time covering up Toni's mosquito bites after the scene.

Mosquitoes weren't our only neighbors. Very often the local Indians would come up to the lodge to watch when we were shooting at night. They were very adept at being quiet; one could be standing right behind you and you'd never know it. But Krissy, my Schnauzer, always knew when someone was coming and she would go nuts. She ruined a lot of shots warning us that Indians were approaching. Her skills would have been more useful had we been making a western.

We were a union production, just barely. The four leads were union, plus the Teamsters, but because Florida is a right-to-work state, many of the extras were non-union. Following us was to be a non-union low-budget film (starring June Wilkinson, I believe) that wanted to use some of the same sets we did after we were finished with them. We filmed a big chase scene in an abandoned warehouse near the Golden Lantern Motel on Tamiami Trail, where we stayed later in the shoot, and the other crew had plans for the warehouse, too. We finished the chase sequence in one evening and everyone was relaxing at the hotel bar when we heard a bit commotion. It turned out that the warehouse mysteriously burned to the ground, I think to prevent the non-union crew from using it.

"Bloodstalkers" is a horror flick so people die in gruesome ways, thanks to the talents of effects director Doug Hobart. Toni Crabtree gets an axe between her breasts in a bloody close-up, and I take a flying sickle right in the throat. The sickle was made of balsa wood but it looked real. It was held in place by wires that went to the ceiling. Doug and his crew put it against in my throat, then added blood and meat so it looked like I had hemorrhaged through my neck. It made the gore hounds really happy!

Even my dog Krissy meets a violent end when her throat is cut by the bad guys. But she wouldn't lie down and play dead for very long, so it was decided that we would fly a vet out to the set from Miami and have Krissy lightly sedated. I agreed only after being assured that there was absolutely no risk that anything could go wrong. When Krissy finally started to fall asleep, the effects crew added the blood and viscera, which really disturbed me because it looked too real. Everyone had to be very quiet because she would move slightly whenever she heard someone talking. But Robert Morgan finally got the scenes he needed and yelled "cut"—

at which point Krissy jumped up and shook blood and guts all over everyone! It was as if she knew the scene was over and that she could move again. She was quite the little actress, and somewhat of a prima donna. She's listed in the credits as Kristina Von Mueller (which is my last name in German). Krissy spent most of the shoot snoozing on a cooler, which was probably the most comfortable spot on the set.

My character was a lounge singer married to a stripper, and Celea Ann and I have a big scene in which I try to get her to quit her job. The producers wanted me to burst into song at that moment, which seemed remarkably dumb to me. Why would I break into song in the middle of the Everglades? I flashed on the painful song sequences in "I Was A Teenage Werewolf" and "Attack of the Puppet People" and decided I really didn't want to do it this time. So I did some fast talking and reminded the producers that they would have to use a standard song and pay royalties, which would cost a fortune. They saw my point and dropped the issue. It would have been a weird transition, anyway.

After the movie was scored by Stan Webb, associate producers Irv Rudley and Ben Morse and I went to the Cannes film festival to market "The Night Daniel Died." I had a wonderful time there; I was treated like a movie star and went to all of the outrageous parties. MGM opened the festival with their big retrospective extravaganza, "That's Entertainment!," and brought over whomever was still available from their stock company. The film opened at the Palais Theater, followed by an invitation-only dinner at a nearby casino. I was invited, and got to sit with some of MGM's best-loved stars from the golden age of musicals, as well as many of the people on the film festival's board of directors. All of the food was brought over from the United States and prepared by the owner of Ma Maison— no expense was spared. There were eight courses, and each course was introduced with a song from an MGM musical. One of the courses was corn on the cob, which proved to be a disaster; people in tuxedos, evening gowns and gloves simply don't like corn on the cob! A number of wines were served, which the French naturally assumed to be theirs. But right before dessert, it was announced that all the wines had come from America, too. Amazingly, several French people walked out in a huff, insulted that MGM had the nerve to bring American wine to France. We Americans were dumbfounded by that reaction, and more than a little amused that the stuffy French couldn't tell the difference between American and French wines until they were told.

We had a booth in the lobby of the Palais Theater, where the festival showed all of the movies nominated for awards. And we got great response to "The Night Daniel Died." We showed it four or five times at various theaters for distributors, and sold it to about thirteen countries. From Cannes I went to Paris, where I was paid by the producers to promote "Daniel." And from there I went to England, where I had the opportunity to renew old friendships.

But while "Daniel" did well on the foreign market, the producers had to distribute it independently in the United States. It played in a few theaters nationwide, but I never saw it. When it finally arrived on video shelves, the title had been changed to "Bloodstalkers." The title change was probably a good idea—horror buffs know exactly what they're getting, and I understand the movie has done okay on video.

Another interesting thing is that Bob Morgan's real love has always been Bigfoot, and it's a subject he's always wanted to make a movie about. He swears he saw a real Bigfoot in Washington state, and at one time he talked to me about being in a docudrama on the subject, but it never materialized. He gave up everything to pursue Bigfoot, and I haven't heard from him in years. The last I heard, he was living with some Indians in New Mexico who are also great believers in Bigfoot.

Chapter 9
FANDEMONIUM!

In my opinion, one of the greatest perks that comes with being a movie and television celebrity is the attention you get from your fans. Though I had been an entertainer for several years in Springfield, I never had real, rabid "fans" until I started appearing in movies and television. Almost overnight, I was seemingly the most popular guy around! I started receiving letters in care of the studios, and the fan magazines started receiving requests for me, which just blew me away. People not only remembered my name, they actually wanted to see more of me!

As the amount of mail I received increased, someone suggested I find someone knowledgeable to organize a Kenny Miller Fan Club. The idea appealed greatly to my ego (what better way to say Movie Star than an actual fan club?), but I had no idea how to go about it. I dropped by a fan club association on the Sunset Strip, but found their way of doing things rather expensive, so I passed. I was making good money, but there was no way I could support a national fan club out of my own pocket.

Then someone mentioned Nancy Streebeck, who was known as both a publicist and a fan club director. I dropped by her office and she told me that she could organize it so that my fan club would pay for itself—music to my ears. Membership cost 50 cents. For that, my fans received two journals a year, four quarterly newsletters and an 8x10 autographed photo. Not a bad deal, really. And Nancy was perfect for this game because she knew all the shortcuts, from inexpensive photo reproduction to value-priced mimeographing.

Around the time I set up shop with Nancy, I already had one fan club in Springfield, which had been started by a sweet gal named Judy

Crabtree. Judy was a big fan and a good friend who spent a lot of her own money to keep things running, but by this time it was getting out of hand for both of us. Judy was spending an outrageous amount of time handling membership requests, and I was dropping more money than I really should have supplying her with photographs. So Nancy Streebeck got in touch with Judy, and they decided to work together on my behalf. The new address for my fan club became the post office box that Nancy used for all of the fan clubs she managed, including June Allyson, Dick Powell, Jimmie Rodgers and several others. After the address was listed in a few fan magazines, the memberships came pouring in!

As time went on, so many people joined The Kenny Miller Fan Club that we decided to form individual chapters. Each had its own president, but everyone received the same newsletter, which was printed in California. I also had a few devoted fans in the Hollywood area who put together the semi-annual journals, which usually included a couple of photos of me suitable for framing. A lot of those journals were compiled by Clem and Marge Poor, who started as fans and became dear friends. Clem always seemed to end up with the unenviable task of editing the journals and putting them together, but in his capable hands they were genuine works of art, and I was very proud of the whole setup. Some of the fans would write articles about various aspects of my career or an incident in which they met me, and these would appear in the journals after Clem transcribed and edited them.

For one special Christmas journal, people from various chapters painted the covers and sent them to Clem for collation. My fans also put together a wonderful tribute to my mother when she passed away in 1959. It was just gorgeous, and included a beautiful poem dedicated in her loving memory. It was things like that that really demonstrated to me how special fans could be, and I always tried to give as much of myself back as I could.

The 1950s saw an amazing proliferation of fan clubs as every actor and actress with at least one flick under his or her belt jumped on the bandwagon. There were councils of fan clubs that met all over the country, allowing fans of different stars to meet and compare notes. It's kind of similar to the autograph and nostalgia shows that now take place around the United States. We would make occasional appearances at these fan club gatherings and do some schmoozing (especially if we had a new movie or album to promote), but unlike the celebrities of today, we never charged for our autographs. Not that I'm criticizing celebs today who sell their signed pix—I do it, too. The autographs of many of yesterday's stars are now valuable, so no one can blame today's celebrities for cashing in. If they didn't, the dealers would. It's a great way to make a little walking-around money or raise money for your favorite charity. But more importantly, it's also a wonderful way to stay in touch with your fans. In recent years I've attended autograph shows in Fort Lauderdale, Miami, Chicago, Memphis, Orlando, Los Angeles and elsewhere, and I'm constantly surprised by the number of people who come up and tell me, "I was in your fan club!" They're like long, lost friends and it's always a pleasure to see them again and catch up on old times.

A lot of people involved in my fan club eventually found their way to California. Babbie Sue Smith, for example, was a fan club president in southern Illinois before moving to California, where she worked on my national club. Another gal named Toni Deal, whom I met at a fan club party, married a California guy named Bob Randall—which made her Toni Randall. And then there was Jack Knox, a professional photographer who often showed up at fan and professional functions. Jack was a first-rate guy and very generous with the photographs he shot. One time he presented me with a photograph of Marilyn Monroe and Rock Hudson after they won the Foreign Press Awards (now known as the Golden Globe Awards). He thought I would like the picture because I was there, too. As I said, I made a lot of friends through my fan club—many of whom I'm still in touch with today—including Annette Vaseloff, who did most of the artwork; Maryanne Poore (no relation to Clem Poor), Buddy Marshall, Don Bastien, Eddie Colbert, Frank Edwards, Marilyn Lamas and John Easton.

It became known among my fans that I liked to wear sweaters, and soon I was literally swamped with outerwear of every type and style. At one point, I had nearly 60 sweaters crammed into my tiny closet. I kept them for a long time, but eventually started giving them away as presents because I couldn't possibly wear them all. "Teen Life" had a contest in its September 1961 issue titled "Should I Dye?" that asked whether I should dye my hair to get more movie roles. I flew to New York to meet the winner, we had lunch at the Russian Tea Room and I presented her with one of my favorite sweaters. Not a spectacular prize, perhaps, but she certainly seemed to enjoy it. I wonder if she still has it?

When my fan club was at its height—at one time I had one of the largest fan clubs with more than 50 active chapters—there was a group of

California fans who somehow always knew where I was going to be, and they would show up with cameras and make a big deal over me. They were a wonderful group and I was very, very flattered by their attention. I was usually there with a beautiful gal who was also in the biz, and my fans would ask if they could take pictures, which usually caught the attention of those who didn't know who I was, and they would start taking pictures, too. These fans even showed up when I just went out to dinner, which never failed to amaze me. I could never figure out how they kept such close tabs on me. They must have had a grapevine going 24 hours a day!

In that crowd were twins named Rita and Collette LaVelle who were quite well known in Hollywood for their near-obsessive fandom. They would go to the big parties and movie premieres, especially if I was going to be there. They also loved Van Johnson and Troy Donahue. I once was told that they had a collection of more than 3,000 color transparencies of me. Whenever they would ask for more pictures, all I could think was, "My God, don't you have enough?" But they always wanted more. Over the years, they gave me quite a few of the pictures they shot, but their obsessiveness always made me a little nervous. I once visited their apartment and was stunned to see life-size blow-ups of Van, Troy and me—a testament, I guess, to how much they loved us. It was surreal. They were always sweet, though some people thought they were a little misguided because they were adults who were living vicariously through me and other celebrities. They never married; we three performers were their life. The Twins were never too tired to attend an event if I, Van or Troy was there. No matter where I was, they were sure to show up. If I was in a parade, for example, they would run up to the car and shout greetings. I appreciated their attention (and that of all my fans), but I have to admit that it became a bit overwhelming after a while. I tried not to let it bother me, but sometimes I would be in late for an important appointment and they wouldn't let me go. That's when the demands of celebrity became more of a burden than a joy.

Were there Kenny Miller groupies? Absolutely. Did I take advantage of their, shall we say, bedroom generosity? On occasion, but not nearly as often as you might think (or I would have liked). The fact of the matter was, most of the girls who threw themselves at me weren't exactly Annette Funicello or Sandra Dee in the looks department. I loved them dearly and greatly appreciated their enthusiasm and attention, but—not to sound shallow—most of them simply weren't my type.

Some people think that fans who hang out looking to attach themselves to their favorite celebrity are a bunch of weirdos, but that's not true at all. Some of them are a little disturbed, to be sure, but most of them just want to get to know their favorite star on a more intimate level. It's all a matter of degree. Some merely want a kiss, while others are genuine starfuckers.

Many of the gals in my fan club were knockouts who should have been in front of the camera themselves. Unfortunately, most of them lived in other states so we were seldom able to get together aside from fan get-togethers, which were hardly conducive to romance.

In addition, I was often with someone when we saw our fans, which made a rendezvous even more unlikely. I did take advantage of a fan's offerings on occasion, but always very discreetly. I made sure there was no one else around, and that the girl I was with could be trusted to keep her mouth shut. Gossip about something like that could ruin my reputation and my career, so I tried to be extremely careful. The opportunities were endless and there were a lot of times when I would have liked to join in the action, but most of the time it wasn't a good idea, and I had to think with my big brain instead of my little one (Mr. Happy). After all, my image was The Boy Next Door.

I also had to be very careful because if I slept with one fan, they might tell the others and I just couldn't handle the resulting jealousy and bad blood. I wanted my fans to believe that I loved them equally—which I did—and it would have been bad all around for me to single one out as special. Besides, I don't think most of the fans who hung around me were really interested in sleeping with me. They identified with me because I was a nice guy who took the time to pose for pictures and sign autographs. Seldom did it become a sexual thing.

Over the years some of the folks in my fan club became dear friends. Ann Marie Van Hausen and her sister Willie Van Hausen, who were the presidents of my fan club in New Jersey, are just two examples. I stayed in touch with them for years, and watched both of them get married and start families. Willie and her husband Neil Marshall are like family to me, and I'm even the godfather of their youngest child, Sheri Mae. Willie gave Sheri my mother's middle name as a token of her love.

Most of my fan experiences were like that—very loving and gracious. But not all of them. I've also had my share of bad experiences, though thankfully nothing really dangerous.

One time I was going to the theater in New York with writer Joyce Becker, who used to be Connie Francis' secretary and president of her fan club. It was opening night and the crowds were terrible. It was a mob scene outside with limos lined up down the street and throngs of people straining their necks to see which celebrities were in attendance. A group of my New York fans were also hanging around, though I have no idea how they knew I was going to be there. One guy had a bunch of stuff he wanted me to sign, but we were running really late so I only signed a few items. After the play, the crowd was so bad that a cop had to help us get to our car. The same guy came up and asked me to sign some more of the stuff he had with him. I said no, explaining that we were in a hurry and on our way to dinner. I was very nice about it, but the guy got pissed off and intentionally squirted ink all over my tuxedo. I was so angry I wanted to clobber him right there on the sidewalk, because it was a vicious thing to do. Some people are obsessed with celebrities, and I guess that guy was obsessed with me. In retrospect it's kind of scary that someone would be so intentionally mean, but at that moment I didn't think about any potential danger. All I could think was, what a fucking asshole! It would have been different if I had ignored him or been rude to him, but I was more than nice by signing a few things before going in, which was more than most others would have done. But you can never do enough for an obsessed fan. They want to own you, and when they realize they can't, sometimes they lash out. There were probably a few other bad fan experiences, but I've tried to block them from my mind. I prefer to dwell on all the nice things my fans have done for me over the years.

(Speaking of Joyce Becker, it was she who started the rumor that singer Judi Meredith and I had eloped! The three of us were hanging around one evening listening to the radio, and Joyce said, "I'll bet you don't know how popular you really are. If I were to call the radio station and tell them you guys had eloped, I'll bet they would put it on the news." I was doubtful, so Joyce called and reported the non-event, telling the DJ that Judi and I had run off to Las Vegas to be married. Much to my amazement—and shock—that story led the 10 p.m. news, and was repeated for the rest of the evening. Not surprisingly, Judi and I were swamped with calls, which was doubly amusing because we weren't even dating. But it did prove that we had our share of popularity. We never insisted on a retraction, and the story finally died as people gradually realized it wasn't true.)

Among my fans, the Twins were a special case. I had to be very careful with them because they were living their lives vicariously through me and they always wanted to be around me. At premieres, there were always other people vying for my attention, but the Twins would get jealous if I had to leave them. They could be very rude, which always upset me, but Nancy Streebeck explained to me that I was their whole existence at that moment and if I didn't give them my time they immediately assumed that I didn't like them. It wasn't that way at all, of course, but that's apparently how they felt.

My fan appeal and my appearances in the fan magazines seemed to feed on each other like a snake eating its own tail until, for a while, my face was seemingly everywhere. At that point, Nancy Streebeck became my press agent, helping to keep my face and name in the right publications where those in a position to give me work could see it. Back then, no matter how talented an actor was, he was nobody in the eyes of the movie studios until he appeared in the newspapers and the fan magazines. Once they realized you had a solid fan base, you became a more marketable commodity. We were pretty much viewed as slabs of meat with nice tans, but that was the nature of the business. So-called "serious" actors who didn't want to play the game generally found themselves back in New York pretty damned quick.

It was amazing how much mail I got at the fan magazines. I think those publications made me more of a celebrity than the movies I was in. Most of the magazines were based in New York, and they would assign people to come to Hollywood to do stories about us and set up photo shoots. Every now and then I would go to New York for interviews on their turf. I would meet the writer for lunch or dinner, and often she would ask me to drop by the offices to say hello. It was a lot of schmoozing, but I didn't mind. Most of the magazines treated me like a big-time movie star, and I just ate up the attention. It was a two-way street, and everyone understood that—I needed publicity, and they needed the hottest names on their covers. There was little hostility (unlike today), and everyone got along well.

The photo layouts were usually set up by a writer or the publisher. Often you didn't know until the last minute who you were being paired with for a photo shoot, but more often than not it was someone you already knew and either worked or played with. I almost never turned down a layout because I didn't want to offend the magazine. Besides, it was great publicity. Some actors didn't want to do fan-magazine layouts because they thought it made them look stupid. But it was a very important thing to the fans and the actors who indulged. I have some very cherished memories and a lot of scrap-books filled with those sorts of things.

In a round about way, it was the fan magazines that made it possible for me to sing with the magnificent Ella Fitzgerald and legendary blues singer Dinah Washington at a party hosted by Jan and Dean for DJ Jimmy O'Neil. I was wandering around the patio when I heard someone say, "Kenny, aren't you going to say hello to me?" I turned around and came face to face with Ella Fitzgerald. I was dumbfounded because I didn't know Ella knew who I was. But it turned out that she was a voracious reader of the fan magazines, and recognized me from some of my photo layouts. We chatted and I became her escort for the evening. A little later, Dinah was playing the piano, and she coaxed Ella into singing. After a song or two, Ella said, "Now Kenny's going to sing for us too!" Dinah started playing "Embraceable You," and suddenly there I was, performing with Ella Fitzgerald and Dinah Washington before a group of 80 or 90 people. It was as if I had found Camelot; I knew I would never have another experience like it.

Ruth Bowshier was one writer who interviewed me often, and we became close friends as a result. Another was Bessie Little, who was the editor of several fan, film and teen-age magazines. One of her most popular titles was "Hep Cats," which featured me quite often. Once, while in Paris, a friend showed me a copy of "Hep Cats" that was practically a Kenny Miller Tribute. I usually appeared in just one or two photos, but this particular issue—and I wish I still had a copy—contained more than 30 photographs. I begged my friend to let me have it, but he wouldn't part with it.

A frequent contributor to "Hep Cats" and other fan magazines was a struggling writer named Rona Barrett. I hosted one of the first parties for Rona when she moved to Hollywood, which would become her regular beat for years, and I invited everyone I knew. We initially planned to have the party at Molly Bee's house, but moved it to the home of a dancer-friend of Molly's named Beverly Sandler because Beverly had a huge back yard. Although employed, none of us was incredibly wealthy, so we made the party a potluck barbecue. Practically every young performer in Hollywood showed up, including Judi Meredith (who was on the Burns & Allen TV show), Barry Coe, Troy Donahue, Nan Morris (who managed a lot of young talent over the years, including Bobby Sherman and Dirk and Dack Rambo), and Stella Stevens, who had just arrived from New York.

Rona was just beside herself as celebrity after celebrity came by to say hi and welcome her to Hollywood. She worked for Bessie Little for a while, then freelanced. That's how she made her living until she made a big name for herself as a gossip columnist. She was ubiquitous in the late '60s and '70s, and became a major influence in Hollywood. She, the woman who was once the teenage president of Eddie Fisher's fan club!

I always invited Rona to the parties I hosted, and she always wanted to know who was on the guest list. If the names weren't impressive enough, she would graciously decline. Sal Mineo was the same way—he primarily wanted to meet people who could help his career. But their attitude cost them dearly when they both declined to attend a party I hosted at Doris Duke's house in the early '60s. It turned out that one of Doris' neighbors was Marlon Brando. He heard music from down the street and dropped by unannounced to check things out. Marlon quickly made himself at home and ended up playing the bongos! He was absolutely wonderful and partied with us until the wee hours of the morning. All I could think was, here's one of the biggest names in Hollywood and Rona and Sal missed him!

One of the perks of celebrity are invitations to be the grand marshall in various parades. The really big celebrities get the really big parades, but I was invited to more than my share of them. The Whittier, California, Christmas Parade, for example, turned out to be one of my most embarrassing moments. A day or so before the parade, I decided to try a product called Man Tan to give me a dark, healthy tan. I slathered it on, and within 30 minutes I looked like Eddie Murphy with blond hair. I was horrified, and worked furiously to lighten it up. After numerous showers and applications of cold cream, I didn't look quite as bad, but I was still a lot darker than I wanted. When I picked up Marianne Gaba, who was my co-host for the event, she commented on my tan, and I lied and told her I had spent some time in Palm Springs. We posed for a lot of newspaper and fan-magazine pictures during the parade, and I swear to God, I looked like something from another planet. My teeth were white and my hair was blond and I had this ridiculously dark tan—darker than George Hamilton on his best day. I showered three times a day in an attempt to get it off, but it didn't work. I just had to wait for it fade naturally, which took weeks.

As the fan magazines worked themselves into a frenzy of hero wor-ship, my friends and I would have a contest to see who could appear in the most magazines in a single month. We would meet at an outdoor newsstand in downtown Hollywood and go through them all, laughing hysterically. I won the contest most of the time because my fan clubs were more active than many others, resulting in a greater demand for my pic-ture. It was kind of like stuffing the ballot box, but I didn't feel bad about it. All's fair in love and publicity!

I was garnering so much publicity through the fan magazines that in 1958, "TV Star Parade" asked me to write a monthly column. They ap-proached me because I was the most partying person, and their idea of Hollywood's best-known promising newcomer. I was a bit reluctant to take the assignment because I was busy and didn't have time to write a monthly column. But Nancy Streebeck thought it was a great idea be-cause (1) it would be good publicity, and (2) we would be paid for it. Nancy offered to ghost the column if I provided the information, which simply meant jotting down notes on the various parties, premieres and other events I attended.

The column was called "The Young Set," and it was read, according to the editors, by thousands of people. As a result, the list of events to which I was invited grew longer and longer, because organizers knew that my attendance might mean some free publicity. I was one of the first celebrities to write a column like that, but certainly not the last. Within months nearly every movie magazine had a celebrity columnist, though most of them didn't last as long as I did. "The Young Set" ran for nearly five years, ending in 1962 when Nancy and I decided we had said every-thing there was to be said. We were beginning to repeat ourselves—same parties, same events, merely different names.

The premiere of "The Greatest Story Ever Told" (1965) is a good example of how the publicity machine used to work in Hollywood. It was a huge, epic film starring everybody and their brother—but word had gotten around Hollywood that it was a real stinkeroo. MGM was going to have a two-night premiere, but the lack of attending movie stars (and who can have a premiere without a lot of movie stars?) forced them to pare it down to just one night.

Disc jockey Johnny Grant was going to be doing interviews at the premiere and he literally begged me to attend. I wasn't that keen on the idea, but I had a brand new red Mustang convertible that I was dying to show off, so I agreed on one condition—that I not have to sit through the whole movie, which was originally a numbing 260 minutes. Johnny had no problem with that. He would interview me, then I would slip out a side exit after entering the theater.

When I drove up under the lights of the theater, my red Mustang appeared to be a hideous orange, which really ruined the cool effect. I arrived just as Zsa Zsa Gabor was being interviewed, and she just droned on forever. By the time I stepped up to chat with Johnny, two or three other celebrities were standing in line behind me. After Johnny was done with me, I was interviewed briefly by Army Archerd, then I went into the theater for a glass of champagne. As the movie started, a group of us went to the side door by the screen and quietly slipped out. Our cars had been brought around to that exit to avoid the crowds outside, so we were able to make a hasty retreat. And that's how we used to publicize movies in the good old days!

The premiere of "Raintree County" (1957) was a bit more fun. I was invited by Morgan Hudgens, who was one of the heads of publicity at MGM at the time. I had met Morgan through Rod McKuen, and he really treated me kindly. Not only did he invite me to the premiere of "Raintree County," which was a sought-after ticket, but he included my name in a full-page ad announcing all the attending stars that appeared in "Daily Variety" and the "Hollywood Reporter." There was Molly Bee and me on a list that also included Elizabeth Taylor, Debbie Reynolds, Gene Kelly, Howard Keel, Jane Powell, Eva Marie Saint, Lee Marvin and other megastars.

After the premiere, Mike Todd hosted one of his outrageous parties for Elizabeth Taylor at the Luau Restaurant in Beverly Hills—and we were invited. It was wall-to-wall stars. Elizabeth and Mike Todd arrived with Debbie Reynolds and Eddie Fisher, and the festivities began. After a couple of drinks, I asked Molly to excuse me and went over and asked Elizabeth to dance with me. Well, actually, I asked Mr. Todd if I could have his permission to dance with her. And he said, "Well, that's up to Elizabeth!" She was already half out of her seat, and said, "Of course, Kenny!" I'll never forget how beautiful she was, in a long black velvet gown with an emerald tiara and emerald and diamond necklace. After a couple of choruses, Fernando Lamas cut in, that bastard!

A little while later, as Molly and I were going through the buffet line, we heard a ruckus in another part of the restaurant. Two women were having a free-for-all. Hair pulling, jewels flying. It was Zsa Zsa Gabor and Gia Scala. The two Hungarian Queens of Hollywood were duking it out like prize fighters. I never found out the reason for the fight, but people on the sidelines were gleefully egging them on. It was like a Roman gladiator spectacle.

I reciprocated Morgan's generosity by bringing young performers of my acquaintance to other MGM events that he arranged. Morgan was a genuinely nice guy who went out of his way to help me make some contacts within the industry. For instance, he was good friends with Hedda Hopper , the renowned gossip columnist, so I would go over to his house and then he and I would pick up Hedda and head off to this event or that. He did that just so I could get to know Hedda, who was one of the two (the other being Louella Parsons) most influential gossip columnists in Hollywood. A mention in her column carried big-time weight.

In 1960, Morgan arranged for me to attend a pre-release studio screening of Alfred Hitchcock's "Psycho." I picked up Hedda Hopper, and when we arrived at the Paramount screening room, I sat on one side of her and Anthony Perkins sat on the other. During the screening, Anthony went on and on about how the movie wasn't any good and how no one would like it. He really hated "Psycho" and felt that the scenes in which he turns into his mother simply didn't work. After the screening, he hugged Hedda and took off because he just couldn't stand to be there anymore.

Hedda was supposed to be the only press person in attendance, though I ended up writing about the screening in my "TV Star Parade" column, noting that star Anthony Perkins didn't think the movie was very good. Of course, history proved just the opposite to be true. "Psycho" became one of Hitchcock's signature movies, and made Anthony Perkins a bigger name than he had ever been. It also typecast him, though he later grew to accept and even capitalize on the film's cult-like popularity.

The studios tightly controlled the publicity of their hottest actors, and went to great lengths to make sure that their stars always appeared in the right places and with the right people. Events were closely scripted, and "dates" were often written about in detail long before they actually took place to meet publication deadlines. That's how my "date" with Sandra Dee came about.

This was the early '60s and I was Mr. Clean—the wholesome boy-next-door that any girl would be proud to take home to Mother. At the time, Sandra was one of the hottest things at Universal. I thought she was a doll, but you almost never saw her anywhere. She had a strict mother and the studio kept a tight rein on her to ensure that she remained America's sweetheart. As a result, she never dated anyone, or at least never went on any dates that made it into the newspapers or fan mags. One day I got a call from one of the publicists at Universal asking if I would take Sandra to the premiere of a movie, the title of which escapes me now. I told Nancy Streebeck about it, and she thought it was an excellent idea—Mr. Clean dates Miss Wholesome. Great publicity.

I agreed to the date, and was told to pick up Sandra at the studio, where she was going to have her makeup and hair done. But Sandra got sick (or backed out at the last minute) so the date never took place. But the studio had already leaked the story that we were dating to some of the fan magazines and newspapers, and many of them printed the tale despite the fact that it never happened. To this day I have yet to meet Sandra Dee, yet it was all over the magazines that we were a duo. I got a lot of ribbing from my friends about that, and it just goes to show you how the studios used various actors to advance the careers of others. From what I understand, Sandra didn't date much until she met Bobby Darin, whom she later married. Had things gone differently, it might have been me!

I've also had a few other embarrassing moments at events I actually did attend, such as an industry showing of Joshua Logan's "Tall Story" (1960) starring Jane Fonda and Anthony Perkins at the Directors Academy Theater. They had a bevy of models dressed up like cheerleaders for the event, all looking very beautiful. I arrived with Connie Stevens and the New York press handling the movie immediately asked me to pose for pictures with the cheerleaders. They assumed I was someone important because my fans were taking pictures of me and making a big deal about my arrival. The picture that ran in the "Hollywood Citizen News" the next day had the caption "Nick Adams attends moving showing!" Nick and I always looked somewhat alike, but it pissed me off that the press didn't even bother to confirm my identity. It's funny now, but it wasn't then, because Nick and I were always vying for similar parts and I didn't want him feeding off MY publicity!

Another time, Nancy Streebeck and I attended the premiere of a movie starring Marlo Thomas. The movie was made in New York, so the New York press was again in attendance. The showing was at a small theater on La Cienga Boulevard, and they had a party tent set up outside. The moment we arrived we were surrounded by camera hounds. Nancy and I just looked at each other and shrugged; we had no idea what was going on. After the photographers were done with us, the head of public relations grabbed us and seated us in the fourth row of the theater. He said, "We're so glad you could make it, Mr. Bridges!" Nancy nudged me and started giggling—they took me for Lloyd Bridges! We thought it would be fun to let the mistake play itself out, so I was introduced to the director of the movie and everyone else as Lloyd Bridges.

Then Marlo, who I had known for years, appeared on the scene. Someone introduced me to her as Lloyd Bridges and she let out a loud yelp, "He's not Lloyd Bridges! He's Kenny Miller!" Even though Mr. Bridges is 20 years older than I am, we do look somewhat alike in low lighting. I always wanted to portray his son in a film, but one of his own sons (Jeff or Beau) would be first in line.

Many of my fellow celebrities went to outrageous lengths to be included in various publicity and fan events. Poet and song writer Rod McKuen, for example, was renowned within our circle of friends for his ambition when it came to getting his name in the papers. Rod is extremely talented and appeared in a couple of teen movies early in his career, but he simply wasn't fan-magazine material and usually wasn't invited to events that I and a lot of other young performers attended routinely.

Example: Louella Parsons, the much-feared gossip columnist, gave a party every year for Jimmy McHugh, the famous song writer. She hosted the get-together around her pool and invited mostly musical people. In fact, just about everyone who had anything to do with music received an invitation because Louella and Jimmy hoped they might use some of Jimmy's old songs as part of their future projects. I had done a few musical things, but Louella invited me primarily because I had appeared as the opening act for Nancy Wilson at the Coconut Grove.

Anyway, the invitation came by telegram. I got one, Tommy Sands got one, and of course Molly Bee was also invited, so we decided to all go together. Rod desperately wanted to go, too, but for one reason or another he wasn't on Louella's list. Eager to hobnob with Hollywood's musical elite, Rod had me read the wording of the telegram to him over the phone, then he went down to Western Union and sent a telegram to himself! With bogus invitation in hand, he asked if he could go with us, so we all went in a huge limousine. The funny part was, it was one of the few parties where no one checked our invitations at the door.

The McGuire Sisters—Phyllis, Christine and Dorothy—were at the party. They were really popular then, so Louella made sure they were invited. I had met them years earlier because they were from a little burg outside of my hometown of Springfield, and their mother was an ordained minister. My mother kept the Sunshine Mission going for another eleven years after my father died, bringing in various ministers and preachers to spread the Lord's word because she was unwilling to get up in front of the congregation and preach herself. One of the preachers who visited us often was the McGuire Sisters' mom.

Phyllis and Christine were sitting next to Louella and Louella's daughter Harriet. Every once in a while, there would be a muted sound, kind of a "pfffftttssss," that no one could place. Phyllis turned to me a couple of times and asked, "Kenny, what IS that noise?" I kept shushing her because the truth was, the sound was coming from Louella herself. She had kidney problems and wore a catheter because she had to pee all the time. That was the sound—Luella Parsons taking a whiz. It was common knowledge around Hollywood, though no one ever mentioned it out of respect.

I couldn't tell Phyllis the truth because Louella was right there, so I invited her to take a walk with me to the other side of the pool. When I explained what was going on, Phyllis almost bust a gut. It struck her as funny in a bizarre way, and we could barely contain ourselves. Phyllis laughed so hard she almost peed herself! Poor Louella couldn't help it, and we didn't mean to be cruel about her condition, but the whole scene was so surreal with Louella peeing into her catheter throughout the party that we just had to laugh. Poor Phyllis had to sit down next to Louella again, and I left the area and walked to the other side of the pool because I couldn't look at Phyllis or we would have started howling again.

During the glory days of my career—and Hollywood itself—the fan magazines and the fans themselves were very important when it came to establishing a budding performer's career. They had a lot of influence because they kept you in the public eye when you weren't working that much. I was usually working, but during the times when I wasn't, the magazines kept me alive in the minds of the movie-going public.

The fan magazines—at one time there were nearly 40 of them— were also a tremendous ego boost because they made you feel appreciated even when it seemed none of the studios wanted you. Nowadays, there is no such thing. Oh, there are couple of magazines that are sort of about TV and movie people, and there are still a few teen magazines promoting the heartthrob of the month, but it's just not the same. The glitz and glamour are gone. Hollywood changed, and so did the public's taste. Unable

to compete with television and the tabloids, the old-fashioned fan magazines went the way of the dinosaur. When I later returned to Hollywood
after five years in Europe, there were almost none left. I was one of those
whose career truly benefited from the fan mags, and I regret that they are
no longer a part of Hollywood.

KM signing autographs in London with a Bobby looking on.

Recording *Stateside* in London with Shel Talmy for EMI.

Shelley Fabares and KM.

Terrea Lea and KM singing
at The Garrett after hours.

Going overseas to entertain the troops in the Far East with Marion Collier, Irish McCalla, Charlie Watts, Donna Reaser, KM, Elizabeth Talbot-Martin and Carol Mitchum.

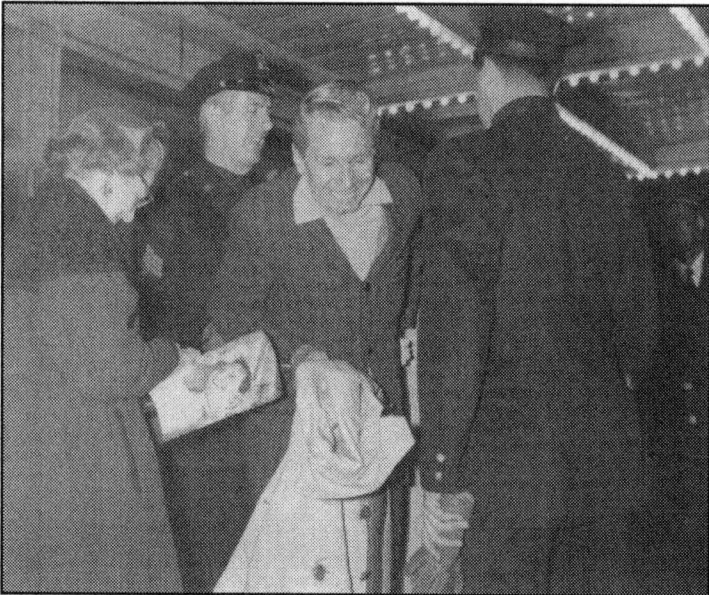

Escaping from fans in NYC with the help of those great guys, the NYPD.

Margarita Sierra and KM doing the cha-cha-twist on Surfside Six. She was a ball of fire!

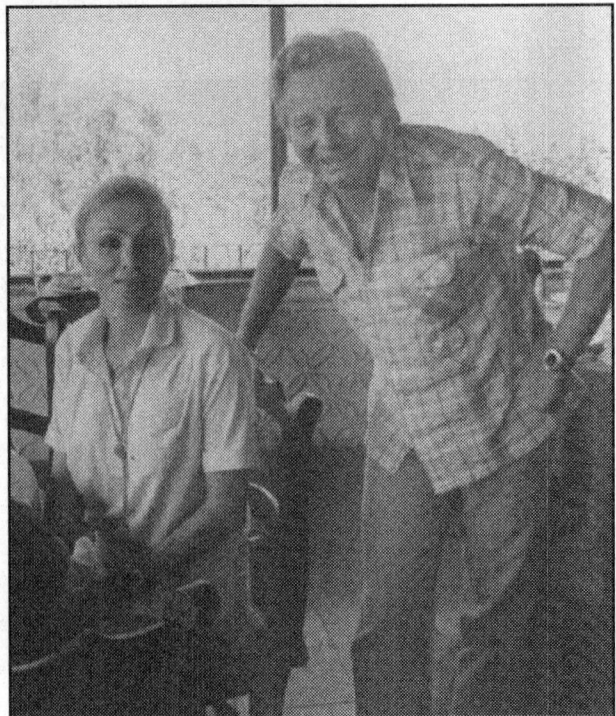

Empress Reza Pahlavi, former wife of the Shah of Iran, and me at Ted Wick's La Ventana de Taxco Restaurant in Taxco, Mexico.

Visiting the delightful Irene Ryan on the set of *The Beverly Hillbillies*. Irene was like a godmother to me.

Appearing at The Pavilion in Madrid, Spain. Backstage with the Flamenco Dancers who were *wonderful*.

With fans after a show in Florida.

Layout for a fan magazine in Hollywood with Bobby Vinton, Lyn Loring, Jackie De Shannon and KM. Breaking in my new motor scooter.

My band (l. to r.) Bob Bowshier, Dick Tull and "Hoppy" Hopkins—all from Springfield, Ohio. I took them to Florida to appear with me at The Golden Falcon.

Doing a TV show in Brighton, England with Lulu, a big UK recording star (sang "To Sir, With Love").

With darling Jo-Anne Campbell appearing in Las Vegas, doing a fan magazine layout at nearby Hoover Dam.

Recording "You Are Love to Me," my first record for Faro in Hollywood.

A publicity shot in my favorite car, a '56 T-Bird.

KM with Kathy Nolan of
The Real McCoys TV show.
She became the first woman
President of the Screen
Actor's Guild.

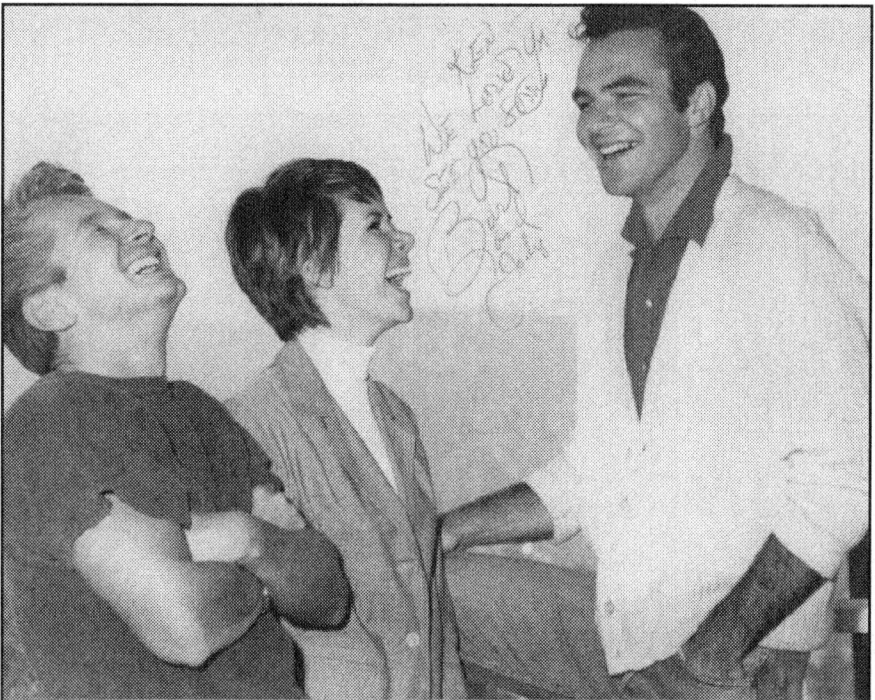

KM, Judy Carne and Burt Reynolds. Boy, we were a happy group!

KM at an autograph collectors' show in New York with Candy Clark,
Will Hutchins and his wife Barbara.

My first autograph show—in
Ft. Lauderdale, Florida, with
wonderful Buffalo Bob Smith.

Ann Robinson and KM.

Lauren Chapin from *Father Knows Best*.

KM and Warren Stevens.

Ken Tobey and KM.

Mark Goddard and KM.

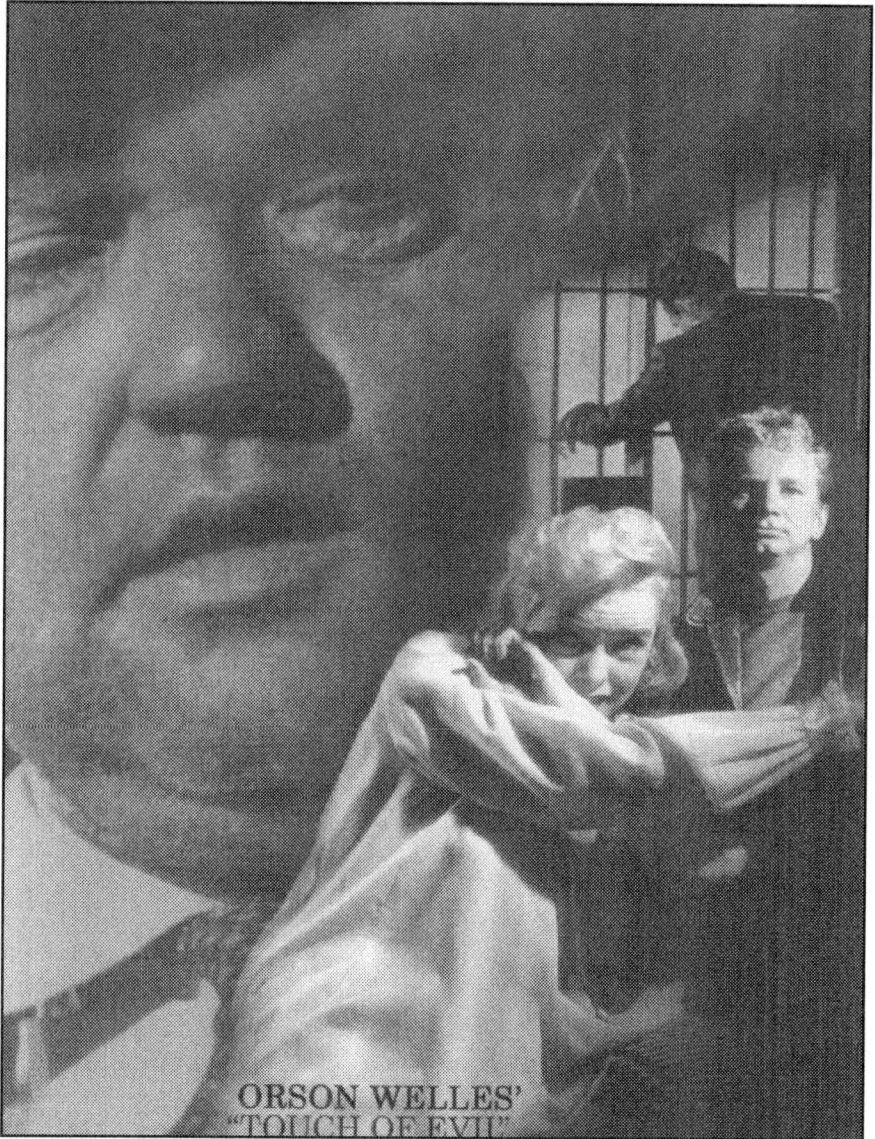

Touch of Evil with Orson Welles, Janet Leigh, Kenny Miller, and Charlton Heston.

Touch of Evil, with Mercedes McCambridge (right).

Surf Party (20th Century-Fox) with Bobby Vinton, Pat Morrow, Jackie De Shannon, Lori Sawyer and KM.

Another scene from *Surf Party*.

Surf Party.

Singing "Pearly Shells" in *Surf Party*. I broke my shoulder surfing in this film!

With Jackie De Shannon in *Surf Party*.

A publicity shot for Surf Party, in Malibu Beach.

Little Shepherd of Kingdom Come, with George Kennedy, Luana Patten, Robert Dix, Jimmie Rodgers, KM. (20th Century-Fox, 1961).

KM as Reuben Turner in Little Shepherd of Kingdom Come.

My favorite movie still. The Search for Bridey Murphy.

The Search for Bridey Murphy.

Chapter 10
TV Daze

Television was just coming into its own when I was growing up. There was no TV station in Springfield when I lived there, but there was a small station in nearby Dayton that covered our area. I was asked to appear on that station's local country-western musical shows several times when I was a teenager. I got to sing and dance—excellent preparation for many of the teen movies I would make years later.

After I moved to Hollywood and had a few movies under my belt, I made three different promotional appearances on the "Ruth Lyons Show," which originated out of Cincinnati. Ruth had been a major Midwest personality many years before, and her show boasted a live audience and its own orchestra. She loved to feature local celebrities as well as nationally-known personalities, and I found myself on Ruth's show whenever I was in the area promoting a new movie or record. When Ruth retired, her announcer, Bob Braun, took over for a while. Sometimes the hosting chores fell on Nick Clooney, who is now one of the on-air hosts on cable's American Movie Classic." He also happens to be the father of George Clooney and the brother of Rosemary Clooney.

One of the initial shows I did upon my release from the military was "The Cisco Kid," starring Duncan Renaldo as Cisco and Leo Carrillo as his faithful sidekick, Pancho. The syndicated western was produced by ZIV Television and was extremely popular during the 1950s—an impressive 156 episodes were made between 1950 and 1956. The show has the unique distinction of being one of the first television series to be taped (most television shows were aired live during the 1950s), and was also filmed in color, even though most stations nationwide could air it only in black and white during its first run.

I was only 19 and still a novice actor, so I was a basket case when my agent sent me to the old ZIV studios to read for casting director Nina Fine. But I guess I did okay because I was immediately offered the role of Jay Jones, a 13-year-old kid who Cisco takes under his wing. Leo as Pancho kept calling me "Yay Yones" in his fractured English, which I always found hilarious. But I also found out later that it was the correct pronunciation in Spanish for "Jay Jones."

Duncan and Leo were older than God when we made "The Cisco Kid" (or maybe it just seemed that way to me because I was so young) but they were troupers in the true Hollywood tradition. They never complained, and willingly did whatever the script required. The makeup they went through every day was amazing, and sometimes you could actually see it start to wilt and drip as we worked long days in the hot California sun. But Duncan and Leo didn't mind; they were just happy to be working on a program that was a bonafide hit, which "The Cisco Kid" was, and still is, especially among children.

One day I saw the wardrobe director cleaning Leo Carrillo's boots and noticed that they looked a little strange. I had never seen boots built up with lifts before, and she explained that they made Leo look taller. This reminds me of an actor friend named Steve Rowland, who was a great-looking guy, but a little too short for a leading man. All of his boots had outrageous lifts in them, and sometimes it seemed as if he were walking on a slant. The standing joke was, "One day, Steve is going to fall off of his lifts and hurt himself." But then, I have no room to talk. I later had lifts put into my boots, but only the ones I wore in my nightclub act. It's amazing how many of Hollywood leading men who are 6-foot and taller still put lifts in all their shoes. In fact, one actor of my acquaintance has lifts built into his tennis shoes!

I appeared in only one episode of "The Cisco Kid," and found it a wonderful learning experience, quite different from motion pictures. ZIV was a small studio, so the budget for the show was extremely tight. You got it on the first take and that was it; there were few retakes. If there was a minor mistake, the producers didn't care. Unless someone really blew a line or fell off his horse, they put it in the can and moved on. Television on a shoestring, but God, it was fun!

Just in case you happen to catch that episode of "The Cisco Kid" with me in it, you may notice that I don't look quite the way I do now.

That's because I didn't have the time or the money then to get my nose fixed after it was improperly set while I was in Germany. I still wince when I see myself BN (Before Nosejob). I doubt if things would have gone as well as they did for me had I not visited a surgeon pronto!

I played a lot of juvenile delinquents during my early TV days. One of the first was on a show called "The Public Defender," starring Reed Hadley as attorney Bart Matthews, a public defender who tried to help the poor and innocent. The show didn't last very long, but it was rather unique because the stories were all based on files from actual public defenders around the country.

To be honest, I remember almost nothing about my work on "The Public Defender." I appeared on the show twice, but my roles were very small and I can't recall one from the other, aside from the fact that in one of them I was a "troubled youth." One thing I do remember is that Reed Hadley was a huge man, and extremely nice to me. He knew I was relatively new to television and went out of his way to make me feel comfortable on the set. But other than that, I'm drawing a blank.

I also recall little of my work on the show "The Halls of Ivy," an early CBS situation comedy that starred screen legend Ronald Colman and his wife Benita Hume. Colman played Dr. William Todhunter Hall, president of the fictitious Ivy College, and Benita played his wife Vicky. I played a student in one episode and I had maybe one or two lines. I remember being in awe of Ronald Colman on the set, though I didn't have any scenes with him and I didn't get to know him at all. It's too bad because I'm sure he could have taught me a thing or two about acting.

"Father Knows Best," on the other hand, remains one of my favorite and most memorable television experiences. I had a small recurring role as a friend of Bud's—I think I was in three or four episodes—and found "Father Knows Best" to be one of the most fun shows to work on because everyone was so nice, yet professional. Robert Young and Jane Wyatt were wonderful to work with, as were Billy Gray, Elinor Donahue and Lauren Chapin, and the set was always happy and carefree. It had none of the tension that infected many of the other sets; everyone did their job and enjoyed doing it. If someone forgot a line or made a mistake, we laughed and got on with it. They treated you like real family.

To me, Robert Young and Jane Wyatt were, in real life, exactly as they appeared on the show—very family-oriented, caring and compassionate. They had a wonderful mother-father quality about them that really came across on television. As for the rest of the cast, visiting the set was more like dropping in to talk with the neighbors. We were all young, so we sat around and talked about the stuff young people talked about back then. I wish all of my television experiences had been as special as "Father Knows Best."

Some of the cast ran into problems after the show ended in 1963. Billy Gray, who played Bud, was falsely accused of having a serious drug problem and it really put a dent in his career. He had been busted for smoking pot, but then word spread that he was also into heroin, which wasn't true. He spent many years trying to get rid of the stigma because the rumor just wouldn't go away.

Lauren Chapin, who played little Kathy on the show, also had her share of problems. She found it almost impossible to get work when the series ended, and ultimately turned to drugs. Unlike Billy, Lauren really was into heroin, and it almost destroyed her life. She did time in prison, mental institutions and various drug treatment programs before getting her life back together with the help of some compassionate friends and a dedicated priest. She even stayed with me and Pat and Frannie for a short time when things were really bad. I ran into Lauren recently at an autograph show in Orlando, where she now lives, and we had a delightful reunion. She has managed to overcome all the adversity in her life and is now guiding the career of her beautiful daughter and working on various entertainment projects.

Elinor Donahue, who played Betty, was the only one of the Anderson children who came away from the series okay. In fact, she did great. Elinor married producer Harry Ackerman, who was very big in the television industry, and she also continued acting in television and theater. We almost worked together in a dinner theater play in Florida, but there was a conflict and we weren't able to get together.

"Dragnet" proved to be one of the most unique television experiences of my career—all because of Jack Webb.

I appeared in three episodes of "Dragnet" (but not as a recurring character) during the early days when it starred Webb and Ben Alexander as his partner, Frank Smith. In one episode I played an arsonist, and in another I was—wait for it—a juvenile delinquent!

"Dragnet" was much different from my other television work because Jack Webb was one of the first to make regular use of the TelePromTer. He wanted the whole rhythm of the show to be just like his no-nonsense character, Joe Friday, so you always had your dialogue beneath the camera, and you were supposed to deliver it in that clipped, just-the-facts-ma'am style. As a result, everyone on the show took on Jack's signature cadence. Mary Beth Hughes appeared with me in one episode, and she had a very hard time getting into it.

Webb was a very nice man to work with, but he was a perfectionist. This included being very tidy, immaculate in his appearance and everything he did. A lot of Joe Friday WAS Jack Webb. I didn't know him very well personally, but I did know Julie London, who was his significant other for a long time. Jack gave the impression of being very rigid. I don't recall any hysterical laughter on that set. It was all business—go in, do it and get it over with.

My grandmother on my mother's side, Mollie Ann Lewis, had a huge crush on Jack Webb, and I was the apple of her eye after I brought her an autographed picture of him. She kept a bunch of framed family photos on a living room cabinet, and right in the center was that signed picture of Jack Webb!

When my family finally got a television set, the only shows my grandmother would watch were "The Tennessee Ernie Ford Show" and "Dragnet." She couldn't get enough of Jack Webb—and she was so cute to watch when the show was on. I returned home for a quick visit one time and got to witness the whole routine.

After dinner, Grandma disappeared into her room and came back wearing a freshly pressed dress and her hair pulled back in a bun. Mom and I were sitting on a couch in front of the television, and there was an overstuffed chair to one side. I invited Grandma to sit with us on the couch, but she said no. When "Dragnet" came on, Grandma moved the chair farther away from the screen so that she had to stretch to see it. Whenever there was a close-up of Jack Webb, she would suddenly straighten up, as if to disappear. I said, "Grandma, what are you doing?" "Oh, nothing," she replied innocently. "I just don't want him to see me."

On the way home I had to smile, but considering my grandmother's background, it made a strange sort of sense. She was a woman who came to Ohio from Virginia in a covered wagon and who didn't really understand how technical things like television worked. She thought that if we could see Jack Webb, then during close-ups looking into her living room he must be able to see us. She wasn't a stupid woman, she just couldn't understand how images could appear out of thin air on a box in her living room. It didn't make sense. To be perfectly honest, I don't understand how television works, either, and I've been on it! I would never allow anyone to tell Grandma any differently.

It's barely worth mentioning, but I appeared on "The Steve Allen Show" when it was just a small local show on Channel 13 in Hollywood. I sang a song or two while Steve accompanied me on the piano, but I wasn't a guest on the couch because at the time I wasn't that well known. The show was done before a live audience and Steve was rapidly developing the devoted following that would soon propel him to national superstardom.

There was a lot of bizarre and wacky humor on the show, which became Steve's trademark when he hit the big time on NBC in 1956. At the time it was no big deal; just another regional show that I hoped would get me some local exposure.

"American Bandstand" was more my style. I first appeared on that show to promote my record, "You Are Love To Me," which was being heavily pushed by Faro Records. But getting on the show was no easy task. I was gaining some exposure through my movies and the fan magazines, but I still wasn't as well known as a lot of other performers.

The whole thing started with a trip to New York. I did the "Joe Franklin Show," which was a big deal in New York at the time, as well as numerous fan-magazine interviews. While there, my road manager, Don Gallasse, got in touch with Dick Clark's people to see if I could make an appearance. At the same time, I called my good friend Connie DeNave, who handled a lot of singers and music people, including Dick Clark. Connie also called Dick's people—and all of a sudden I was booked! We went to Philadelphia by train and I did the show. It was fun, but not earth-shattering because, quite frankly, the song wasn't earth-shattering. Dick was very nice and I got to know him a little better through my friend Jo-Ann Campbell.

My three appearances on "The Rat Patrol" were the result of good timing and strong connections. The show was filmed near Almeria, Spain, and I happened to be dividing my time between Madrid and Marbella at the time, doing a little singing and other odd jobs. One day I ran into a friend of mine named Stan Schpetner, who was a co-producer of "The Rat Patrol," and who had once dated an agent of mine named Audrey Baer. Stan mentioned the show, I mentioned that I was free and one thing led to another.

Chris George was the star of "The Rat Patrol," which concerned four young commandos fighting Rommel's special Afrika Korps in North Africa during the early days of World War II. It was a good series with a lot of action and more than a little humor. The bone-dry flats around Almeria looked just like the desert of Northern Africa, and the show was able to use sets left over from the filming of several World War II flicks, including "The Great Escape" (1963) and "Battle of the Bulge" (1965).

Working with Chris was a ball because we had known each other for years, but the locations were absolutely hellish. Almeria itself was a very nice, quaint little town, but the surrounding areas were, in my opinion, the armpit of the world. Blistering hot, sandy and extremely uncomfortable.

The producers thought taking the show to Spain would help cut costs as well as provide the perfect backdrop, but found out the hard way how difficult it is to bring Hollywood sensibilities to another country. Aside from the top echelon, most of the production crew was Spanish, and they just didn't move that fast. Constant communication problems and differences in customs plagued the show and often made filming extremely difficult.

I remember one time the show needed a certain kind of train, which had been located in Madrid, hundreds of miles from Almeria. Knowing how long these kind of things can take, the production company ordered the train two full weeks before it was needed. But even with that kind of pre-planning, the train arrived a week late—and it wasn't even the right kind of train! It was from the wrong year, for one thing, and had several other things wrong with it. But what could the producers do? If they sent it back, it would be another three weeks or more before the correct train arrived—if it ever arrived at all. So the art directors refurbished the train so that it looked more like it was supposed to.

On the average work day, lunch usually wasn't served until around 2 p.m., which was customary in Spain. The director tried to get as much accomplished as possible before lunch because the catered meal was like a feast, and we usually drank a lot of wine because the water was so bad. Combine alcohol consumption with the desert heat and it was no wonder that everyone was exhausted by mid-afternoon. Whatever was done after lunch was hardly worth doing. They should have just let us go home because our get-up-and-go usually got up and went.

I had a recurring role on "The Rat Patrol," and my character died wonderfully in my third episode because it was revealed that I was really a double agent working for the Nazis. When Chris's character, Sgt. Sam

Troy, realizes what's going on, he sneaks up behind me as I'm shaving, grabs my razor and slits my throat with it, spewing blood everywhere. It was a glorious scene, but when they sent the dailies back home the network found it a little too brutal for television at that time and edited it a lot. In the televised version, they just showed Chris coming up behind me, grabbing my razor and cutting my throat, then a quick shot of my mouth agog. They cut out all the blood and gore, which was sad because I felt the scene as shot was very, very powerful.

I had a little apartment in Almeria and one of my neighbors was Clint Eastwood, who was there making a western with Italian director Sergio Leone. Clint was miserable at the time because of the heat and the Spartan conditions that came with making a relatively low-budget film overseas.   Clint was sort of typecast by his stint on the TV series "Rawhide" and had a hard time finding work when he left the show. He was very happy to be working with Leone, and was confident that the movie would help jump-start his career. And boy did it! Spaghetti westerns made Clint an international star and he's been riding high ever since.

Clint's wife, Maggie, was with him and I ran into her first at a little cafe in downtown Almeria. She was excited to see me because she, too, was starting to get tired of the rustic side of Spain, and the daily grind that Clint was under. The apartment building in which we were all living was on the beach—but not the nice part. Instead of the Mediterranean's famous azure waters, we faced what was essentially an open toilet because that's where the town's sewage went out. We didn't spend much time on our beach-front balconies because the stench was unbearable.

Chris George, on the other hand, was housed in an upscale hotel because he was the star of "The Rat Patrol." I used to visit Chris every chance I got because it was such a nice place—and because Chris was a genuinely nice guy with a great sense of humor.

ABC-TV filmed "The Rat Patrol" in Spain for only one season because the savings didn't pan out as planned, and because the region was just a nightmare in which to film a weekly series. The weather often didn't cooperate and the producers were frequently unable to get even the basics needed to shoot a television show. I'm sure Spain sounded like a good idea at the time, but the reality proved entirely different. The show's second and final season was primarily filmed in the California-Nevada desert.

It was while working on "The Rat Patrol" that I met a German actor named Hans Gudagast. Hans later changed his name to Eric Braden and achieved stardom in the soap operas. We were chatting on the set of "The Rat Patrol" one day and he told me, "I'm going to Hollywood to become a big star!" Years later I ran into him in Santa Monica, and he had indeed made it big on the soaps. "I'm in another world of motion pictures," he told me, "but it pays so well that I'm going to stay with it as long as I can." Eric and the soaps proved to be an excellent match—he's made a fortune and is extremely popular.

I'm kind of envious of Eric's success on daytime television because I've always wanted to work in the soaps, but never had the opportunity. Most of my agents didn't want to bother with soap operas, and I never understood why. The money is good, and it's an excellent acting experience. No matter how schlocky and melodramatic the stories are, you're still in front of the camera, learning and working. I've never even been interviewed for a soap opera, nor have I ever met a casting agent for one. Like anything, I guess it's just a matter of being in the right place at the right time.

In the early '80s I acted in a few episodes of a syndicated show called "Guilty or Innocent," which featured attorney Melvin Belli and was filmed at the new Dallas Communication Center in Texas. I was visiting my niece and nephew, Barbara and Gene Mendenhall, in Dallas at the time and contacted the casting people, who immediately signed me up.

"Guilty or Innocent" was a combination drama/game show that presented dramatizations of real cases before a jury that was supposed to determine whether the defendants were guilty or not. The jury was kept for one week, and if they were correct enough times, they won prizes. It was a strange hybrid of a show and I'm not even sure if it ever made it on the air. I played a murderer in one episode, a car theft victim in another, and a husband with a philandering wife in a third. Belli was the show's host, and proved to be just as flamboyant in person as he was on television.

I became involved with "BL Stryker" in 1989 through my long-time association with Burt Reynolds, who was the star of the Florida-based detective show. Burt called one day and told me they were going to be filming the show in and around Palm Beach County. I hadn't heard from Burt in a while and I was surprised at the news. He asked if I would mind working in production and I said no, of course not.

After the production company had set up its offices locally, Burt brought me in to meet with the producers. "I don't know what kind of deal they'll make with you," he said, "but would you mind starting out as a production assistant?" The job meant being a glorified "gofer" but with better pay. It wasn't exactly what I wanted, but again I said yes. "I just want to help you find your rainbow," Burt added with sincerity as he led me into the offices of producer Charles Floyd Johnson. It was a touching moment after years of little contact.

So I became a production assistant and worked like a dog. For five or six months, I did everything, including sweeping up dog shit on location so that the cameras could be placed. Plus, on my own, I did things like getting up at 4 a.m. so I could arrive at the location sites to show the cast and crew where to park in the dark. Only one person, casting director Peggy Kirton, noticed my hard work and thanked me when it was all over. But despite the drudgery, I really loved being part of the industry again after being away from it for so many years. It's like a drug you just can't kick.

One day, assistant director Melanie Grefe told me that Burt wanted to see me on The Bus. No one went on The Bus; that was Burt's personal transportation. I went inside and Burt told me what a good job I was doing and to hang in there because things would work out. He called me into The Bus several times after that for one thing or another, which really baffled the other workers on the set because they had no idea that Burt and I had been friends for so many years. They thought I was just another production assistant and I never corrected them because to me it wasn't a big deal.

The highlight of my association with "BL Stryker" occurred on a day when we were shooting a scene in front of the Boca Raton Police Department. Melanie came up to me again and told me that Burt wanted to see me on The Bus. I joined him as soon as I could, and he handed me a package. Inside was a red leather script holder with my name on it. This was a gift Burt gave only to guest stars who appeared on the show, so the message was clear—I was being promoted from production assistant to performer in due time! Carol DePiazza, who was head of catering, went with me behind the craft services truck, where I had a good cry as this was a very emotional moment for me. Dutch Hardie, one of the lead production assistants, found us and gruffly told me to get back to work. He had no idea what had happened. Dutch and I had some problems at first, but later resolved our differences.

My much anticipated screen appearance didn't happen until the last show of the second season. By then, I had been promoted to head of publicity, thanks to some expert advice from Stanley Brossette, who had been Elvis Presley's personal PR man and publicist on many major motion pictures. Stanley had always told me that I should become a publicist, and Burt thought I'd be perfect for the job.

One day I got a call from my cherished friends Carol Wood, who was the show's art director, and scenic director Dean Metzner. They got the scripts before anyone else because they had to design the whole show, and they started to read the description of a particular character. Then they started screaming on the phone, "It's you! It's you!" I could hardly contain myself, but I couldn't tell anyone Carol and Dean had told me about it because I wasn't supposed to know. Later that morning, I received a call from Charles Floyd Johnson, our executive producer. He handed me a script and said, "Burt wants you to do this part." I quickly perused the script and realized it was a co-starring role, and that I would be a regular on the show from then on. Charles contacted my agent in Beverly Hills and got the ball rolling.

The episode, titled "Night Train," was directed by Burt, and proved to be a magnificent experience—even though I was involved in a car accident the day before shooting started and had to do the whole thing with a crushed collarbone. My shoulder was tightly taped and I had a wonderful nurse on the set with me, so I managed to get through it pretty well. My character gets shot and falls down an escalator, but that was done by a stuntman.

I played the part of Wally Wardell, an over-the-hill lounge singer with a gambling problem. My long-time friend, wardrobe director Norman Salling, dressed me wonderfully for the part; I really looked like a contemporary mobster. Wally owes $40,000 to gangsters so they call in his chips by making him kill a young girl who has some incriminating evidence against them. But Wally doesn't have the balls to do the job, so he hides her and just tells the hoods that he had killed her. I get shot but not killed, and one of the last scenes of the show is me confessing everything to my brother, played by series regular Alfie Wise. The whole episode took place on a train. Lindsey Alley, who had worked previously on television as a new Mouseketeer, played the little girl I was supposed to kill.

The icing on the cake is that I won the Crystal Reel Award from the Florida Motion Picture and Television Association in the best supporting actor category for that role. It's one of the highlights of my career, and I'm extremely proud of it.

"BL Stryker" wasn't renewed for another season. I was again a victim of the Anthony Quinn curse from "The Buccaneer"—big promises that never went anywhere. "Stryker" had a hard time finding an audience because the network kept moving it around and alternating it with other shows, which is death for any series. Burt begged for a more regular schedule because the series really was wonderfully done and deserved another chance, but ABC declined. Interestingly, "BL Stryker" had a strong following in Europe and a few episodes were shown as full-length features because they were shot as two-hour shows.

In retrospect, it's a wonder that I didn't have a nervous breakdown while working on "BL Stryker." I pushed myself to the limit in every job I had with the show because I really wanted to prove myself to Burt, the others on the team and, most importantly, myself. But "Night Train" made it all worthwhile, with the help and support of Carol Wood, Dean Metzner and my darling friends Debi Hand Thomas and Beverly McDermott, who had been my agent years before and now is working as a television casting director.

Long before "BL Stryker," I appeared in a syndicated television special called "Take Me Home Again," produced and narrated by Merv Griffin, that was all about Burt. It was shot in and around Palm Beach County, and I was living on Burt's ranch at the time. It detailed Burt's life and career, and I sang "Lonesome Road," which was one of Burt's favorite songs.

My association with Burt even extends to the theater. Burt used to have a dinner theater in Jupiter, Florida, and I performed there in a production of "The Odd Couple" with Charles Nelson Reilly and Daryl Hickman as Felix and Oscar. I played Felix's and Oscar's accountant, Roy. The production was directed by Broadway legend Nancy Walker, and it was such a huge success that Showtime taped it for airing on that network. That was the first time a theatrical production was filmed in its entirety and shown that way on Showtime or any other network, and I was proud to be part of it.

What a challenge it was working with Charles Nelson Reilly eight times a week. You certainly had to be on your toes because Charles, God love him, occasionally would take a few liberties with the script and add his own shtick, which the audience loved. Sometimes it seemed like an eternity before we'd hear our cues for the next line. But being the consummate professional, Charles always eventually got back to the script. There was a scene in "The Odd Couple" in which Charles, as Felix, drags me, as Roy, out of the bathroom, so Felix can commit suicide. One time I bent over so Charles could grab me by the neck, as he was supposed to do, and he accidentally dragged part of the toilet out on stage with me! The audience went into convulsions of laughter, and Charles just milked the situation for more than five minutes. I laughed so hard tears came down my cheeks. It was one of the most fun times I've ever had on stage.

Dom DeLuise is a good friend of Burt's, so he was a frequent guest at the Burt Reynolds Dinner Theater and even did a stint on "BL Stryker." Dom, Charles, Burt and I have had some side-splitting adventures together over the years because Dom is a genuine character and he possesses one of the quickest wits I've ever seen. For example, I went to California a few years ago to take care of some business and stayed with my nephew Keith. I tried to reach Dom in Malibu so we could have lunch, but he wasn't in so I left Keith's phone number on Dom's answering machine. When Dom called back, Keith answered the phone.

Dom: Hello, Kenny. This is Dom.

Keith: I'm sorry, Kenny isn't in right now.

Dom: You sound just like him. Who is this?

Keith: This is his nephew.

Dom: Oh yes, of course you are. And what is your name?

Keith: Keith Miller.

Dom: Oh, isn't that nice. You don't even have to change the monogram on your towels!

Acting in television is quite a bit different from acting in motion pictures. You tend to work harder and faster in television because you don't have the luxury of time. A series has to produce a show a week, and once one is in the can, you immediately move on to the next. It's hard work and the limitations can be frustrating, but most of my television experiences have been happy ones, and I've made a lot of great friends along the way.

In the end, no matter how you slice it, it's all about acting. I have put as much energy and dedication into my television work as I have in my biggest movies. To me, that's what being a professional is all about.

Chapter 11
Famous Friends & Fun Times

Whenever I reflect back on my career, I'm amazed at the number of movie stars, celebrities and other international figures with whom I became good friends. I crossed paths with—and often got to know quite well—some of the biggest names in filmmaking, politics and royalty. That such a thing should happen to a dirt-poor preacher's kid from Ohio never fails to astound me. Even now, decades later, I marvel at the path God chose for me to follow.

There was, for example, the time I taught Jackie Kennedy to do the Twist.

This was early in 1961. I was in New York and had just signed with manager Don Seat, who handled a number of well-known performers, including rock singer Jo-Ann Campbell. I became close with Jo-Ann because she was like the social director of the New York recording crowd. Her apartment was a popular hang-out and you never knew who would be there when you dropped by.

Don worked closely with Dick Clark who, eventually married Don's secretary, Loretta Martin. Whenever Dick was in town, the four of us—Dick, Loretta, Jo-Ann and I—would go out and hit the latest clubs. One day Jo-Ann told us she had discovered an outrageous club on 45th Street called The Peppermint Lounge, which was attached to a hotel. The crowds there were doing a wild new dance called the Twist, backed by the house band, Joey Dee and the Starlighters. We checked it out one evening and the place was packed. The New York society crowd had discovered the Peppermint Lounge, and limos were pulling up every five minutes. It was an incredible scene.

We started going to the Peppermint Lounge quite often. Dick Clark talked with Joey Dee and the Starlighters, and was instrumental in getting them a recording contract. They did one of the first big Twist songs, "The Peppermint Twist," which made them famous. At the same time, the Twist became THE hot dance craze in New York, and Twist parties were the vogue. I was often asked to teach people how to do the dance, and Susan Littlefield, who was a close friend of Connie DeNave, became one of my Twist partners.

One day I got a call from my friend Gary Filosa, who gave great parties in Beverly Hills and who was now living and working with Eric Javits. Gary and Eric invited Susan and I to come to a how-to-Twist party at the apartment of Eric's mother, Lily Javits. Susan and I attended three Twist parties in three days, and it was at one of these parties that I first met Jackie Kennedy and taught her how to do the Twist.

I started getting some exciting club gigs upstate and would do shows with Jo-Ann Campbell and others, usually with an orchestra. I really enjoyed performing, and the income generated by these shows kept me going for some time. I went home to Ohio for Christmas, and learned that International Harvester, which employed about half of the people in Springfield, was planning a big holiday party at Memorial Hall. My brothers and several other family members worked for IH, and they asked me if I would entertain at the Christmas party. I readily agreed (how could I say no to a request like that?) and ended up doing the Twist with my young niece, Vicky, and my nephew, Jimmy. But the show-stealer was my five-year-old nephew Keith, who hit the dance floor and out-Twisted us all. He brought the audience to its feet and soon the whole place was Twisting while I sang my heart out. I loved every minute of it!

When we returned to my brother George's home that evening, Don Seat called from New York to tell me he had landed me a gig in Florida. "Can you get down there and bring a band?" he asked. It was a big request, especially since I had just three days to make it happen. Luckily, my sister-in-law Carol's brother, Dick, was in the band I had worked with at the Christmas show for International Harvester and they quickly agreed to go with me. So we piled into a van and traveled all night to Florida.

The gig was a nightclub called the Golden Falcon in Pompano Beach, and it was like heaven there after spending a week in the sub-arctic Ohio winter. I did my usual nightclub act, with one portion devoted to the Twist. That dance craze hadn't reached Florida yet, and it took off like a rocket. The management even made the dance floor bigger in front of the stage so people could Twist while I sang.

I opened on December 22, 1961, and Dick Clark and Loretta Martin came by to offer their support. That was pretty cool, but not as cool as what happened next. Midway into my show, the club owner came over to tell me that Jackie Kennedy had arrived unexpectedly, and the Secret Service was quietly casing the joint. The dance floor was packed. I looked through the teaming mob and saw a man bringing Jackie to the dance floor directly in front of me. Without missing a beat I stepped down to the floor and Twisted with Jackie. You'd think there would have been a mob scene, but no one was really paying much attention because it was dark and they couldn't see who she was. Jackie was there with her sister, Lee Radziwill; they had been shopping in Bal Harbour and just dropped by for a very quick visit. They didn't stay very long; Jackie danced a bit, threw me a kiss and left as quickly as she had arrived. Stephanie Javits, who bears a striking resemblance to Jackie Kennedy, and her husband, Eric, also came by a little later in the evening and stayed until the wee hours.

I didn't really think much about Jackie's quick hello. But within hours her innocent visit, which had been witnessed by hundreds of people including members of the local press, become a huge scandal because Joseph Kennedy was ill, and people were shocked that the First Lady was out partying during this trying time. Not surprisingly, the Kennedy camp immediately denied the whole thing ever occurred; Pierre Salinger said it wasn't Jackie at the Golden Falcon because she was with her family at the Kennedy compound in Palm Beach.

I immediately started getting calls from newspapers, radio and television stations all over the world regarding Jackie's appearance. There were even messages from Russia! But I was told that before I talked to anyone, I should talk to Pierre Salinger at the Kennedy compound in Palm Beach. I called and Salinger said: "Please Kenny, don't say anything! Tell the press it wasn't Jackie, just someone who looked like her or something like that."

Unwilling to embarrass the Kennedys or cause a huge international scandal, I grudgingly did as Salinger asked. I didn't exactly deny the incident, but I didn't push it either. The official line was that the woman dancing with me was Stephanie Javits, not Jackie Kennedy. But that story didn't hold up very well under scrutiny because Jackie and Stephanie were there at the club at different times and a lot of people knew that. Adding fuel to the fire were news reports that a police officer in nearby Hillsboro had stopped Jackie's limo for speeding. Of course, when he realized who he had stopped, he let the driver off with just a warning. The cop informed reporters that Jackie had told him they were speeding because she had stopped at the Golden Falcon and they were running late.

I'm telling you right here and now: Jackie Kennedy did the Twist with me at the Golden Falcon. She was right next to me; I even held her hand. Besides, if it wasn't Jackie Kennedy, why would the Secret Service check out the place first? No matter what the White House claimed, I know the truth because I was there.

The Twist became a great thing for me. The band and I played the Golden Falcon the whole season of '62 and quickly became the headliners. Jerry Van Dyke opened for me and asked if I would tour with him, but it was out of the question because I was booked solid. After the Jackie Kennedy episode, the lines to get into the club were longer than ever. I moved into a suite at the hotel, and the club gave me a Corvette to drive. I was definitely living the good life!

During that time, William Paley, the head of CBS, invited the band and me to perform at a private party at the Taboo restaurant in Palm Beach for an outrageous fee. The party was on a Monday, which was usually our day off, so we accepted the invitation. Mrs. Paley and Sam Peterson, then the owner of Taboo, had redecorated the place with a circus motif specifically for the party, and it looked great.

I was very pleased to see Jackie Kennedy there. The Kennedy clan spent a lot of time at the family compound in Palm Beach during the winter months, and Kennedy sightings were always big news. I said hi to Jackie and she told me she was going to another party and and then on to a club called the San Souci (at least I think it was the San Souci). We chatted for a minute, but neither of us brought up the Golden Falcon affair. What really happened that night was an unspoken secret between us.

I did a 30-minute set at the Paley party—including the Twist, which became my signature song for a while—and got people up to do the dance. After the show, I headed over to the San Souci at Jackie's invitation. The place was packed and so loud it was nearly impossible to hear the person sitting next to you. Jackie and her group invited me and my manager to join them at their table, but we weren't able to converse very much.

Jackie and I weren't best pals or anything like that. I knew her only socially, and we never had the opportunity to talk on anything but a superficial level. But she loved the Twist, and I look back on our "dance relationship" with great fondness. I'll also never forget her voice. Jackie Kennedy had one of the most beautiful voices I've ever heard, unusually soft and sweet. When she spoke, it was like listening to an angel.

I returned to California for a year or so, and in 1964 I was signed by an independent producer to do a movie in Munich, Germany. I decided to use the trip to visit some old friends in England, including a fellow named Shel Talmy, who always had a thing for music. He had gone to London and made a name for himself as a record producer, and was instrumental in discovering The Who, Chad & Jeremy and several other big rock acts. I dropped by his office and we had a lot of fun catching up. A little later, Ann Hallam, who worked for Shel, made me promise that I would return to London after I finished the movie in Germany because Shel really wanted to record me. It was something he had wanted to do when we were in California, and now he was in a position to make that dream come true.

The whole situation was very serendipitous because while I was in London I also looked up a guy named Tony Ponte, a friend of Nan Morris who was then working as an entertainment manager. I told Tony about Shel's recording offer and asked if he would like to manage me. Tony was excited at the prospect because he was confident he could launch me as a major celebrity in the United Kingdom.

With a recording contract waiting for me in London, off I flew to Munich. I arrived a day or two before everyone else and contacted the assistant director. "We have bad news," he said. "The film has been postponed because of problems with the star. He's out." I won't reveal the actor's name here because it would serve no good purpose, but the fact of the matter is, he had a serious drinking problem. I stuck around for a couple more days at the AD's urging, only to be told that the whole project had been scrapped because the financial backers wouldn't agree to any of the stars suggested to replace their first choice. I was sorry to hear that the film had been canceled, but I was delighted when they gave me two weeks' pay. That gave me a little walking around money.

So I returned to London, which I found very friendly and supportive; the people there really took me under their wing. I met with Shel again and he found me a nice apartment that I could rent by the week. Then I met again with Tony and we signed the management contracts while Shel looked for material for me to record. He got me a recording contract with EMI Stateside, which owned Capitol Records in the United States and was one of the biggest recording companies in England. The Beatles and other major acts recorded for them.

While the wheels of my burgeoning British recording career slowly turned, Tony signed Bernard Delfont, one of England's top agents, to represent me. His brother was impresario Sir Lew Grade, and the two of them were big shakers-and-movers in British television, theater and motion pictures.

I really wanted to record one particular song which had been floating around among various recording managers, but Shel didn't think it was right for me. The song was "It's Not Unusual," and a few months later it became Tom Jones' first major hit. I could have performed that song, but I don't think I could have brought the energy to it that Tom did. He really turned it into something special.

Shel finally found a song he thought was perfect for me—"Restless," written by Allan Fielding, who composed many of rock star Billy Fury's biggest hits. I came into Shel's office to hear the demo and I loved it. It was like a Gene Pitney song with a big orchestra behind it. Conductor/arranger Arthur Greenslade came up with an arrangement that just blew me away. I recorded the song early in 1965 and it proved to be a success 'for me in England and Europe.

At the time, England didn't have any Top 40 radio stations, but there were numerous illegal pirate stations playing the rock songs the kids wanted to hear. Most of the pirate stations were housed on boats just off shore, and I visited a couple of them to promote "Restless."

One of the biggest legitimate stations was Radio Luxembourg. It broadcast all over Europe and popularized my record throughout the continent. "Restless" did so well that I lived off that one record for nearly a year. It generated a tremendous amount of publicity for me, and helped me land some television gigs in England and elsewhere. I also did some great radio shows, including one that allowed me to sing "Restless" with the London Symphony Orchestra. Talk about the big time!

England was awash with daring new music during that period, sparked by the astounding popularity of The Beatles. There were numerous live musical television shows, plus people listened to the radio all the time—much more than they did in the United States.

As a result of the huge success of "Restless," the Delfont Organization started booking me throughout the UK. My first gigs in England were in "workman's clubs," where laborers came to relax, have a drink and be entertained after work. A lot of American star singers strived to be booked into workman's clubs because it was great money and an enthusiastic audience. The shows were usually early, around 6 or 6:30 in the evening, because the workers couldn't stay out late; they had to go to work the next day. So they would come in, down a few pints, have a great time and go home. After the entertainment was done, the club would close until the next evening.

My first show was at a workman's club in Manchester. The place was packed and really noisy. In fact, the crowd was so boisterous that I didn't think they would even listen to me. My opening act was a wonderful girls' trio which later appeared on "The Benny Hill Show." But I guess the crowd had heard them several times before because they paid them little attention. I was sitting in my dressing room, listening to the whole thing through my monitor speaker and worried sick that I would bomb. The noise of the crowd was so loud that right in the middle of the girls' big song I heard a voice over a loudspeaker yell, "Have a little respect for the artist! Have a little respect for the artist!" I thought, if they do that for me, I'll just fall through the floor.

But I quickly found out that if an English audience likes you, they love you. That boisterous crowd quieted right down the moment I took the stage. You could have heard a pin drop. I performed a selection of older songs, as well as "Restless," which drew a rousing response.

I got into a regular pattern of appearing at workman's clubs in the early evening, and regular night clubs later the same night. Most of the workman's clubs were outside of town, so a driver would pick me up and take me to whatever night club I was appearing at that week. Sometimes I opened, and sometimes I was the featured performer. One week I worked with a wonderful singer named Vera Lynn, who had a lot of hits during World War II, including "Auf Wiedersehen, Sweetheart." She was a terrific lady, and a marvelous talent even in her later years.

Dashing from workmen's clubs to night clubs every evening became grueling after a while, but I got a lot of exposure, met some wonderful people and had one of the greatest times of my life.

Whenever I worked outside of London, I stayed at what were known as digs—private homes that specifically housed visiting entertainers. In Manchester I stayed at the Astral House, which was sort of split, with supporting acts such as the dance team and the comic on one side, and the "stars" on the other. Even meals were split, with the stars eating in one dining room and the other acts eating in another. The lady who owned the Astral House was an old vaudevillian with a million great stories to tell. I was too young to be in vaudeville in America, but in jolly old England I got the closest thing to it. Also living in the house were some of the stars of the longest running soap opera on British television, "Coronation Street," and since I was a "star," I often got to have breakfast and dinner with them. They were a lively bunch, lots of fun and very friendly.

Everyone in England treated me wonderfully, though you never knew what to expect from one club to the next. At one club in Leeds, there were just two people in the audience! It had an odd layout, too. The stage was about three feet high, and the orchestra was behind me. The audience was on the right and left—and immediately in front of me was a huge mirror. It was very disorienting because it forced me to look at my reflection while performing. I always moved immediately to my right or to my left because I preferred to sing to the audience, not to myself.

As my popularity in England grew, I made several television appearances, including "Ready, Steady, Go" and "The Three O'Clock Club," which did a special on me. The theme was "Surf Party," so the show went to Brighton, which is on the seashore. Unfortunately, Brighton doesn't have that much surf. It was also very overcast and cold. They couldn't use regular surfers, so the producers dressed up the show with race boats and guys on water skis. I got to be good friends with Lulu while making that show. Her recording career was starting to blossom, and she would soon appear with Sidney Poitier in "To Sir, With Love" (1967). What fun she was!

After I came back from my whirlwind tour of northern England, I was booked into the Celebrity Club in Piccadilly. I was billed as "The American Sensation," which was pretty heavy. The place was owned by Paul Raymond, who has a lot of London strip joints as well as legitimate night clubs. The Celebrity Club was a legitimate place, and it had a Las Vegas-type revue of dancers and nudes. I did only one show a night, but the dance troupe put on four grueling performances at four different clubs every evening! I'll never forget the specialty dance team, a nude man and woman who sprayed their bodies gold so they looked like statues. They would start at one club and end the evening at the Celebrity Club, which was the big show. By then, back stage you could see where the paint was starting to wear off. I was afraid they would get sick from the body paint, but they both seemed pretty healthy. They wore long velvet capes—and nothing else—as they were transported in the cold from one club to the other. After the show they would leave the club still painted gold and go home to clean up. It was a hell of a way to make a living, but the audiences loved them.

It was also while I was in England that I got to meet the great singer Hildegarde, who was appearing at a theater club near my apartment. She had once been an international star, but her career was starting to fade at that point, though she didn't want to admit it. Hildegarde arrived with her personal manager, Mary Collins, and thirteen trunks full of clothes and costumes. She was booked at the Theater of the Arts, which she thought was a big theater, but which was actually just a small private club. When she finally saw the size of the venue, she was crushed. She had been booked by an American producer who didn't know what he was doing, and her proposed tour of England died before it even got off the ground.

I really felt sorry for Hildegarde because she still had it as a performer, and Mary and I tried desperately to cheer her up. Then the fates intervened and Hildegarde was asked to headline at the Talk of the Town, where many of the biggest entertainers appeared. She replaced a comic who had become famous on British television, but was a disaster on stage. My agent, Bernard Delfont, got Hildegarde the gig and she was very well received.

Hildegarde stayed in London for quite a while, so we became very close. Mary loved to cook, and in November we invited our British friends over for Thanksgiving turkey, which was a real novelty for them. Turkeys were hard to come by, so we went to Harrad's department store and paid a fortune for one. I admired Hildy very much—no matter how cold or nasty the weather, she went to mass every morning.

I was in England off and on for about four years. To maintain my worker's green card (or the British equivalent), I had to occasionally go out of country and then come back. It was a righteous pain in the ass, but my situation was made easier by one young lady who was huge fan. Her mother worked in the main immigration office, and she arranged for me to keep my worker's green card simply by going to Paris for a day and then coming back to England. It's nice to have fans in high places!

Tony Ponte, my manager, was a ladies' man and a great looking guy. Women were all over him. He was good friends with Linda Christian, who was married to Tyrone Power at one time. Linda was the star of several big-budget films made in the United States as well as a big social butterfly in England and Europe. She wanted to meet me because Tony had told her all about me, and she liked "Restless."

Through Linda and Tony I met Her Royal Highness Muna al Hussein, the Queen of Jordan. She was English by birth (real name: Toni Gardiner) and hers was a fairy tale that all of England adored. As a result, Muna was almost as beloved and respected as the Queen of England herself. Muna was in town with King Hussein's sister, Princess Basma, who was going to school outside London. I found Muna to be very down to earth and extremely beautiful, and we became very good friends. I was a nervous wreck when I met her, but she put me completely at ease in about two seconds.

Muna took me under her wing and we had a lot of great adventures together over the years. The King was seldom around, so I escorted her to various parties and other functions. Not that we were alone—we were usually in the company of Jordanian security officials, the director of protocol and other members of the royal entourage.

One night we all went to the theater and sat in the Royal Box where the Queen of England had been the night before. At intermission, Muna and I couldn't help but laugh because the staff hadn't cleaned up the private room next to the royal box and there were glasses and used napkins everywhere. The servant who served us looked around at the mess as he took our order and muttered, "Forgive me, Your Highness" to Muna. Moments after he left, two maids showed up to clean the room. I really thought the Queen would have been a little more tidy!

Discos were at their height in England during the 1960s, so Muna and I visited some of the classier establishments when we had the opportunity, always in the presence of her security guards and other hangers-on. I remember going to one popular disco and running into three of the Beatles (John was absent that night). It was the kind of place where stars and royalty just hung out. I even got to dance with Hayley Mills!

When things briefly slowed for me in England, I went to Paris to work. One of my first gigs was at a little club off the Champs Elysees called the Gaslight, part of a chain of private clubs that originated in Chicago. It was managed by a Canadian named J. Duncan Newton. The place was unique because nearly all of the staff were American gals who waited on tables and also performed. But in a bizarre twist of irony, the musicians in the club's Dixieland band were all French—and they were tremendous. There were a lot of small clubs on the Rue d'Colisee, where the Gaslight was located, many owned by African-American entertainers who had fled to France to avoid persecution and inequality. It was a really cool street and I had great fun hanging around there after I finished my last show at the Gaslight.

One evening, King Hussein visited the club with his entourage. He didn't know I was performing there, and he was very charming. We had a cordial relationship and I don't think he ever minded me entertaining

Muna because he knew our relationship was strictly platonic. It took me a long, long time to get over the fact that I was running around with the beautiful wife of the King of Jordan and their family! My parents would never have believed it.

Muna and I got together again in New York after I returned to the states around 1967— and almost provoked an international incident.

She and the King, who she fondly referred to as HM (His Majesty), were staying at the Waldorf Astoria Hotel. King Hussein had to leave for some reason, so Muna found herself accompanied by another member of the royal family who she didn't particularly care for. We were going out to dinner, and planned it so the other family member wouldn't be included. But we were still accompanied by the Jordanian head of protocol and a handful of American Secret Service agents, who were assigned to assure Muna's safety.

I suggested to Muna that we have drinks with a writer friend of mine named Jim Boshier. Jim and his wife asked to meet Muna over dinner because they didn't believe I really knew her. When I walked into the restaurant with Muna on my arm, Jim and his wife were completely speechless. Our schedule was to have dinner and then hit some clubs, but Muna had other plans. After returning from the rest room, she decided it would be more fun to ditch the Secret Service and go club hopping on our own!

We somehow diverted the Secret Service agents and took off in a cab. "Now we can have fun!" Muna said as we sped through the city. We went down to Greenwich Village and hit a bunch of trendy discos and night clubs. In one of them, you had to go down a slide to get in. We met Jim and some friends at a little club for a nightcap around midnight, then I brought Muna back to the Waldorf.

Needless to say, the Secret Service and the head of Royal Protocol were furious with me. I got a stern lecture on the dangers of touring New York without security, and how it would have been entirely my fault if anything had happened to Muna. I was also told I could have sparked an international scandal by escorting the Queen around town without a chaperone. But I don't regret a minute of it. We had a wild time, and Muna really appreciated the chance to let her hair down for a while.

Also while we were in New York, I invited Muna to see Connie Stevens, who was appearing at the Plaza. Muna readily agreed because she was a big fan of Connie. That afternoon, I went to see Connie and her sister-in-law, Ellen Ingolia, who is very New York. Ellen kept fretting about how to greet the Queen. Should she bow or curtsy? Should she call her Her Highness? I finally said, "Ellen, don't do anything. Just be yourself."

Connie was so cool that night, dedicating the show to Muna without actually mentioning her name. But our cover was blown before we even sat down. As we arrived at the Plaza to go into the show room, the maitre d' asked my name, then looked over at Muna and actually fell to his knees! It turned out he was Jordanian and there he was, facing his Queen. Muna whispered, "Get up! Get up! Please!" The poor guy was shaking all over. He sat us at our table and fawned over Muna almost all night. The one time in a million that Muna wanted to go unnoticed, and she runs into a fellow countryman!

Afterward, Connie, Ellen and Connie's sister, Ava Megna, came out to meet Muna. Ellen was so excited that she was literally shaking. She bowed and said, "Oh, it's so nice to meet you, my lord!" Muna just laughed and hugged her. Afterward she told me, "That's the first time I've been called a lord!"

Muna is one of my closest friends in the world. During the Six Day War between Israel and Egypt, she wrote me beautiful letters detailing what was going on in the Middle East. I treasure those letters. She also gave me a beautiful gold medallion to replace one I had lost while swimming in Spain earlier that year.

That's actually a funny story. While living in Marbella, I had become good friends with a group of gypsy entertainers. One day they invited me up into the hills above Marbella for a lunch of paella and sangria. It was a very hot day and after lunch we decided to go wading in a nearby stream. The gypsies, having no inhibitions whatsoever, removed all their clothing. That seemed like a pretty good idea to me, and soon we were all frolicking naked. I was laying back on some rocks and I realized my medallion was gone. I explained to the gypsies what had happened and we searched feverishly for it, but the current was strong and we never found it. I was devastated because I had owned the medallion for many years; it was a gift from one of my fans. That night I went to dinner with some Spanish friends and I told them the story. They all started laughing, and one of them said, "You think that chain was broken by a rock? Those gypsies are so clever they probably yanked it off your neck without you ever noticing it!" I asked him what they had done with it since they were all naked, and he said, "One of them probably swallowed it. And tomorrow, there will be a deposit!" I'm sure my eyes grew wide; that medallion was as big as a silver dollar!

Muna called me in Marbella from London shortly after, and I mentioned the loss of my medallion. About two months later, I received an overnight parcel from London and in it was a beautiful gold medallion with my initials on the front and a passage from the Koran in Arabic on the back. Muna also included a note with the translation in English. A few months after that, she sent me an English edition of the Koran with that particular passage highlighted. The leather box it came in was almost as impressive as the medal and chain inside it. The box was inscribed "By appointment to Her Majesty The Queen." Muna had the medallion made by Queen Elizabeth's personal jeweler.

Sadly, I don't have that medallion anymore, either—and this story is far from funny. I went to New York to visit Nancy Streebeck a few years later, and was mugged by two guys as I returned to my hotel. The thieves knocked me down a stairwell, beat me up and yanked off all my jewelry, including my Rolex watch. But I don't miss any of that stuff as much I regret losing the medallion Muna had given me.

Muna came to Georgetown, Connecticut, with her sons, Prince Abdullah and Prince Faisel, to see me sing with the United States Coastguard Band on Loyalty Day in September 1974. The boys were considering going to school in Connecticut, which gave us a great opportunity to catch up on our busy lives. Prince Abdullah is now His Majesty King Abdullah of Jordan.

Muna was also able to visit me at Burt Reynold's ranch in Jupiter, Florida, a couple of months later. She really wanted to stay at the ranch, which was a fabulous place, but the Secret Service nixed the idea because of security concerns. My friend Trink Gardiner invited Muna and her family to stay in her beautiful mansion in Palm Beach, and the local newspapers went nuts. So did the paparazzi, which was kind of annoying. We dealt with it as best we could.

Muna eventually was divorced by King Hussein. He gave her the palace as part of the settlement and they remain very close friends. Muna and I are also still close and we chat on a regular basis. She now lives back in Amman, Jordan, and every year she sends me a picture of her family. Muna has two boys and twin girls, Princess Zein and Princess Aisha, and I'm like their unofficial American godfather. All of the kids are married now and have families of their own. In the most recent picture, Muna is seated with her many grandchildren. But she's just as beautiful as the day I first met her in London.

Muna wasn't the only member of royalty that I met through Tony Ponte. It was because of him that I also got to sing with Princess Grace while he and

I were visiting Monaco for the International Red Cross Gala in 1966.

Tony and I were staying in a villa owned by Tony's father located just above the town of Menton. During the day we hung around a wonderful place on the Mediterranean called The Point, which had a swimming pool. It was THE place in town to go for lunch and a swim. We saw Princess Grace there frequently with her two youngest children, which always struck me as odd because she lived in a palace. But apparently it was a palace without a swimming pool

During our stay in Monte Carlo I became acquainted at one of the many cocktail parties with a wonderful gal named Judy Balaban. She was married to actor Tony Franciosa, who was in Rome at the time making a movie. Judy was probably Grace's closest friend, and one night she invited Tony Ponte and I to join her and a few others at an out-of-the-way cafe for a quiet evening. It was a charming place with tables splashing out on the cobblestone streets. Judy arrived and much to our surprise and delight, Grace was with her. We sat around drinking champagne, chatting and enjoying the resident guitar player, who was an excellent musician. After a few drinks we all started singing some silly songs, and then Grace asked me to sing "Fly Me To the Moon," which was one of her favorites. I tried to beg off because I had never sung "Fly Me To the Moon" in public and I wasn't sure of the lyrics, but Grace wouldn't hear of it. So, with a lot of help from the guitar player, I sang the song, making up lyrics when I couldn't remember the actual words. And Grace just loved it. She had a very sweet voice, but was shy about singing alone. We sat in that little cafe, drinking and singing, until around 2 a.m. I always thank Judy for that wonderful evening because to me she's a princess herself.

Speaking of international royalty, I also got to know Shah Mohammed Reza Pahlavi of Iran shortly after he was deposed in 1979, though I knew his wife, Empress Reza Pahlavi—more commonly known as Farah Diba— a bit better.

I was visiting Cuernavaca, Mexico, with some friends from Palm Beach at the time. Cuernavaca is a very elegant place; a lot of wealthy people visit and live there because you can hire servants for practically nothing and live like a king for pesos a day. The Shah and his family were staying in a villa there, having been kicked out of their own country by followers of the Ayatollah Khomeini.

Our group was staying in another villa outside of town owned by Palm Beach socialite Judy Grubb. She lived in Cuernavaca during the summer and had frequent guests because it was such a lovely place to vacation. The area was a little slice of Eden located in a lush green valley between two dormant volcanos.

A gentleman named Jesus Vargas was Judy's major domo, the guy who managed the villa's thirteen servants and made sure everything ran smoothly. Vargas spoke fluent Spanish and English, and because of his flawless reputation, the Shah's people contacted Judy to find out if they could borrow him part-time. Judy gave her okay because her place was completely staffed and she was pretty much settled in. So Vargas divided his time between the two villas, keeping a close eye on both.

One day Judy received a call from the Shah's Head of Protocol inviting her to a birthday party for the deposed ruler as a way of saying thanks for her hospitality and generosity, and Judy invited me to go with her. The Shah's villa was absolutely gorgeous, as might be imagined, with a lot of children running around and security guards keeping a watchful eye. I was introduced to the Empress and put her at ease right away by mentioning our mutual friend Muna, who had asked me to say hello. Farah Diba and I chatted for several minutes about Muna, the Middle East and other things, and got along very well.

The Shah wasn't feeling well that day, but he put up a brave front. He looked thin and pale, but smiled often and tried to keep up with the festivities and his children. Farah Diba asked me to sing "Happy Birthday" when they brought out his cake, which I did. Then Farah Diba told the Shah that I was a professional singer, to which he replied: "Then you sing!" I tried to say no, but he really had his heart set on hearing some rock and roll. So, lacking a band or even a record player, I sang "Kansas City" a cappella for the Shah and his guests. It was a bit awkward, but everyone had a great time and I was pleased that I could give him a few minutes of happiness. The children helped my performance by clapping hands and making funny noises behind me.

A few days after the party, I decided to travel to Taxco, Mexico, to visit my friend Ted Wick, who had managed Tommy Sands, Nancy Sinatra and others. Ted used to be a big player in Hollywood, but left it all behind upon his retirement for a quieter life in Mexico. He had lived there for several years, and had built a beautiful restaurant outside Taxco called La Ventana de Taxco, which overlooks one of the town's famous silver mines. You can see the whole village from the restaurant's terrace, and it is a very popular place with tourists and locals alike.

I made the trip with Judy Grubb, American socialite Lyn Rubin and a wonderful sculptor named Colin Webster Watson. Our plan was to drive into town to look at jewelry, then have lunch at Ted's restaurant. I called Ted when we arrived and he said, "You're not going to believe who's coming to town!" I said, "Farah Diba?" Ted was stunned. "How the hell did you know that?" he asked. I explained that a few nights earlier she had told me she was coming to Taxco, and I suggested she eat at Ted's restaurant. Ted then asked if I could drop by a little early because he was really nervous.

We arrived at the restaurant a few minutes before Farah Diba and her entourage, and were stunned to see them pull up in a van painted wild, psychedelic colors. It looked like something straight out of "The Partridge Family." Apparently the van was one of the Shah's primary modes of transportation, the assumption being that no terrorists would ever dream the Shah's family was inside. Our mouths hung open as the van pulled into the patio and Farah Diba and the children piled out, followed by their security guards. It was a scene straight out of a John Waters movie.

Lyn was very excited and asked if I could introduce her later to Farah Diba, who had nodded to me as she came in. Ted also asked me to introduce him and take a few pictures. But I didn't want to bother Farah Diba while she ate with her family, so I told them to wait a bit.

The whole nation of Mexico seems to have a problem with flies, and Ted's restaurant was no exception. Everything was spotlessly clean, but flies just came with the territory. As we were eating, a couple of flies crawled on Lyn, who slapped at them on the hard marble table. Lyn has big hands, and the splats sounded just like gunshots. When the sound echoed through the restaurant, the security men knocked Farah Diba and the kids to the floor and whirled around, guns drawn. There was a moment of stunned silence, then the security men helped Farah Diba up. The kids started laughing, followed by Farah Diba, and soon all of us were roaring. Lyn was so embarrassed by the incident she almost melted into her chair. But Farah Diba and the security guys took it all with good humor.

As they finished their meal, one of Farah Diba's security guards came over and told me that Farah Diba would like to see me when we were finished. I went over alone and chatted with her for a few minutes, then asked if she would mind posing for a few photos with friends. She readily agreed and they killed off about four rolls of film because everyone wanted their picture taken with Farah Diba and then with me. It reminded me of the good old days when I was overwhelmed by camera-bearing fans!

We were one big family by the time everyone had to leave. As Farah Diba's driver pulled away from the plaza, he accidentally knocked over a big stone fountain with the van. Farah Diba got out and started to pay Ted for the damage, but he told her to forget about it. Farah Diba apologized profusely to Ted, then she hugged me and for some unknown reason said, "Thank you, dear Kenny, for everything." A moment later, she and the kids rode off into the Mexican dust, raucous rock music blaring out the windows of their Partridge Family van. That was the last time I ever saw Farah Diba. The Shah died the following year.

While we're on the subject of Cuernavaca, it was while visiting Judy Grubb there on another occasion that I talked the great actress Gloria Swanson into walking my dog, Krissy.

I had known Gloria for a long time, having met her through Al Anthony, and she and her husband, pianist Bill Dufty (who at one time was an accompanist for the great Billie Holiday) decided to spend a few days in Mexico with Judy and me.

Gloria liked to get up early and exercise by walking around Judy's pool. My suite opened up onto the pool area and Krissy, who sensed that Gloria wasn't fond of her, would start barking whenever Gloria walked by. Gloria would then start yelling at Krissy, and soon they were both going at it.

I suggested that Gloria make friends with Krissy so that there would be no more yelling or barking and I could a few extra minutes of sleep in the morning. Gloria agreed, and that afternoon she became one of Krissy's best friends. Every morning thereafter, Gloria would quietly open the door to my suite and take Krissy walking around the pool with her. I'll always remember peering out my window and seeing Gloria Swanson, one of cinema's greatest actresses, marching around the pool with my little Krissy two steps behind.

Gloria was a health-food nut and very particular about what she ate, so she brought her own food with her to Mexico. Judy's cook would whip up some great Mexican dish for us at dinner, and Gloria would make something healthful for herself and Bill. One day Judy, Gloria and I were driving somewhere and Judy said to me, "We're going to have one of your favorite foods tonight—oso buco!" Gloria heard this, grabbed Vargas, who was driving, and exclaimed, "I love oso buco! It's one of my favorites, too!" I thought Judy was going to die right there because she had bought only enough lamb for our small group, expecting Gloria to eat her usual health food. When we got back to the villa, Judy had Vargas rush down to the market for one more lamb shank, and Gloria ate as much oso buco as I did, if not more. She really loved the stuff.

Gloria and I stayed in touch over the years, and I could always count on her to call on New Year's Eve—no matter where I was. She had an absolutely uncanny gift for locating me anywhere in the country. One New Year's I was a guest at a party at the Flagler Museum in Palm Beach and in the middle of the festivities I was told I had a call from Gloria Swanson! Gloria was a good and inspiring friend and, in my opinion, one of Hollywood's genuine superstars.

This chapter has taken us around the world a bit, so let's return to London, where my singing career was still doing well. My follow-up to "Restless" was a nice little song titled "When the Earth Was Green," backed by a little-known musician named Davy Jones, who Shel Talmy was also trying to record, though he had trouble landing Davy a contract. Davy looked like a little cherub and was extremely talented. At night he used to play his guitar on the sidewalk in the theater district and people would throw money into his guitar case. We became buddies and would occasionally have a pint or two in a pub across from Shel's office.

After I left England, I lost track of Davy. But a few years ago I was talking with Annie Hallam, Shel's assistant, and she asked, "What do you think about Davy Jones?" I said, "I don't know. What happened to him?" Annie looked at me like I had just arrived from Mars. She said, "Don't you know, love? He changed his name and is doing quite well. He calls himself David Bowie now." I couldn't believe my ears. I would never have recognized David Bowie as the little fellow I knew way back then! Some day I'd love to visit him backstage and say, "So, I guess you made it!"

I also spent a lot of time in France during this period because I was in big demand, thanks to "Restless." I sang at various clubs, and eventually was booked on the popular "Anna Marie Peyson Show," the number one talk-variety show in Paris. It was sort of a French version of the "Ed Sullivan Show," and I was supposed to sing two songs.

I chose the old Dion Warwick hit "Don't Make Me Over" and "For Me, For Me, For Me Formidable," which had been made famous by Charles Aznavour. I wanted to sing these songs in French, and I worked for nearly four weeks with J. Duncan Newton's secretary, Loretta, who was fluent in that language, to make sure I got it right.

The "Anna Marie Peyson Show" had a live audience and a full orchestra. I was a little nervous because French is a difficult language to learn, and I'd been studying for only a month. I came out and sang "For Me, For Me, For Me, Formidable" first, and it went great. Then I sang the first two lines of "Don't Make Me Over,"and after the second line I heard people starting to snicker. Evidently I had mispronounced a word, and the audience found that amusing. That shook me up and I mispronounced more words, which made the audience laugh even harder.

I was furious on the inside, but I knew there was no turning back so I decided to turn my set into a comedy routine by intentionally mispronouncing words. The audience started clapping and roaring, and gave me a standing ovation when I was done! I ran off stage and my European agent, Bernard Hilde, said, "Kenny, go back! Go back!" But I just couldn't. I was mad as hell because I had worked so hard to learn the song in French, and the audience only wanted to make fun of me. I swore I would never sing in French again, and I never have. I made the best of the situation and it could be argued that I came out on top by bringing the audience over to my side. But it was still a disheartening experience because I wanted the song to be a beautiful ballad, not a joke. The incident also didn't improve my opinion of Parisians. The French as a people are wonderful, but it's been my experience that the Parisians just don't like Americans and never miss an opportunity to prove it.

During this period I was really burning the candle at both ends. I was working all night, up half the day, and my health was starting to suffer. My friend Richard Harrison, with whom I had appeared in "Battle Flame," showed up at the Gaslight with his wife Loretta, and he said, "You look like death warmed over." I loved the entertainment scene while working at the Gaslight, but I knew I needed a break. I had a booking at the Casino Estoril in Lisbon, Portugal, but I had a couple weeks to kill so at Richard's insistence I vacationed at his villa on the Mediterranean in Marbella, Spain. Richard had a housekeeper and a handyman, neither of whom spoke English, so we communicated primarily by sign language. That's when my acting skills really came in handy! I fell in love with Spain during that trip and would later spend a lot of time there. After a couple of weeks I felt great again, and headed off for my gig at the Casino Estoril, which was the largest casino in Lisbon.

Afterward, Richard suggested I come to Rome, where he lived, for a possible film role. That job didn't work out, but it did give me a taste for the international film scene and introduced me to a number of prominent people who would later become good friends.

One of the many people I met while in Rome was Anna Korda, a relative of renowned movie producer Alexander Korda. She and I met at a party at the home of Italian director Federico Fellini, and Anna later proved helpful in getting me film work in Spain and elsewhere. For example, I worked on "Custer of the West" (1968), a Spanish-American production that employed nearly every actor in Madrid. It was an unfortunate mess that suffered from serious script problems, but it featured a lot of talented performers, including Robert Shaw as Custer, Jeffrey Hunter, Lawrence Tierney, Robert Ryan and Ty Hardin. Not a great movie, but a wonderful experience for me.

It was while I was living in Spain in the mid '60s that I almost became reacquainted with Charles Bronson. I say "almost" because Charles proved less than friendly upon our meeting, which was a tremendous disappointment. I met Charles, or Chuck as we called him, when I was attending the Hollywood School of Drama. One of my instructors there was a guy named Steve Messina, whose wife was singer Kitty Kover. Kitty was extremely talented, and appeared in night clubs around Hollywood and in Las Vegas. I became very close to her and Steve and we socialized quite a bit. One evening they were going over to a friend's house for dinner and cards, and they invited me to go along with them. Lo and behold, the friends were Charles Bronson and his wife. Chuck was a super guy but mad at the world because he wasn't working that much. And when he did work, he was usually cast as the heavy. We spent many Friday nights over at Chuck's house playing cards and just talking.

I lost touch with Chuck over the years and kind of forgot about him. Then his name came up while I was living in Spain. He had gone the international route, too, and his career was really starting to take off. I finally ran into him at the Castellana Hilton Hotel in Madrid, which had become THE hang-out for American actors living and working in Spain. He walked into the lounge, where I was chatting with some other actors, so I went over to say hello—and he didn't recognize me. I couldn't understand that because we had spent many an entertaining night together at his house shooting the bull.

A few days later Chuck came by the lounge again, this time with Jill Ireland, so I stopped by his booth once more to say hello and got an equally icy response. Success hadn't gone to his head—it had gone way over it. Chuck was behaving very much like James Dean at his worst, refusing to acknowledge a friendly greeting. I can't handle that kind of put-down, so I never approached him again. I understand from others that he's mellowed out, but back then he was anything but friendly.

I returned to Marbella around 1977 for an extended stay. I had become somewhat of a celebrity in Spain because of my television and night club appearances, and one day I was asked by a wealthy Marbella couple named Fernand and Jackie Gillis to open a restaurant with them there. They wanted to capitalize on my fame and connections and promised great rewards if I would go into business with them. Having nothing better to do and intrigued by the possibilities, I agreed, even though I knew absolutely nothing about the restaurant business.

The restaurant was called La Bonne Auberge, and we had a fabulous Belgian chef and an equally talented Spanish chef. But, like many things, it just didn't work out. Fernand had roots in the Belgian Congo, which was in the middle of a vicious civil war at the time, and he and Jackie spent a great deal of time trying to get their possessions and money out of the country. That meant they weren't around a lot, which, to be honest, was fine by me. Fernand was not a particularly pleasant person to work with, and he had the annoying habit of sitting down with visiting royalty and being an obnoxious jerk with a stinking cigar, which wasn't good for business.

One day Jackie left to join Fernand in the Congo and didn't come back. They were upset with me because I refused to introduce them to my high-society friends, which I was forced to do because of their boorish behavior. They just didn't fit, and I wasn't going to let them ruin my reputation just so they could weasel their way into the in-crowd.

I had no money, but everyone in town was wonderful to me. The area butchers and shop-keepers let me run a tab so I could keep the restaurant open, but my credit finally ran out and I was forced to close the doors. I ended up with practically nothing but some wonderful memories.

Fernand Gillis was a man of grandiose dreams and a complete lack of ability to turn them into reality. He had some land above Marbella and wanted to built a western-themed resort, sort of a Spanish dude ranch. He asked me to go to New York to establish some contacts who could provide materials, and I readily agreed because I was getting a little home sick. While in New York, I saw my darling Connie Stevens in "Star Spangled Girl," with Richard Benjamin and Anthony Perkins. She was brilliant in it, and we had a wonderful reunion afterward.

It was during that visit that Connie told me she was in love with Eddie Fisher. My heart sank because I had met Eddie years before and I thought she could do better, but I put on a happy face for Connie's benefit. She introduced me to Eddie and I have to admit that he seemed really nice. More importantly, he seemed genuinely in love with Connie, and was very generous and attentive to her. He even offered me his limo because I was conducting a lot of business meetings around town in connection with the proposed resort in Spain.

One day, Connie was doing the "Perry Como Show" in New York, and she invited me to come backstage and then on to an engagement party for her and Eddie at Buddy Hackett's house. Connie and I had a few minutes together before the show, and she said, "I know you're not happy about this, but it's the right thing. You'll see—Eddie's a wonderful man." I told her I was sure he was, and that I wished them nothing but happiness. I rode with Connie, Eddie and his sister and brother-in-law, and we picked up author Paddy Chayefsky along the way.

I couldn't believe how gorgeous—and huge—Buddy Hackett's house was! I thought, why didn't I become a comedian?! When we walked through the door there must have been at least 250 people inside. It was a mind-blowing party, and one of the highlights was Eddie singing to his beloved mother.

As we were getting ready to go, Connie took me aside. We sat on the stairs and she said, "We're not going back to the city with you. Eddie and I are staying here for the night." They were leaving the next day for Bermuda to be married and wanted to get some rest before they left. I still didn't feel quite right about the whole thing, but I smiled and told her everything would be fine. Then I kissed her goodbye and the rest of us rode back to Manhattan.

The resort in Marbella was never built. The Gillis' couldn't get their money out of the Congo and they eventually dropped the whole idea. But at least I got a trip to New York out of the deal!

I hope this chapter doesn't sound like an exercise in name-dropping, because that certainly isn't my intent. Hanging with the rich and famous was lots of fun, but in the end the names, titles and outrageous parties meant nothing compared to the many dear friendships I came to cherish through the years. And as corny as it sounds, those were the memories I clutched to my heart most as the '70s and '80s slipped away and my life and career followed new directions.

The Search for Bridey Murphy. Brad Jackson and Eileen Janssen get married, with me as best man.

The Young Guns.

Little Laura and Big John. Left to right: Karen Black, Fabian, Lee Warren, KM and Bob Rossi.

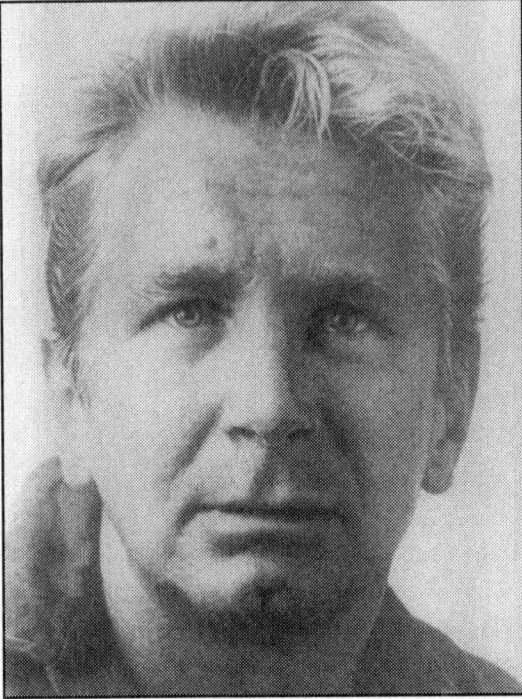

Little Laura and Big John, Crown International Pictures, 1973.

Little Laura and Big John, Crown International Pictures, 1973.

My death scene in *Little Laura and Big John*.

The Nun and the Sargeant. Robert Webber is in front of me, taking a hill in Korea, and I still got shot!

KM as Marine Private Oliver Quill in *The Nun and the Sergeant*, United Artists, 1962.

KM and Scott Brady in *Battle Flame*, Allied Artists, 1959.

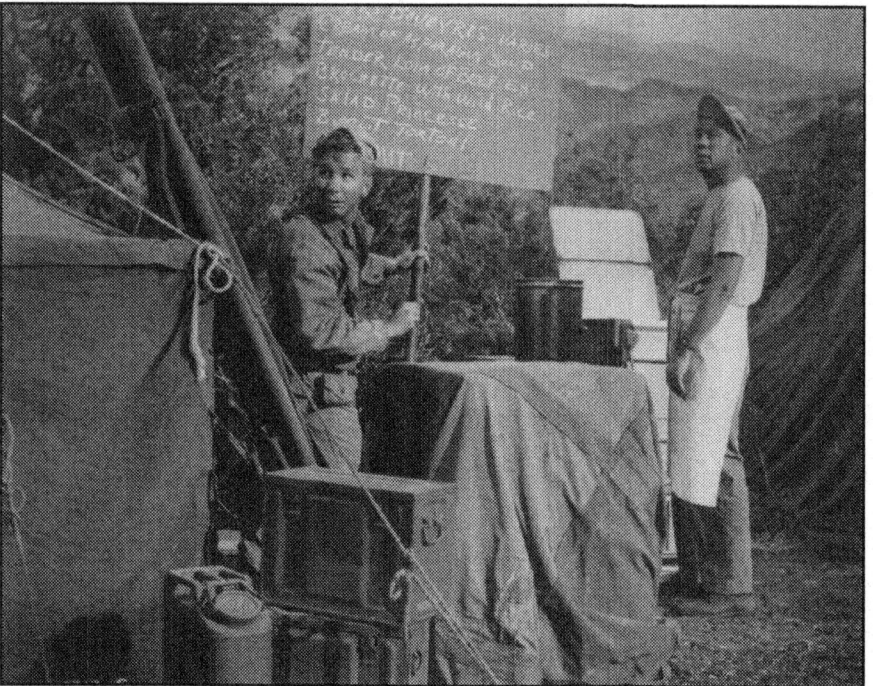

KM and Anthony Redondo in *Battle Flame*, Allied Artists, 1959.

Bill Goodwin and KM in *Going Steady*, Columbia Pictures, 1958.

Left to right: Susan Easter, Molly Bee, Alan Reed, Jr., and KM in *Going Steady*.

Still *Going Steady*.

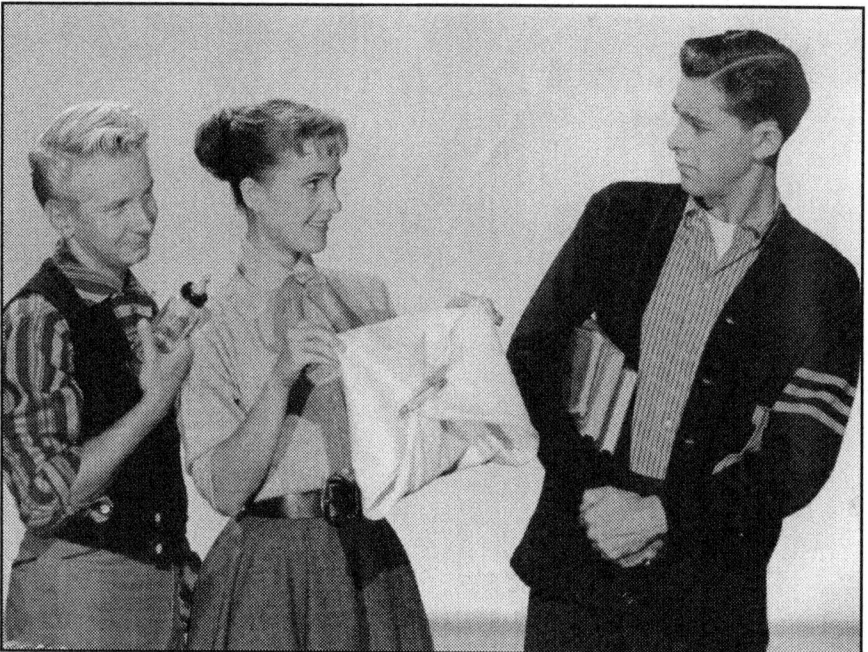

KM, Susan Easter and Alan Reed, Jr. in *Going Steady*.

Singing and dancing with Cindy Robbins in *Rockabilly Baby*,
20th Century-Fox, 1957.

Gary Vinson, Tony Marshall, Jimmy Murphy, Jim Goodwin, Barry Truex,
and me in *Rockabilly Baby*.

Rev. & Mrs. James M. Miller (Bessie Lewis).

Chapter 12
Do You Know The Way To San José?

As much as I hated to leave the warm and sunshine of Florida, I needed work, so I contacted an entertainment agency in Frankfurt, Germany. I was told that they could book me into military clubs and other venues, so off I trudged to dreary Frankfurt, where I stayed with some German friends.

While I was there, I was asked to headline a review that would play military installations throughout Germany, the Middle East, the Far East and conclude in California. The review consisted of six dancers, a dance team, a comedian and myself. We did our first show in Frankfort, and afterward there was a big party at the home of the general who oversaw the project. I returned to the Frankfurter Hof early because I wasn't feeling well. It was a cold, snowy night, and as I got out of the car I slipped on the ice and hit my head on a fire hydrant. I was taken to the hospital, where they discovered I had a clot at the base of my brain. The treatment consisted of long needles stuck into my head to help disperse the clot. During this period, the review continued around the Frankfurt area as they waited for me to recuperate. After about four weeks, I felt I was up to performing. I rejoined the show at a base outside of Frankfurt—and passed out cold while singing. The tour left Frankfurt without me, and after a few more weeks of therapy, the only place I wanted to be was home.

I returned to Springfield and stayed at my brother George's house. One evening my friend Joe Maccora called to tell me that Molly Bee was appearing at a nightclub in Dayton called Suttmillers. Wild horses couldn't keep me away from going to see my little Molly. I didn't call her as I wanted to surprise her. I arrived in the middle of the first show and was surprised to see how much Molly had changed. After much hugging and kissing, she told me of all the bad things she had been through. That night, we decided that she should come back to Springfield and stay at my brother's with me the last three days of her engagement. She was up half the night and barely slept. As I put her on the plane for California, I was very concerned.

As soon as I was well enough, I decided to return to Hollywood. Unfortunately, Hollywood didn't want me. I found myself completely rejected. I had been gone for more than five years and I know that I had changed, but Hollywood had become a foreign place to me. Not just in the way it had deteriorated physically, but the heart of that once glamorous film capital was gone. Nearly all of the young stars I had known during the television boom were working in real estate or had fallen by the wayside. For most, it was a tremendous blow to be sought after one minute, and then so quickly to find out that nobody wanted them anymore. Many of them just couldn't handle it. I searched desperately for old friends in the business, but to my disappointment I found only a few. The studio system had changed — all of the casting directors I had known were gone, and the new breed of casting director had made themselves as important as producers.

The look of Hollywood had changed drastically. Beautiful Hollywood Boulevard with its Hollywood Walk of Fame had become a dreary collection of souvenir and porno shops, not unlike a carnival midway with young men and women hanging out on the corners selling their bodies to exist until they could be "discovered." The Sunset Strip that had once been so elegant with designer shops, luxurious restaurants and famous night clubs like Ciro's, Mocombo and Leon and Eddie's had been replaced by rock and roll joints, record shops and fast food restaurants. It was hard to believe that just a few years earlier I had been the last singer to appear at world-famous Ciro's before it closed. Now it's a comedy club. Even the big Hollywood sign up in the Hollywood Hills had been vandalized.

I finally signed with agent Arthur Driefus, a wonderful gentleman who had been a well-known producer many years before. He felt sure he could reintroduce me to the studios and get me work. We made a new demo tape of scenes from my better movies, took new photos, redid my resume and cut out more than half of my film credits because Arthur felt that more than 20 films was just too many for casting directors to digest. Arthur, bless his heart, worked hard on my behalf, but I couldn't even get in to read for the new casting people—they didn't remember me and didn't care.

I realized that Hollywood had nothing left for me, that I would have to flee the city that I used to dream of being up in the heavens. For me, the shining star had fallen out of the sky. I wouldn't allow it to destroy me as it had so many of my talented friends.

While I tried to decide what I was going to do with my life, Molly's mom, Lou, called from Las Vegas. She asked when I would be coming to Vegas again because it was very important that we talk. I drove up the next week, and we met for dinner. What happened then was the beginning of something I've never told the complete truth about in all these years.

While I had been running around Europe, my little Molly had been living the high life in the fast lane. She had become a big Las Vegas star, and finally moved there permanently. She had also had a big romance with one of America's top entertainers, as well as a long line of other beaus. And why not? Molly was a beautiful, exciting and talented young lady. I knew she still loved me, but in a more brotherly way.

It also seems that Molly had started living the script to a film we had done together, "Going Steady." In the movie, she and her boyfriend ran away to Nevada to get married. The only difference now was that she didn't have to run away—she already lived in Nevada. And she was pregnant.

Nowadays, famous people live and have babies out of wedlock, and it's all quite acceptable. Back then, it was frowned upon, plus Molly's upbringing weighed heavily upon her. She needed me to marry her, and it was one of the most difficult decisions I ever had to make. I flew back to Hollywood and discussed the wedding with two of my closest friends, who begged me not to do it. Nancy Streebeck, my press agent, didn't know the whole story, but she approved of the wedding.

The next week, I flew to Macon, Georgia, to be with my close friends, Cindy and J.L. Parker, who I had met when they built Burt's home at the ranch in Jupiter, Florida. Cindy, J.L. and their children, Gayle and Wayne, had become a very special and important part of my life. Burt, a wonderful friend named Miko Mayama, and I would often spend weekends at the Parkers' beautiful home in Macon when we weren't working our butts off at the ranch. This particular time, I was flying back for the dedication of a beautiful country church called the Little Church in the Wildwood, where I had often performed. It had also become an emotional part of my life because of the many young people who were a part of it. My whole family flew in for the dedication, and it was a day I'll never forget. J.L. and Cindy had purchased two of the pews in the church and had plaques engraved for them, one for his mom and dad, and one for my mom and dad. The day before the dedication, a few of us went to the church to see the new organ that Cindy and J.L. had bought to replace the church's old piano. It brought tears to everyone's eyes.

I had told the Parkers about the marriage, and they were very excited for me. I didn't tell them the true story, however. They knew that I had spent a lot of money over the previous months, so they insisted on taking me to their jeweler to pick out wedding bands for Molly and me—which they paid for. And that's not all. J.L. said he had to go by his tailor, but when we got there, he had already arranged for me to be fitted for the wedding.

As you might have guessed, I had decided that I was going to go through with the wedding to Molly no matter what the repercussions. After all, she was one of my closest friends and now she needed me. We were married at the Wee Kirk of the Heather in Las Vegas in the middle of the night so no press would attend. A few months later, Molly gave birth to a gorgeous little girl. I flew from Los Angeles to Las Vegas to be with her during that blessed event. Her baby had a name and a father, even if she wasn't mine.

Things went down hill from there, though. Our renewed relationship—which had been on shaky ground from the beginning—went from bad to worse. We were divorced a couple of years later. I haven't seen Molly in years, and doubt I ever will again.

I continued my search for work in Hollywood and my friends there were very supportive. I was lucky on another front, too—I had Connie Steven's little daughters, Joely and Tricia Leigh Fisher, to help fill the void. Connie had divorced Eddie Fisher, so I got to spend a lot of time with my two precious adopted nieces.

I finally became completely disillusioned with Hollywood, however, and decided to seek greener pastures. I stayed with Burt's folks, Burt Sr. and Fern, in Florida for a while and then I got booked on various cruise ships out of Miami. I really enjoyed singing on the ships, but after six months I became weary of the sea. Plus, as an entertainer, I had to be "on" the minute I left my stateroom. It was a full-time job. The passengers wanted to be with me all the time because I was a celebrity. They were with me for meals, cocktails, parties—everything. The only way I could find some space of my own was to sneak off to my stateroom. Don't get me wrong—it was great fun and the passengers were a wonderful audience. They came on the ship to have a good time and by golly, no matter what, they were going to have a good time. I eventually became a very good sailor and learned to perform even when the ship rocked nauseatingly back and forth. Sometimes members of the audience would get sick, though, and I would have to leave the stage to avoid throwing up, too.

I rented a home on Seaspray Avenue in Palm Beach right after I signed up to appear in the film "Too Soon to Laugh, Too Late to Cry" (later retitled "Little Laura and Big John"). A man named Frank Wright called and welcomed me to Palm Beach. He had been a public relations man in the area for many years, and was a great help to me in almost everything I did there. In fact, he set up my first newspaper interview with the Palm Beach Post. Susan Hixon, the reporter who interviewed me, did a great two-page story and we became fast friends. Susan later married and was known as Susan Kennedy, one of the top writers in South Florida. Her interview started my phone ringing and when I got home from shooting, I was amazing at the number of people who had called. One was a photographer who wanted to represent me and "introduce" me to Palm Beach society. I had to laugh because I didn't need to pay someone for the invitations I was already getting for free. My mailbox was chock full of invitations to luncheons, cocktails, dinners, galas and balls from people who just wanted to meet me. I thought I was back in Beverly Hills. Thank God I had Frank Wright to advise me, and he didn't charge me a cent. But I repaid him ten fold over the next few years by singing gratis at the Round Table and other charities in which he was involved. My biggest payback to him, though, was when I sang a song someone else had written specially for his anniversary party at the Flagler Museum. The song was to his wife, Eleanor, and was titled "Sweetie Pie." Yes, "Sweetie Pie." Here I was, at the prestigious Flagler Museum with a full orchestra and more than two hundred people in front of me dressed to the hilt, and I had to sing "Sweetie Pie" to Frank's wife with a straight face. Well, that paid off every favor Frank had done or ever would do for me in this lifetime!

To say I was in demand in Palm Beach would be a gross understatement. I was having the time of my life. The more publicity I got, the more photographers wanted to take my picture. Then it dawned on me—Palm Beach was like an extension of Hollywood. Here I was, going to functions, being photographed for all the magazines and papers, and being catered to like a celebrity—and loving every minute of it. There was only one difference: No one asked me for my autograph. But I didn't care.

Palm Beach is the richest place on Earth during the season. The residents are all stars of one magnitude or another and they create their own world. Their magazines and newspapers are solely about them. Nothing but society happenings and photographs and photographs and more photographs. It's the good life like no where else in the world. I also defy anyone to tell me of any other place that gives more to charity during the season.

Another thing that makes me love Palm Beach so much are the wonderful people who are connected to show business. It's home to many great beauties who married well and entertain like royalty from their luxurious mansions. They also have a great sense of humor. One of my favorites is Celia Lipton Farris, who was a musical comedy star in her native England. Celia thinks nothing about flying in at her own expense two hundred film stars for one of her charity galas. And bless her heart, she always invites me along with the other stars. Some time ago, Celia called and asked if I would like to be Sarah Churchill's escort for the premiere of "Young Winston" at the Paramount Theater in Palm Beach. I quickly accepted because I had met Sarah briefly in Rome and found her to be great fun. That weekend included not only the premiere, but the International Red Cross Ball, various cocktail parties and other events.

For a little relaxation, I took Sarah, her companion Jewell Baxter, Celia, her husband Victor and their two children, CeCe and Marion, on a picnic at Burt's ranch. Sarah absolutely loved it, and ended up jumping into the lake by the tree house clothes and all. I thought it wise not to mention that the lake was rumored to have alligators in it.

Another favorite Palm Beacher is Gregg Sherwood Dodge, who was a Copa girl, then a famous cover girl and then a movie actress. She married Horace Dodge, heir to the Dodge fortune. Gregg is a wonderful writer and has an outrageous wit. When a friend called her recently to inquire if she was going to attend a reception for Prince Charles, Gregg replied: "No, darling. That's the day I get my legs waxed!"

A few other Palm Beach fixtures include Dame Alma DuPuy, an actress and former Samuel Goldwyn Girl who travels around the world like you and I go to the supermarket. Mary Hartline, the blond beauty who was the star of television's "Super Circus" with Burt Parks, and who later turned in her baton for a tennis racquet. Cathleen McFarlane, who graced the Broadway stage and appeared in numerous films. Helene Reynolds, who starred in many 20th Century Fox musicals with Alice Fay and Betty Grable. The Trump Girls, Ivana and Marla Maples, who I saw on Broadway in the "Will Rogers Follies." Helene Tuchbrieter, who was involved in the theater in Chicago and who has chaired numerous charity balls in Palm Beach and elsewhere. Helene told me one night at a party that she was having new resumes made and at the top of the resume she was putting "Balls I Have Held."

I lived briefly with Ann Hamilton, George's mother, in a beautiful mansion that her son Bill had designed. Both Bill and George were in California, so Ann asked if I would stay with her for a few months because she didn't want to be in the big house alone. I stayed in Bill's part of the house and my door opened onto the pool and beach. It was a perfect place for Krissy and me. One day Ann was being interviewed for a television show in London. I had gone out and arrived later in the afternoon to find them filming by the pool. Ann asked me to stay close by, so I watched from the den. At one point, Ann commented, "Oh yes, I recently had my breasts done." I almost fell off my chair! She continued, "George said it was ridiculous at my age, 76, and besides he said, who in the hell is going to see them? Well, I think hope springs eternal, don't you? If I don't find my prince charming, when I die I will insist on an open casket, and I will be topless!"

While I was living with Ann, I was booked into a new supper club in Palm Beach called the Piedmont, which had been remodeled and was truly elegant. On opening night, they had to turn away more than 60 people. Colin Webster Watson, my international sculptor friend, was in town and asked if I would hold my show until he got there with movie star Carroll Baker, who was appearing at the Royal Poinciana Playhouse. I was more than an hour late, but no one seemed to mind except Ann—who came back to my dressing room and said, "Kenny, you get out here now! Who do you think you are, Marilyn Monroe?!" The show went well and everyone was extremely happy. Which reminds me of another opening night in Palm Beach that was a true disaster.

Albin Holder had booked me at the prestigious Poinciana Club to do "A Salute to Cole Porter." It was just an orchestra, a dance team and me. Plus I had asked some of the "stars" of Palm Beach society to sing with me. It was supposed to be spontaneous, but we did rehearse.

However, things went anything but smoothly. First, they had oversold the Poinciana Club by some 50 reservations, so they had to set tables up in the lobby and anywhere else there was room. Albin rented a new sound system so I could be heard clearly in both rooms. It was a hot, humid southern night but the new seating arrangements prevented the wait staff from getting through to serve many of the Palm Beachers. Then the air conditioning went out. Just before I was to go on, Albin came to my dressing room to tell me that Joseph Ricardel's orchestra drummer had suffered a heart attack on the stand, and the paramedics were taking him to the hospital. The bass player went with him because he was the drummer's son. Oh God—no drummer and no bass player!

But the show went on. After I was introduced, it took me almost as long to get from the back of the room to the stage as it did for Cleopatra to enter Rome. Then when I started to sing, nothing happened. Somehow the paramedics had disconnected the new sound system. I used the old system as a back up, and only half of the crowd could hear me. The show went fairly well, though, and my "guest stars" came through with flying colors. Oh yes, I forgot—when the dancers were introduced, they had to fight their way from the back of the room just as I did and when they arrived on the dance floor to start their number, there was no dance floor. It had been covered by chairs, tables and people. The dancers obviously couldn't dance, so they just left. But even with all these disasters, guests such as Douglas Fairbanks Jr. and his wife Mary, Senator Jacob Javits and his family, Sen. Ted Kennedy and family and the creme de la creme of society all seemed to have a wonderful time. Fortunately, my darling friend Mike Lund was ringside and when I looked over at her smiling face, I knew everything was okay.

I went with Mike for a couple of years, and it was one of the happiest times of my life. She was a beautiful blonde with a great sense of humor, and a laugh that came right from her toes. She should and could have been in movies, as she had been married to a Hollywood producer, but she wanted no part of show business. We did the Palm Beach scene in great style and the two of us became Palm Beach's "little darlings." We were invited to everything. After a couple of seasons, that became a little rough, plus I was starting to drink too much. So we decided not to be so available. Just then, an old friend of Mike's, Len Mercer, took over the Taboo on Worth Avenue. I had met Len briefly in Fort Lauderdale and we all became good buddies. His friend, Jesse Lacey, another gorgeous blond, helped him run Taboo. They asked Mike and I if we would be in the photo for their newspaper ads. We finally agreed and from then on we had carte blanch at Taboo. Talk about entertaining! Mike, whose real name was Ann, had to move to New York full time due to a job change. And as fate would have it, I started preproduction work on "The Night Daniel Died." That got me away from life in the fast lane, and missing Mike—at least for a while.

During my early days in Palm Beach, I met a couple who are now a part of my family, Danielle and Peter Basil. They gave the most extravagant, fun parties in Palm Beach, and asked me to sing at them. Danielle and I had instant rapport, so we decided to adopt each other. Danielle is my sister and if anyone denies it, she immediately sets them straight by telling them we are brother and sister related through love.

Danielle didn't tell me until much later that she, her sister Francine Snyder, mother Lorraine Freimann, and her father Frank, lived in Beverly Hills when she was younger. She grew up knowing nearly all of the Hollywood stars and their families. But then, why not? Her father had been the head of Magnavox.

Danielle gave me the most cherished living gift that I have ever received, my little Schnauzer Sassifrass. My other Schnauzer, Krissy, had been gone several years and Danielle felt it was time I had another companion. She and her granddaughter, Courtney Refkin, gave her to me in a big box with red ribbon in the lobby of the Waterview, where Danielle lived. We all got down on the floor and she opened the box and an eight-week-old puppy, clipped and groomed, trotted out and promptly bit me on the nose. That truly was love at first bite! Sassy travels with me everywhere and she also co-starred with me in a TV docudrama we did for PBS in Texas and Palm Beach.

Jan McArt, who had been on Broadway and the concert stage, opened a wonderful little theater in Boca Raton called the Royal Palm Dinner Theater. We had become friends through Bob Freund, the entertainment editor of the Fort Lauderdale News. Jan kept begging me to do a show at her theater, but I was having too much fun in Palm Beach. Finally, I decided to pull myself together and consider it. I was playing with the rich folks, but what I had forgotten along the way was that I wasn't rich. The bills kept coming in and the rent had to be paid. So I said yes when she called and offered me a part in "Promises, Promises." Along with a salary and meals, I also got a charming little house with a pool that I shared with two young ladies, Helena Grenot, who was the star of the show, and Nanette Gordon. The rehearsals were torture, but Bob Bogdanoff, the director, and Jan were patient with me. I hadn't done live theater in years, and my discipline was very lax. No more cocktails at 5 o'clock. The show turned out fine and I was happy to be back in theater.

Jan later produced "How To Succeed In Business Without Really Trying," and she wanted me for J. Pierpont Finch, the role made famous on Broadway by Robert Morse. The show was great fun, but very hard work. At first I was a little concerned because the theater was negotiating with Rudy Vallee for the other lead role, which he had done on Broadway. I had heard all kinds of stories about him, especially his demands and needs. There's nothing wrong with that, but I wanted this to be a fun project without a lot of hang-ups. My fears were for naught, though, because negotiations fell through with Vallee. Jan would not agree to everything he wanted, plus Valley was in ill health. They signed another fine actor, Marvin Teicher, for the role and he was wonderful to work with.

"How To Succeed" was a great success and a terrific learning experience for me. I'll never forget Sally Ricci, who played the boss's mistress. Her performance brought down the house. Friends from Palm Beach came down by the busload to see the play. I even did a one-man show on my night off called "A Love-In," and more than half of the audience was Palm Beachers.

I was back in the swing of things and I got booked into Club Gigi in the Fountainbleau Hotel in Miami Beach. It was a beautiful club that reminded me of a set from an MGM musical. Some of my friends actually came down in their Lear jet to see me perform there. One review in a Miami newspaper said, "Meet Kenny Miller, the international film star. The debonair, continental, blond American singer with the infectious smile springs from Springfield, Ohio, but has found the world a happy stage, singing, performing, entertaining, recording, touching on every facet of the theatrical world and scoring in every one. His warm, ingratiating personality and easy, winning style finds him an all-embracing audience that loathes to see him go." I have to laugh when I read that—reviews like that can go to a guy's head!

Two hardworking, talented people, Ruth and Ward Everitt, took over an old movie theater on Clematis Street in downtown West Palm Beach and, with their own sweat and tears, turned it into a wonderful, legitimate theater called The Stage Company. Fabled Broadway director Jose Quintero came to direct their first production, "Ah, Wilderness." Ruth and Ward approached me about starring in Bernard Slade's "Tribute," which Jack Lemmon had done on Broadway and in film. I agreed to play Scottie Templeton because the part is a tour de force. The cast was superb in every way, from Nancy Hassinger, Conni Adkins, Iris Acker, Bernie Fridkin and David Haller to darling Monika Kelly, daughter of that famous clown, Emmett Kelly.

On opening night a long line of limousines and Rolls Royces came over the bridge from Palm Beach. Allan Endries, a long time friend and former radio personality from Chicago, gave me a never-to-forgotten opening night party at the Colony Hotel in Palm Beach. Allan owns the Ol' Town Florist on Palm Beach, and never in my life have I seen so many orchids on the centerpiece of each table. My devoted ex-fan club president and cherished friend, Wilma Marshall, had even flown down from New Jersey to see me. The run of "Tribute" went much too fast, and on closing night one of the thrills of my life happened when legendary film star Janet Gaynor came back stage. She hugged and kissed me and told me how much she loved me in the show—even better than Jack Lemmon! Boy, did that make my night! Miss Gaynor was opening the following week at the Stage Company in "On Golden Pond," her last public appearance.

The next week I was booked in the Palm Beach Hilton by owners Leonard and Sunny Sessa. I was to become their resident performer and good will ambassador. Sunny, Lenny and I were on the cover of society magazines and newspapers practically everywhere. I loved singing at the Hilton, but whoever designed the dining room hadn't expected a band or any other entertainment because a stairway came up in the middle of the room. It made it very hard to get close to the audience. Leonard eventually put the bandstand on the side.

While I was appearing at the Hilton, I was asked to sing at the wedding reception of Ralph Levitz, the furniture magnate, and his beautiful wife, Peggy. You never knew what was going to happen at the Hilton. One night after their show at the Poinciana Playhouse, Martha Raye, Rosemary Clooney and Kay Starr came in and sang with me and each other. Later, Maggie—Martha Raye's nickname—and Rosie Clooney cooked pasta in the kitchen. Two other wonderful people came to see me at the Hilton almost every night, Count and Countess de Bothuri. The Countess had been a famous actress in France and Montreal under the name Elaine Bedard, and her husband, Alexandre, was a world famous artist. We became instant friends and our experiences have taken us to all parts of the world. They too are an important part of my life.

After my stint at the Hilton, I became involved with plans to build a plush new resort in the Caicos Islands in the Grand Turks, which are between Florida and Cuba. It sounded great and I wanted to be a part of it. The backers wanted me to go see the actual site, so we decided to fly there for the weekend on a private plane. I asked Bonnie Walker, a close friend, and a couple of others to go along with us. What a paradise it was! No tourists, no cruise ships—and lobster for breakfast, lunch and dinner if you wanted it! I had lobster prepared every way known to man, though my stomach wasn't ready for lobster omelette for breakfast. Snorkeling and diving off the reef was underwater heaven.

At the end of the weekend, we reluctantly returned to the island air strip where ours was the only plane. I was seated by the door. About fifteen minutes into the flight, I was casually looking at the schools of sharks below me when suddenly—POW! The door next to me flew open! The other passengers grabbed me as my wallet, papers, sunglasses and part of me were sucked out into the air. Mom had always told us to wear clean underwear when we left home. When that door ripped open, Mama's warning was history! I was quickly pulled back into the cabin by my panic-stricken cohorts. Bonnie was screaming and everyone was yelling. The pilot, Chris, yelled for us to be quiet and stay calm, which wasn't easy. He explained that no one was in danger because the wind against the door prevented it from opening any wider. He banked against the wind and we finally got the door latched. Thank God I had my seat belt on! We begged the pilot to turn back to Caicos, but he said no because there were severe storm warnings and we had to continue on to the mainland. To say that was the longest flight of my life would be the understatement of the century! All I could think of as we flew through the fog and clouds was those schools of sharks below eating my wallet, my papers and my sunglasses. But not me, thank God.

When the plane landed, I kissed the ground, I kissed the plane, I kissed Chris, I kissed the Customs officer and everyone else I could find. I had never been happier to be on solid ground in my life!

Later that year, I was asked back to The Stage Company to play Sancho in "Man of LaMancha." What made it even more enticing was that internationally-famous opera star Adria Firestone was flying in from New York to play Dolcenia. What a joy she was! She was so beautiful and such a great talent. We became inseparable during the run of the show. I often get notes from Rome, Rio, Cairo, Milan—wherever Adria is appearing. She's a free spirit just like me. On closing night of "La Mancha," I received a plaque that I'll always cherish. It reads, "Kenny—We like him—our Sancho! What a gift of love you give to La Mancha. From the Cast and Crew."

Next I was booked in a plush new club in Vero Beach called The Regency Room. It was the closest thing to a Las Vegas showroom that I've ever worked, and I got to sing with Bill Claypool's orchestra. I stayed at the hotel where the supper club was located, which turned out to be a mistake. Again, lots of people drove up from Palm Beach for the opening night. My good friend Dona Kay Waterman even drove up from Miami, a distance of more than one hundred miles. I think Dona has been to every opening I've ever had in Florida whether it was a nightclub, stage or whatever. She's a very special person in my life.

The Regency Room was a thrilling place to appear at first, but then one of the employees took more than a platonic liking to me. She was always around, and I finally began to feel like a prisoner. I knew she meant well, and I respected her feelings toward me, but I just wasn't attracted to her. I started slipping into the Paddock Room, a lounge next to the supper club, and having a few belts between shows. That wasn't like me at all, and it also affected my performance. I finally couldn't stand all the attention and I gave my two week notice. I had to get away so I could find my own space.

I went home to Palm Beach just in time for Jimmy Moore's 25th birthday party. Normally, a 25th birthday party isn't that unusual, but this party was for Jimmy's 25-year-old Rolls Royce limousine! My attorney, Bryant Simms, helped Jimmy organize this unusual but fantastic event. The limo, which was parked in front of the door of the Poinciana Club, had a special hood ornament with a huge diamond in the middle of it. Jimmy normally kept the ornament in his bank deposit box. There was a six-foot cake to serve the 250 guests and the champagne flowed. But that's Palm Beach for you!

Since I wasn't working and had nothing better to do, I got back into the social swing of Palm Beach. The thing I enjoyed most was being invited by Barbara Gault to the Royal Poinciana Playhouse's gala opening nights. Every opening was like a Hollywood premier. The theater patrons were a show in themselves—the men dressed in black tie and the women in their beautiful gowns and sparking jewels (all of which were real!). Of course, the photographers were always there, along with reporters from the local television stations interviewing "the Palm Beach stars" as they arrived, which was shown on the 11 o'clock news later that evening.

I appeared at the Royal Poinciana Playhouse several times, but one of the most fun shows was "The Palm Beach Follies." Sheilah Haisfield called and asked me if I would appear as a guest star along with George Hamilton, Lynda Day George and Ethel Smith. The rest of the show was made up of Palm Beach residents, and they rehearsed for more than two months. I shared a dressing room with George Hamilton, who had his Argentinean valet, Jorge, with him. The show ran for three fun-filled performances, and the theater was packed every night.

God has blessed me with some extraordinary friends, and several families have adopted me as their own. I've been offered some wonderful places to escape—some far away and some close by. When I really want to get away, I fly off to Judy Grubb's villa in Cuernavaca, Mexico. That's truly paradise to me, and the pampering I get from Judy's servants doesn't hurt.

Judy told me that years ago her family lived in San Antonio and once drove about 200 miles to a plush Mexican resort built especially for wealthy Texans. She and her family packed two cars and even brought one of their servants, a handyman named Clarence. Clarence had lived and worked all his life for Judy's family, and had never been outside of San Antonio. But he was miserable in Mexico and Judy's father had to arrange to have Clarence driven home. All the other servants wanted to know what Mexico was like, but all Clarence would say was, "I tells you one thing—in Mexico, if yous in a hurry, yous all by yo'self!"

The pressures of show business can be brutal; it isn't all fun and games, though it often appears that way. When things get especially harrowing, you need the warmth of close friends, people you can just talk to. That's when Sassy and I pile in our car and drive over the bridge to visit my caring friend, Margie Hough. She's always there for me, no matter what. So are Eleanor and Charles Sims, Bryant's folks. When I visit them in nearby Winterhaven, it's truly like going home again.

Another place I can relax and enjoy myself is the home of Margaret Sanders, the feisty daughter of Colonel Harland Sanders of Kentucky Fried Chicken fame. At one time Margaret had two penthouses, one for living and one that acted as a studio for her sculpting. She has a million outrageous stories about her life and that of her father. Maggie is very spiritual and swears that we were very close friends in a past life, which I don't doubt. We have a special luncheon every so often that usually includes Limburger cheese and a big slice of raw onion on dark rye bread with horseradish mustard—and a cold beer! The old saying is true: Once you get past the smell, it's really delicious!

I returned to Hollywood a couple of times to see if I could get work, staying with my nephew, Keith, who has his own computer company in Newport Beach. If I could have stayed there all the time I would have been happy, but I had to drive to the Valley to see my agents. I also was representing several books and scripts that I hoped to have made into movies or television mini-series. The drive on the LA freeway is a nightmare no matter what time of day you take it. Quite often traffic was so bad that I had to stay in town with my good friend Nedra Ware, who lived just two blocks from the old Republic Studios, which is now MTM Studios. Nedra has been a special friend since my early days in Palm Beach, and we have gone through all kinds of traumas together. She's a fantastic gourmet cook, and wrote a cook book titled "Scraps from the Emperor's

Table." She's crazy for Napoleon. Her daughter and son-in-law, Baron and Baroness Wilhelm and Laura Shurtleff, live in a town home next to her.

I believe the main reason my nephew, Keith, likes for me to visit him is because he really loves my dog, Sassy, and Sassy loves him. The only other person besides Keith and I that Sassy goes absolutely bananas over is my business manager, Duane Caylor. Duane never warmed up to my first Schnauzer, Krissy, but Sassy was able to win him over in no time flat. Sometimes I think Duane believes Sassy is half his, which works out great when I have to travel and can't take her with me. Duane has taken care of my business affairs for several years now, and even when there's no business to take care of, he's a tremendous friend.

In Malibu, I ran into an old friend of mine, producer/director Tom McGowan, who produced the film "Born Free" (1966). He was working on some projects and wanted me to be part of them, along with another friend of mine from Palm Beach, Alfons Landa. Tom put all the other projects on hold when he decided to do a docu-drama based on a National Geographic article on what happened to the people west of the Pecos in Southwest Texas after the oil boom ended. The location was the barren, hot, God-forsaken desert and the circumstances worse than the Florida Everglades when I made "The Night Daniel Died." Our first location was in the town of Pecos and we stayed in a modern Holiday Inn. The second location was in Girvin, Texas—population 5! The only motel there was also the worst motel I've ever seen in my life. It was so dirty I covered the floor and nightstands with towels and even put towels on the floor of the shower. I carried Sassy in and out of the room so she wouldn't have to walk on the filthy floor. Thank God the bed liners were clean. However, the people were wonderful and our producer, Herb Taylor, made life bearable. Herb, Tom and our cinematographer, Bud Holderson, found a great gourmet restaurant about five miles in the other direction in McCamey, Texas. It was absolutely unbelievable.

Sassy was in every scene with me and became a real pro. In fact, when we finished in Texas and came back to Palm Beach to shoot more footage, Tom had changed the script to make Sassy the star. Well, almost. There is an old proverb in show biz: Never work with children or animals because they'll upstage you every time. And Sassy's living proof!

Whenever I had time, I tried to resurrect "Sunshine Mission," a medley of gospel songs I started years before to say thanks for the wonderful life I've had. It's dedicated to my Mom and Dad, who had created the Sunshine Mission back home in Springfield. I gathered some background tapes of some of the old, wonderful gospel songs and hymns that were sung at the Mission when I was growing up, such as "In The Garden," "I'll Fly Away," "Precious Memories" and "Amazing Grace." The concert is arranged to be performed in hospitals, retirement homes, nursing homes and churches.

On December 11, 1995, I almost met my maker at the Gardens Mall in North Palm Beach. It was a beautiful, sunny day as I drove along the perimeter road behind the mall on my way home. Suddenly, out of no-where, I saw the cab of a huge truck bearing down on me. I tried to accelerate, but it was too late. The truck turned me around, crushed me in my car and careened into a nearby lake. I was knocked unconscious for a minute or so, and when I came to the pain in my body was almost unbearable. I was also blinded by blood in my eyes, which resulted when my head shattered the driver's side window. I yelled for help, and the crowd that had gathered around my car tried to console me as the ambulance pulled up. My car was so mangled that the paramedics had to cut me out of it with the Jaws of Life. The force of the impact had thrown me under the passenger side dashboard, even with my seatbelts on! The angels were certainly there looking after me—the driver's side had been crushed to a height of just three feet! Thank God my dear Sassy hadn't been with me. She almost certainly would have been killed.

Everyone on the scene, myself included, thought I was going to die. I can't begin to describe the pain of my injuries, or the feeling of helplessness as I lie there waiting to be pulled to safety. I prayed like I've never prayed in my life, and I guess the good Lord heard me. The paramedics tried to call in a trauma helicopter, but it was at another accident, so rather than wait they shoved me in an ambulance and raced me to the emergency trauma center at St. Mary's Hospital in Riviera Beach.

My friend Helen Picket, who works at St. Mary's but was off that day, came to the hospital as soon as she heard what had happened. I was so battered that she didn't recognize me when they told her where I was. Another good friend, Debi Thomas, didn't recognize me, either. She went back to the nurse and said the guy in the room wasn't Kenny Miller. The doctor had to assure her that it was me.

My injuries were so extensive that it's no wonder no one could recognize me. My scapula was smashed down to my buttocks, I had cuts and scrapes all over and my body was drenched in blood. I begged the ER docs for some pain killers, but they wouldn't give me anything until they had completed all of the X-rays because they were certain I had also suffered brain damage. I heard the doctor ask Debi if I had a living will. She said she didn't know, and immediately called my attorney, Bryant Sims. Bryant was in such shock that he couldn't find it, so his secretary, Glenna Henwood, immediately typed up a new one and rushed it to the emergency room. I couldn't sign it, so a nurse took my hand and scrawled an "X" on the document. Debi and Helen witnessed it and Glenna notarized it on the spot.

I found out later that my injuries were worse than initially believed. In addition to a crushed scapula, I had seven broken ribs, a collapsed left lung, several broken bones in my left shoulder, a punctured ear drum, internal bleeding and my whole left side from my head to my toes was crushed and looked like raw hamburger.

Dr. Richard Weiner, the head of the St. Mary's Trauma Unit, took special care of me, aided by all the other doctors. I was in Intensive Care and then Step Down for quite a while, and a lot of concerned friends came to visit me—or so I was told. I was on so much pain medication that I don't remember receiving many visitors.

One visitor I do remember was Princess Susan Troubetskoy, wife of my late friend, Prince Youka Troubetskoy. Susan brought me one of my favorite foods, Beluga caviar with all the fixings—chopped egg whites, chopped onions, sour cream and toast halves. After much coaxing, the head nurse finally agreed to let me taste it. She placed some in my mouth, and it was like ambrosia. Of course, I missed the chilled Russian vodka to wash it down, but Susan couldn't bring everything! That's just one of the many pleasant memories I have from that absolutely miserable experience.

My doctor released me a couple of days before Christmas with the stipulation that I have someone with me at home full-time plus a home-care nurse. My dear friend Helen said she would stay with me as long as needed. My doctor ordered a special hospital bed for me and all the other necessities I would need for my recovery. My homecoming was something I'll never forget. My neighbors, Cindy and Barry Shapiro, had taken my little Sassy into their home, and their children, Staci and Ethan, even had Sassy sleep with them. They had put Sassy in my townhouse, knowing that I was coming home that day. When my pals Bryant and Dick Ayscue brought me home and put me in my wheelchair, a lot of my neighbors came outside to say hi, and Sassy heard my voice through the gate. They finally let her out, and she leapt into my lap and made the most outrageous noises you've ever heard coming from a dog! She kept licking my face because she missed me so much. It hurt like hell, but I didn't stop her; I had missed her just as much.

The next few weeks were a nightmare for me. I couldn't sleep in the hospital bed or in a chair, so I was constantly exhausted. Margaret Sanders even sent over a special mattress, but it didn't help very much. I finally tried a special heavily padded chair that Helen got from St. Mary's, and that helped a little. I was able to get a couple of hours of sleep each night. Many friends came by with food, and Nancy McDaniel, a long time friend, was always there whenever I needed anything at all. Christmas came and went, but I was so drugged that I barely remember it at all. My brother and sister-in-law, Dick and Katie, and my nephew Keith, came down right after Christmas to look after me. And when they had to leave, my other brother George took a shift. Thank God I had so much family and so many friends to see me through that trying time.

On those long, lonely nights, sitting in my chair waiting for the sun to come up, I had a lot of time to think, meditate and pray. I also reflected on my life and career. Show business is a really tough business. You can go to school and study to be a doctor, lawyer or architect, and when you get your degree that's what you are. You can study drama, dance and singing, but when you get your degree there's no guarantee you'll ever be in show business. The best thing to do is practical work—appear in front of an audience as often as you can, whether it's on stage, a local television station or a street corner. It's practical experience that pays off, so you'll be ready when your times comes, if it comes.

I remember one day being in Burt Reynolds' dressing room with Carol Burnett, and Carol made the comment that she almost had to believe in reincarnation. She knew so many talented people—some even more talented than her—but no matter what they did, they never got a break. They never got that one play or movie or television show that would have started them in the business. She said she had to believe that they hadn't gotten to their highest spiritual plateau, as perhaps she had. In their next life, they would be on a higher plane and success would finally come to them. I thought of all the really talented people I knew who had never achieved any success at all, and suddenly Carol's idea made a lot of sense.

I've never thought of myself as star. Yes, I've "starred" in some films, some TV shows, some plays and musicals on stage, and I've headlined nightclubs throughout the world, but being a star never meant that much to me. All I ever wanted was to entertain people as a singer and actor. I've always wondered why it's so hard, after you've proven to all that you have talent, to get the chance to do what you love so much. Maybe in my next life, if there is such a thing, I'll be able to entertain to my heart's content. Talking about heart, there's an old saying I've found to be true: "It is only through the heart that one sees rightly."

I have never judged life or people by material possessions. I have lived like a king at times, and at others I didn't know where my next meal was coming from. That must be the challenge of life. I think all performers, maybe without even realizing it, are in show business in a large sense to be loved and accepted. We're a strange breed that seems to need more love than others. I've been so very lucky. I have been and am loved by so many, and my love for the people who have crossed my path in life fills the heavens. Love is life to me. To be loved and to love is truly the greatest success I have ever known. No superstar in Hollywood could have any more than I have! If the only thing anyone remembers is "Kenny Miller was truly loved," then when I leave this life I can walk tall with my angels.

Filmography

MOTION PICTURES

FEARLESS FAGAN (1952) MGM, 79 min., B/W. D: Stanley Donen. S: Carleton Carpenter, Janet Leigh, Keenan Wynn, Richard Anderson, Ellen Corby, Barbara Ruick, Kenny Miller.

THE HUMAN JUNGLE (1954) Allied Artists, 82 min., B/W. D: Joseph M. Newman. S: Gary Merrill, Jan Sterling, Paula Raymond, Emile Meyer, Regis Toomey, Chuck Connors, Lamont Johnson, Claude Akins, Kenny Miller.

EAST OF EDEN (1955) Warner Brothers, 115 min., Color. D: Elia Kazan. S: James Dean, Julie Harris, Raymond Massey, Jo Van Fleet, Burl Ives, Richard Davalos, Albert Dekker, Kenny Miller.

RUNNING WILD (1955) Universal, 81 min., B/W. D: Abner Biberman. S: William Campbell, Mamie Van Doren, Keenan Wynn, Walter Coy, Kenny Miller, Kathleen Case.

THE SEARCH FOR BRIDEY MURPHY (1956) Paramount, 84 min., B/W. D: Noel Langley. S: Teresa Wright, Louis Hayward, Nancy Gates, Kenneth Tobey, Richard Anderson, Kenny Miller.

THE YOUNG GUNS (1956) Allied Artists, 84 min., B/W. D: "Albert Band" (Alfredo Antonini). S: Russ Tamblyn, Gloria Talbott, Perry Lopez, Scott Marlowe, Kenny Miller.

DINO (1957) Allied Artists, 94 min., B/W. D: Thomas Carr. S: Sal Mineo, Brian Keith, Susan Kohner, Joe DeSantis, Penny Stanton, Frank Faylen, Richard Bakalyan, Kenny Miller.

I WAS A TEENAGE WEREWOLF (1957) AIP, 70 min., B/W. D: Gene Fowler Jr. S: Michael Landon, Yvonne Lime, Whit Bissell, Kenny Miller, Vladimir Sokoloff, Guy Williams.

ROCKABILLY BABY (1957) 20th Century-Fox, 85 min., B/W. D: William F. Claxton. S: Marlene Willis, Gary Vinson, Virginia Field, Kenny Miller, Irene Ryan, Cindy Robbins, Ellen Corby, Douglas Kennedy, Gene Roth, Susan Volkman, Caryl Volkman.

ATTACK OF THE PUPPET PEOPLE (1958) AIP, 78 min., B/W. D: Bert I. Gordon. S: John Agar, John Hoyt, June Kenney, Marlene Willis, Kenny Miller, Laurie Mitchell, Scott Peters, Susan Gordon.

THE BUCCANEER (1958), Paramount, 121 min., Color. D: Anthony Quinn. S: Charlton Heston, Yul Brynner, Claire Bloom, Charles Boyer, Inger Stevens, Henry Hull, E.G. Marshall, Kenny Miller, Lorne Greene, Fran Jeffries, Woody Strode.

GOING STEADY (1958) Columbia, 79 min., B/W. D: Fred F. Sears. S: Molly Bee, Alan Reed Jr., Kenny Miller, Bill Goodwin, Irene Hervey, Bryon Foulger.

RALLY 'ROUND THE FLAG, BOYS (1958) 20th Century-Fox, 106 min., Color. D: Leo McCarey. S: Paul Newman, Joanne Woodward, Joan Collins, Jack Carson, Dwayne Hickman, Tuesday Weld, Kenny Miller, Gale Gordon.

TOUCH OF EVIL (1958) Universal, 107 min., B/W. D: Orson Welles, Harry Keller. S: Charlton Heston, Janet Leigh, Orson Welles, Akim Tamiroff, Marlene Dietrich, Mercedes McCambridge, Kenny Miller, Dennis Weaver, Zsa Zsa Gabor, Joseph Cotten, Ray Collins.

BATTLE FLAME (1959) Allied Artists, 78 min., B/W. D: R.G. Springsteen. S: Scott Brady, Elaine Edwards, Robert Blake, Kenny Miller, Gordon Jones, Wayne Heffley, Richard Harrison.

THIS REBEL BREED (1960) Warner Brothers, 90 min., B/W. D: Richard L. Bare. S: Gerald Mohr, Mark Damon, Rita Moreno, Kenny Miller, Dyan Cannon, Jay Novello, Eugene Martin.

THE LITTLE SHEPHERD OF KINGDOM COME (1961) 20th Century-Fox, 108 min., Color. D: Andrew V. McLaglen. S: Jimmie Rodgers, Luana Patten, Chill Wills, Kenny Miller, George Kennedy, Neil Hamilton.

THE NUN AND THE SERGEANT (1962) Warner Brothers, 74 min., B/W. D: Franklin Adreon. S: Robert Webber, Anna Sten, Leo Gordon, Kenny Miller, Hari Rhodes, Robert Easton, Dale Ishimoto, Linda Wong.

SURF PARTY (1964) 20th Century-Fox, 68 min., B/W. D: Maury Dexter. S: Bobby Vinton, Jackie DeShannon, Patricia Morrow, Kenny Miller.

CUSTER OF THE WEST (1968) U.S.-Spain co-production (released in U.S. by United Artists), 140 min., Color. D: Robert Siodmak. S: Robert Shaw, Mary Ure, Jeffrey Hunter, Robert Ryan, Ty Hardin, Kenny Miller, Charles Stalnaker, Robert Hall, Lawrence Tierney.

LITTLE LAURA & BIG JOHN (1973) United (distributed through Crown International), 82 min., Color. D: Luke Moberly, Bob Woodburn. S: Fabian Forte, Karen Black, Kenny Miller, Ivy Thayer, Paul Gleason, Cliff Frates, Evie Karafotias, Phil Philbin, Margaret Fuller, Terri Justin.

THE NIGHT DANIEL DIED (released on video as BLOODSTALKERS) (1975) Vidmark, 75 min., Color. D: Robert W. Morgan. S: Kenny Miller, Jerry Albert, Toni Crabtree, Celea-Ann Cole, Herb Goldstein, Robert Morgan, John Meyer, David Faris, Stan Webb.

TELEVISION SERIES
(Exact air dates of Kenny Miller's appearances unavailable)

AMERICAN BANDSTAND (ABC) Music.
Host: Dick Clark.
First telecast (Evening series): October 7, 1957. Final telecast: December 30, 1957.

B.L. STRYKER (ABC) Detective Drama
Cast: B.L. Stryker: Burt Reynolds
     Oz Jackson: Ossie Davis
     Lynda Lennox: Dana Kaminski
     Chief McGee: Michael O. Smith
     Oliver: Alfie Wise
     Kimberly Baskin: Rita Moreno
First telecast: February 13, 1989. Final telecast: August 4, 1990.

CAVALCADE OF STARS (Dumont) Comedy Variety.
Regulars: Jack Carter, Jerry Lester, Jackie Gleason, Larry Storch, Art Carney, Pert Kelton, June Taylor Dancers, Sammy Spear/Charlie Spear Orchestra.
First telecast: June 4, 1949. Final telecast: September 26, 1952.

THE CISCO KID (Syndicated) Western.
Cast: The Cisco Kid: Duncan Renaldo
     Pancho: Leo Carillo.
Produced: 1950-1956 (156 episodes).

DRAGNET (NBC) Police Drama.
Cast: Sgt. Joe Friday: Jack Webb
     Sgt. Ben Romero: Barton Yarborough
     Sgt. Ed Jacobs: Barney Phillips
     Officer Frank Smith: Herb Ellis (1952)
     Officer Frank Smith: Ben Alexander (1953-1959)
     Officer Bill Gannon: Harry Morgan (1967-1970)
First series: January 1952-September 1959. Second series: January 1967-September 1970.

FATHER KNOWS BEST (CBS, NBC, ABC) Situation Comedy
Cast: Jim Anderson: Robert Young
　　　Margaret Anderson: Jane Wyatt
　　　Betty "Princess" Anderson: Elinor Donahue
　　　James "Bud" Anderson: Billy Gray
　　　Kathy "Kitten" Anderson: Lauren Chapin
First telecast: October 3, 1954. Final telecast: April 5, 1963.

FLASH GORDON (Syndicated) Science Fiction
Cast: Flash Gordon: Steve Holland
　　　Dale Arden: Irene Champlin
　　　Dr. Zarkov: Joe Nash
Produced: 1953-1954 (39 episodes)

GUILTY OR INNOCENT
Proposed syndicated series, apparently never aired.
No production information available.

THE HALLS OF IVY (CBS) Situation Comedy
Cast: Dr. William Todhunter Hall: Ronald Colman
　　　Vicky Hall: Benita Hume
　　　Alice: Mary Wickes
　　　Clarence Wellman: Herb Butterfield
　　　Dr. Merriweather: Ray Collins (1954)
　　　Dr. Merriweather: James Todd (1954-1955)
First telecast: October 19, 1954. Last telecast: September 29, 1955.

THE JIMMIE RODGERS SHOW (NBC, CBS) Musical Variety
Host: Jimmie Rodgers
Regulars: Connie Francis (1959), Kirby Stone Four (1959), The Clay
Warnick Singers (1959), Buddy Morrow Orchestra (1959), Frank
Comstock Orchestra (1969), Burgundy Street Singers (1969), Lyle
Waggoner (1969), Vicki Lawrence (1969), Nancy Austin (1969), Bill
Fanning (1969), Don Crichton (1959).
First series: March 1959-September 1959 (NBC).
Second series: June 1969-September 1969 (CBS).

THE PUBLIC DEFENDER (CBS) Crime Drama
Cast: Bart Matthews: Reed Hadley
First telecast: March 11, 1954. Last telecast: June 23, 1955

THE RAT PATROL (ABC) War Drama
Cast: Sgt. Sam Troy: Chris George
      Sgt. Jack Moffitt: Gary Raymond
      Pvt. Mark Hitchcock: Lawrence Casey
      Pvt. Tully Pettigrew: Justin Tarr
      Capt. Hauptman Hans Dietrich: Hans Gudegast
First telecast: September 12, 1966. Last telecast: September 16, 1968.

THE STEVE ALLEN SHOW (CBS, NBC, ABC) Musical Variety
Host: Steve Allen
Regulars (1956-1961): Louis Nye, Gene Rayburn, Skitch Henderson, Tom Poston, Don Knotts,   Pat Harrington, Bill Dana, Buck Henry, Jayne Meadows, The Smothers Brothers, Tim Conway.
First series: December 1950-March 1951 (CBS). Second series: June 1956-December 1961 (NBC, ABC)

RECORDS

"**You Are Love to Me**" b/ "**Zombeeshee Blues**" (Faro)   Released: 1958
"**Spring Vacation**" b/ "**Teenage Bill of Rights**" (Imperial)   Released: 1960
"**You'd Better Believe It**" b/ "**The Letter**" (Viking)   Released: 1961
"**The Young Guns of Texas**" b/ "**A Rollin' Stone**" (20th Century-Fox)
    Released: 1962
"**Surf Party**" (LP Album) (20th Century-Fox)   Released: 1964
"**Pearly Shells**" b/ "**If I Were An Artist**" (20th Century-Fox)   Released: 1964
"**Restless**" b/ "**Take My Tip**" (EMI Stateside)   Released: 1965
"**When the Earth Was Green**" b/ "**Don't Take Your Love From Me**"
    (EMI Stateside)   Released: 1966

THEATRE

TRIBUTE
DARK OF THE MOON
FINIAN'S RAINBOW
ROOM SERVICE
LIGHT UP THE SKY
GOOD NEWS
PROMISES, PROMISES
HOW TO SUCCEED IN BUSINESS WITHOUT REALLY TRYING
THE ODD COUPLE
MAN OF LA MANCHA
A FUNNY THING HAPPENED ON THE WAY TO THE FORUM

NIGHT CLUB ENGAGEMENTS

YE LITTLE CLUB	Beverly Hills
THE MANOR HOUSE	Fort Lauderdale
THE CRYSTAL ROOM	New York
P.J.'S	Hollywood
CIRO'S	Hollywood
ACE OF CLUB	Leeds, UK
LONDON HILTON	London
THE PAVILION	Madrid
HOTEL DON PEPE	Marbella, Spain
FORUM	Dayton, OH
FONTAINBLEAU	Miami Beach
STARDUST	Las Vegas
CASINO ESTORIL	Lisbon, Portugal
GOLDEN FALCON	Pompano Beach, FL
DANNY'S SUPPER CLUB	Fort Lauderdale
PEPPERMINT LOUNGE	Ocean City
COCONUT GROVE	Los Angeles
KING & QUEEN OF HEARTS	England
CELEBRITE CLUB	London
GASLIGHT CLUB	Paris

REGIS HOTEL	Vero Beach, FL
THE CASINO	Marakesh, Morocco
RENDEVOUS ROOM	Estepona, Spain
DIPLOMAT HOTEL	Hollywood
THE PIEDMONT	Palm Beach
THE BREAKERS	Palm Beach
THE PALM BEACH HILTON	Palm Beach

BearManorMedia

P O Box 750 * Boalsburg, PA 16827

Plain Beautiful:
The Life of Peggy Ann Garner

The life story of one of Hollywood's most beloved child actors, whose performance in *A Tree Grows in Brooklyn* won her the Oscar.

$19.95   ISBN 1-59393-017-8

Spotlights & Shadows
The Albert Salmi Story

You know the face. You know the credit list: *Lost in Space, Escape from the Planet of the Apes, Gunsmoke, Bonanza, Kung Fu, The Twilight Zone* and hundreds more…But who was Albert Salmi?

Sandra Grabman's biography is a frank and loving tribute, combined with many memories from Salmi's family, friends, and co-stars, and includes never-before-published memoirs from the man himself. From humble beginnings—to a highly successful acting career—to a tragic death that shocked the world—Albert Salmi's story is unlike any other you'll ever read.

$19.95   ISBN: 1-59393-001-1

visit www.bearmanormedia.com
Visa & Mastercard accepted. Add $2 postage per book.

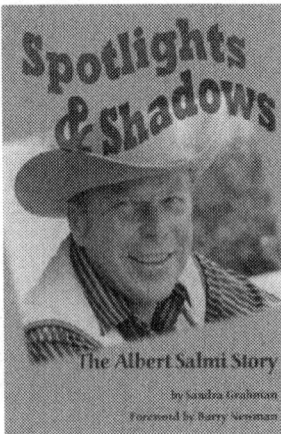

CHECK THESE TITLES! BearManorMedia.com

P O Box 750 * Boalsburg, PA 16827

Comic Strips and Comic Books of Radio's Golden Age
by Ron Lackmann

From Archie Andrews to Tom Mix, all radio characters and programs that ever stemmed from a comic book or comic strip in radio's golden age are collected here, for the first time, in an easy-to-read, A through Z book by Ron Lackmann!

$19.95   **ISBN 1-59393-021-6**

The Old-Time Radio Trivia Book
by Mel Simons

Test your OTR knowledge with the ultimate radio trivia book, compiled by long-time radio personality & interviewer, Mel Simons. The book is liberally illustrated with photos of radio stars from the author's personal collection.

$14.95   **ISBN 1-59393-022-4**

How Underdog Was Born
by creators Buck Biggers & Chet Stover

The creators of Total Television, the brains behind Underdog, Tennessee Tuxedo and many classic cartoons, reveal the origin of one of cartoon's greatest champions—Underdog! From conception to worldwide megahit, the entire story of the birth of Total Television at last closes an important gap in animated television history.

$19.95   **ISBN 1-59393-025-9**

Perverse, Adverse and Rottenverse
by June Foray

June Foray, voice of Rocky the Flying Squirrel and Natasha on Rocky and Bullwinkle, has assembled a hilarious collection of humorous essays aimed at knocking the hats off conventions and conventional sayings. Her highly literate work is reminiscent of John Lennon, S.J. Pearlman, with a smattering of P.G. Wodehouse's love of language. This is the first book from the voice of Warner Brothers' Grandma (Tweety cartoons) and Stan Freberg's favorite gal!

$14.95   **ISBN 1-59393-020-8**

The Writings of Paul Frees

A full-length screenplay (The Demon from Dimension X!), TV treatments and songs written for Spike Jones—never before published rarities. First 500 copies come with a free CD of unreleased Frees goodies!

$19.95   **ISBN 1-59393-011-9**

Daws Butler — Characters Actor
by Ben Ohmart and Joe Bevilacqua

The official biography of the voice of Yogi Bear, Huckleberry Hound and all things Hanna-Barbera. This first book on master voice actor Daws Butler has been assembled through personal scrapbooks, letters and intimate interviews with family and co-workers. Foreword by Daws' most famous student, Nancy Cartwright (the voice of Bart Simpson).

$24.95   **ISBN 1-59393-015-1**

For all these books and more, visit www.bearmanormedia.com or write info@ritzbros.com
Visa & Mastercard accepted. Add $2 postage per book.

CPSIA information can be obtained
at www.ICGtesting.com
Printed in the USA
FSOW03n1115231016
26471FS